MW01127835

FOOL

Identifying and Overcoming
Character Deficiency Syndrome

Second Edition

FOOL

Identifying and Overcoming
Character Deficiency Syndrome

Garry D. Nation

TATE PUBLISHING
AND ENTERPRISES, LLC

This book is designed to provide accurate and authoritative information with regard to the subject matter covered. This information is given with the understanding that neither the author nor Tate Publishing, LLC is engaged in rendering legal, professional advice. Since the details of your situation are fact dependent, you should additionally seek the services of a competent professional.

The opinions expressed by the author are not necessarily those of Tate Publishing, LLC.

Published by Tate Publishing & Enterprises, LLC
127 E. Trade Center Terrace | Mustang, Oklahoma 73064 USA
1.888.361.9473 | www.tatepublishing.com

Tate Publishing is committed to excellence in the publishing industry. The company reflects the philosophy established by the founders, based on Psalm 68:11,
"The Lord gave the word and great was the company of those who published it."

Book design copyright © 2015 by Tate Publishing, LLC. All rights reserved.
Cover design by Junriel Boquecosa
Interior design by Honeylette Pino

Published in the United States of America
ISBN: 978-1-62902-462-2
1. Religion / Christian Theology / Ethics
2. Self-Help / Self-Management / General
15.04.23

To my parents
who led me early in the way of wisdom

Contents

Preface to the First Edition

HUNDREDS OF MINOR CHARACTERS DART IN AND OUT THROUGH THE PAGES OF THE BIBLE. Few are more vividly drawn, are more timeless, or are more tragicomic than "the sluggard," the quintessential lazy guy. Have you read this Bible story or told it to your children? The Scriptures portray a day in his life, and it is as though we are watching the flickering, choppy scenes of a silent comedy two-reeler.

Scene one: Interior, bedroom

It is morning. While the rest of the world wakens and is bustling to its workday, Sluggard is sound asleep, snoring with gusto. He flops over in his bed like a door on its hinges. Time passes. Now at midmorning, every attempt to waken him fails. Others come in trying to stir him, but he mutters back to them (or to himself), "Just a little more sleep, a little longer nap, a little folding of the hands."

Scene two: Interior, kitchen, late morning

The camera pans the kitchen, and we see bags of unloaded groceries, spoiled food and milk, sink piled high with unwashed dishes. Sluggard, having dragged himself out of bed, finally makes it to the table after laboriously performing—and failing to finish—the simplest of cooking tasks, but he is too sluggish to eat. He cannot even get the food from the plate to his mouth because he keeps falling asleep in mid-bite. He makes repeated excuses why he should not go to work—hysterical, outlandish arguments about how he will get killed by a wild animal wandering loose on the streets. Are his excuses as clumsy and exaggerated as they sound, or do they mask a current of real fear that runs through his life?

Scene three: Exterior, Sluggard's house

On his way to work at last, Sluggard has to wend his way through the suburban jungle that is his front lawn. The yard is overgrown with an impossible tangle of weeds, brambles, and unkempt shrubs. There is a garden, and it hosts a wonderful crop of thistles and dandelions. The fence is in awful shape, and the gate through which he fumbles his way is so broken that it scarcely keeps anything either in or out, other than to impede his progress in going to work.

Scene four: Exterior, on the job

When Sluggard finally makes it to work, strife swirls all around him, yet he seems either oblivious to it or is baffled why everyone is always yelling at him. He does not see himself for what he is—an argumentative, do-nothing know-it-all, irritating to co-workers and exasperating to his boss, who cannot even think of him without grinding his teeth. Curiously, he always seems to have obstacles and difficulties—never his own fault, of course—which keep him from doing his job properly or finishing by deadlines.

*   *   *

There is a terribly sad ending to this otherwise humorous picture of an individual stumbling and bumbling through life. Since he does not really want to work and since no one really wants to hire him, he has neither the comfortable present he daydreams about nor the secure future he longs for. He will not get out and work in the uncomfortable weather of early spring, and as a result, he will go hungry in the bitter cold of winter. Perhaps his hunger will prove to be his friend, for it may be his only motivation to work. Alas, if that fails, then his self-centered desires and slothful habits of life will finally be the end of him: poverty, homelessness, hunger, cold, disease, death.

Where in the Bible, you may ask, is this story found? If you have missed it, it is probably because it is found not in a single passage in a straightforward telling, but in at least eighteen richly evocative verses scattered about in no particular order throughout the book of Proverbs.[1]

I admit that I had missed it also, even though I grew up steeped in the stories of the Bible and prided myself on my knowledge of them. As for Proverbs, I knew several of them well enough to quote or at least to paraphrase, but I did not have any real comprehension of the significance of the book among the other scriptures. I regarded it as a collection of moralisms—some of them useful, some obscure—but as a whole a sort of side dish to the main courses of Scripture.

When I signed up for a college course on the poetical literature of the Old Testament, I was sure the meat of the course would be in Job and Psalms. To be sure, Job and Psalms did not disappoint, but what surprised me was Proverbs, and much of that had to do with the approach of our professor, a saintly Baptist nun (she cheerfully called herself an "old maid aunt"), Dr. Rowena Strickland. The day she gave the lecture on "One Day in the Life of the Sluggard," she imparted to me an unexpected appreciation and delight for the poetry and power of Proverbs. (I still have my notes, along with the memory of the twinkle in her eye and the rueful shake of her head at the conclusion of the story.) But she also introduced me to a new method of synthesizing the proverbs, an approach that goes beyond lining up verses in topical categories. It brings proverbs together thematically and examines them both separately and as a whole. It looks beneath each proverb to gain insight for its foundation and perspective and then looks beyond the proverb to make full use of its implications as a forecast for the future. It then brings the collected proverbs together to see how they relate and if the picture they form as a whole is even clearer than the several parts.

Years later, after a good measure of life experience as a husband, father, pastor, teacher, school administrator, and counselor—and of course, with years more experience dealing with my own foibles—I returned to Proverbs for no better reason than to mine it for material for a midweek Bible study. In particular, I was drawn to look more closely and systematically at the proverbs concerning fools and their folly. It started with a word study. That word study yielded connections and insights I had not anticipated, touching issues that went far beyond conventional topical treatments of wisdom and folly. These insights were surprising, exhilarating, disturbing—and of far greater significance in the context of biblical revelation than I had ever thought. I taught the material in the Wednesday night Bible study in my church and adapted it also to teach to students in our Christian school. Eventually, this study became the basis for an essay and then a script for the Probe Ministries International radio program.[2] Finally, after several more years of study, oral presentation, writing, and rewriting, it became this book.

I feel obliged to explain certain aspects of my approach. As indicated above, the core of this book is a word study, but that is only the starting point. It would be more accurate to call this book the study of a *theme*. The primary focus is on Proverbs, but it casts a net also into the wider body of wisdom literature in the

Old Testament (specifically Job, Ecclesiastes, and certain of the Psalms), and into some of the prophets as well. Guided by the doctrine of the unity of Scripture, I have looked also to pertinent passages in the New Testament so as to compare and to fill out some of the teachings that are but briefly sketched in the Old.

As to my method, it is essentially driven by a careful exegesis (analysis) of the scriptures—an approach you will find in any good commentary. What makes my approach distinctive, however, is that I have brought scattered verses together to see them synthesized and arranged in context with one another. Some may object that this is a misuse, even an abuse of Holy Scripture. I would argue that my effort to arrange the diverse proverbs into a thematic unity is completely within the intention of the human author/editor, and of the Holy Spirit as well whose inspiration is the source of their authority. The apparent randomness of so much of the wisdom literature *requires* the reader to do this kind of work, to put things together on his own. The book of Proverbs in particular may be seen as a large literary jigsaw puzzle. A small portion of it has been preassembled by another hand, but most of the pieces are scattered out over the table. Unlike a jigsaw puzzle, each piece makes sense as its own picture. But like a jigsaw puzzle, the pieces fit together to form a larger, global view. Part of the trick—and part of the fun—is to see the inherent relationships between the different parts and fit them together without forcing them.

For this reason, collecting the verses that speak to a specific topic is only the first step in the process. Each verse, each proverb must be analyzed for itself and then appropriate connections made to other proverbs in the set. Sometimes the connections are plain, other times intensely subtle and not easy to grasp right away. What is most immediately obvious is that the connections between the proverbs have little or nothing to do with their sequential location in the book—*usually*. Some verses have multiple possibilities for interconnection. With due consideration for all these issues, I have set the small picture pieces into a larger, more complex arrangement. The pattern that has emerged from this arrangement forms the central thesis of the book.

As to the translation, it is (except where noted otherwise) my own rendition, rooted for the most part in the King James Version or the American Standard Version, 1901 (the version favored by Prof. Strickland). Such revisions as I have made are not for the sake merely of "customizing" the scriptures, but for improving their accuracy, clarifying their expression, and sharpening their impact. I make no pretense of being a Hebrew or Greek scholar, but sometimes I have been bold enough to make substantive revisions of these classic translations. To do so, I have relied on a variety of linguistic and interpretive resources. It is an audacious project, but I believe my offerings are valid and will stand up to scrutiny. As to the stylistic revisions, I have relied on my literary training and my ear for poetry—such as it is. If some rendition of mine (to which I jokingly refer as the NRV, "Nation Revised Version") seems to duplicate another current translation that is unreferenced, the similarity or duplication is purely coincidental (and perhaps inevitable, since we are all trying to produce an accurate translation from the same text). Bracketed words in the biblical texts are there to amplify or clarify the translation, and especially to distinguish between the different Hebrew words for fool. The appearance of italics in some Scripture quotations indicates my own emphasis and is not necessarily a reflection of something in the original text.

The reader is free to disagree with my constructions—and encouraged to make his own. I make no claim to infallibility, nor that the authority that properly belongs to the Scriptures should be adduced to my efforts. I have sought only to do justice to a rich yet neglected portion of Scripture. I have done so to my own satisfaction, and I hope to the reader's satisfaction and edification as well.

It is fair to ask what I hope and intend to accomplish with this book. (Indeed, that is the question with which every reader should open every book.) When I first began writing, I probably would have answered along the lines of, "I want to help people understand and solve their problems." That is not an unworthy motive or intention, and I do still hope that occurs, but that is not my *chief* aim in offering this book to the reading public. *My main goal and my heart's desire is that this book will meet a strategic need in the kingdom of God for the present age.*

What is Christianity, the Christian faith? Is it a system of doctrine? A set of moral standards? A relational experience? No, it is something larger than any of these, which incorporates all of these into a comprehensive trinity of life. *Christianity is truth, operating simultaneously in three dimensions:*

1. *Objective,* or *factual truth* (both specific doctrines and the larger theocentric worldview into which they fit);
2. *Imperative,* or *volitional truth* (the life of obedience and faith that is expected and demanded of those who believe);
3. *Subjective,* or *relational truth* (the believer's personal experience of God in worship, guidance, and fulfillment through faith in Jesus Christ).

There are churches, even whole denominations, which appear to emphasize one aspect of the "trinity" described above to the effectual neglect of the other two. Few are the churches that consciously seek a balance between all the elements of a serious faith. Fewer still are those that achieve it. It is an ancient problem, but one that we cannot afford to indulge in this perilous era.

The reader who is expecting a devotional commentary that will focus on developing his own personal walk with Christ may be disappointed. So also may the reader who is looking for a book on character building or on morality-based therapy. So may be the one who seeks a dispassionate expository treatment of a biblical theme. I rather hope, though, that each one of these will find *more* than what he expected and not less, for there are elements of all these things making up the content of this book. I have written a biblical commentary with a worldview consciousness. The intent is to address the mind, the conscience, and the heart of the reader. It is a serious book directed toward the nurturing of serious Christianity. I know it is an ambitious vision for a little book—I hope it is not grandiose.

Preface to the Second Edition

The second edition to this book does offer some significant revisions from the original. Some of the dated references have been updated or deleted. There are also some new materials, some minor corrections, and some clarifications.

The most important change is the addition of an extended guide for personal and group study at the end of each chapter. Each study guide contains two sections. "The Gist" brings forward a bullet-point summary of key ideas. The section titled "For your consideration" offers a selection of questions to help the reader make applications of the scriptures. They are designed for either personal use as the reader reflects on the chapter, or for discussion with a small group. Some of the questions are intentionally provocative—even as some of the proverbs are provocative.

I pray the updates and additions will be helpful for those who have read the first edition and of enduring value for all who engage and use this book.

The Gist

The nature of this book. It is the study of a theme, namely folly (a.k.a. Character Deficiency Syndrome).

The method of this book. The author seeks to provide a commentary on the Scriptures with a worldview consciousness. It begins with a rearrangement of verses from proverbs that puts them in context with one another, and then explores the meaning of the scriptures (exegesis) in order to derive principles for application.

The objective of this book. The author intends to enable the reader to think biblically about issues of character, to develop scriptural convictions, and to learn how to act on those convictions.

For your consideration

In the opening pages of the preface, a certain kind of character is profiled from a composite of scattered proverbs. *What is that character?*

The author compares the book of Proverbs to a jigsaw puzzle. *How might looking at the book this way change the way you look at individual proverbs?*

"Christianity is truth, operating simultaneously in three dimensions." *What are the three dimensions of truth?*

I

Diagnosing Our Disorder

They seem to come with some regularity now: the news stories about shootings and suicides; about massive data thefts and frauds; about misdemeanors committed by political officials and scandals falling on religious leaders; about violence against this group and oppression against that group. They disturb the nation's soul and leave everyone calling for *somebody* to do *something*, while polarizing people according to their opinion about what that *something* ought to be.

We have no problem identifying the symptoms and dimensions of our social crisis: drugs, gangs, violence, racism, poverty, divorce, AIDS, illegitimacy, social and political polarization. In addition, for every element of social crisis, there seems to be a corresponding personal crisis among individuals—anxiety, fear, anger, low self-worth, addiction, depression, compulsion.

The question is, how do we diagnose these problems? (Leave aside for now the roster of issues over which our society divides when it even tries to define the problem, e.g., abortion, gay rights, capital punishment.) We must identify a cause before we can pinpoint a solution.

The Answers of Humanism

Humanism has historically met these issues with two basic categories of answers. I use the term "humanism" here descriptively, neither to commend nor to disparage. Humanism is a worldview that begins and ends with human understanding and capability. It is a philosophy that says that if man causes a problem, he can fix it. At least, he had better be able to fix it, because there is no one else out there who can.

There are two basic humanistic answers concerning why there is so much disorder and hurt in our society, and solutions are proposed accordingly. One approach that surfaces regularly is behaviorism.

The behaviorists, who are variously in and out of vogue, have supplied us with a sociological buzzword that is still with us today, telling us that human problems are essentially "dysfunctions." We have dysfunctional families, dysfunctional relationships, dysfunctional institutions—dysfunctional people. I confess to you that while I have occasionally used the word "dysfunction," I do not like it. It seems to connote almost a mechanical difficulty, implying a mechanical solution. What you need here is an expert technician in human behavior that can come in and repair the problem with the human machine. Behaviorism always has its proponents and practitioners, and its history suggests that even if it is not the current dominant view, it will be back.

From the beginning of the modern era, an ever-popular diagnosis of human disorder is the "disease" model, which treats people's problems as illnesses. In this approach, all abnormality is essentially the sign of a sick person. Destructive behavior must not be punished. Rather, the perpetrator can and must be cured by the right therapy or, increasingly, by the right drug. The old commercial slogan, "Better living through chemistry," takes on a new meaning in a day when people with disorderly behavior and unruly moods are given a prescription and sent to the pharmacy. Psychology has lost its soul, *pyche* has been absorbed by *soma*, and human redemption is found in a gelcap.

Closely aligned are those who affirm that our behavior is almost entirely the product of our chromosomes. Laboratory study of the human genome has progressed phenomenally in very few years. Every new discovery brings forth some spokesman who calls it certain that all behavior is genetically determined, persuaded that our new knowledge is the key to the peace of the millennium. Once we know that a particular gene is the "cause" of a certain behavior, that behavior can now (or soon) be directed through genetic engineering. In the never-ending battle between Nature vs. Nurture, whichever has the upper hand at any given time, the loser always seems to be human dignity and meaning.

Do not misunderstand the point here. Both models—the behaviorist and the physiological—undeniably do have some practical usefulness. To a certain extent, the methods based on them seem to have had enough pragmatic success to draw some very conservative Christians to their clinics. It is even possible to utilize their techniques within a Christian frame of reference. Nevertheless, as models they both share two fundamental weaknesses, and consequently their results will always be faulty if we try to rely on them for *the* definition and explanation of the human problem.

For one thing, whether we speak of diseases or dysfunctions, we are trying to analyze personal problems and personal choices by using impersonal models. As a result, if we say that someone behaves as he does because he is sick, we have allowed that he is a patient but not a person.

Someone may object here that a patient *is* a person. No, a patient is a subject under medical treatment. Therapy focuses not upon the person but on the disease that produces behavior problems, as though the behavior were separate from the person. The *person* is not really under consideration, but rather constitutes the field in which the abnormal or diseased condition occurs. Of course, all treatment is done to benefit the person, but the patient is responsible neither for his own condition nor for his own recovery, except that he must cooperate to some extent with the professionals who administer the therapy.

In the same way, the very use of the term "dysfunction" inevitably dehumanizes the very person we're trying to help. It implies that we are dealing merely with the complexities of a system, not a soul. Once again, it is the professionals who are the key to the subject's recovery.

In the second place, both of these diagnoses tend to magnify victimhood at the expense of human responsibility. If Joe is sick or if he is the inevitable product of a dysfunctional environment, how can Joe be held accountable for his actions? Much of the psychotherapy of the past two or three decades, with some notable exceptions, seems to have been consumed with laying blame and diverting responsibility. If the 1970s began with the theme "I'm okay, you're okay," the 1990s devolved into, "I'm not okay, and it's *your* fault." With recent advances in genetic technology, an increasing number of troubled people are claiming that it's their *chromosomes'* fault. Whether the double helix becomes the new scapegoat of the twenty-first century remains yet to be seen.

Some go further to blame evolution, and buttress their claims with animal studies that supposedly shed light on human behavior and ethics. For example, some years ago, a zoologist published a book that caused a brief and entertaining (if unedifying) national flap, coming as it did in the midst of the Ken Starr investigation of President Clinton. It purported to show that infidelity is both natural and beneficial among nine out of ten mammal and bird species that mate for life—including humans. The driving force for the cheating is not lust, said the study. Lust is only the means to an end. The real explanation is the drive for species' survival. Males spread their sperm around to try to sire as many offspring as possible, while females search for the best possible genetic prospects to fertilize their eggs. What a comfort to every spouse who has been cheated on and to every child affected by a broken home: Darwinian forces have everything under control! Cold comfort indeed.

The last third of the twentieth century up to the present has witnessed the upsurge in the Western world of a more ancient, Eastern style of humanism that appears to turn our Euro-American categories on their head. Psychology seemed to recover its soul in the writings of best-selling authors like M. Scott Peck and Deepak Chopra. New age philosophies propose that our problems result from our failure to recognize our innate unity and identity with God, even our own divinity. The self-actualization techniques of Eastern mysticism are mined for everything from sublime enlightenment of the spirit to sublime sexual gratification. In this scenario, *psyche* now absorbs *soma*, and human redemption is achieved individually through the *bodymind*.

There is a semblance of personal responsibility in this scenario: the individual must lay hold of his own identity with the universe, conceived in spiritual terms. A closer inspection, however, shows this apparent sense of responsibility is, in fact, only a mirage. The monistic worldview undergirding this philosophy makes no more distinction between the individual and the impersonal forces of the universe than the naturalistic theories we have considered above. If everything is ultimately one, then not only is the distinction between the person and the universe lost, so also is the distinction even between good and evil.

The Answer of the Bible

The Bible, on the other hand, approaches human problems and the complexities of individual and social life through a moral realism.

It asserts that the true crisis we face is neither educational, nor economic, nor political. At the root, the problems we face are moral and spiritual in nature.

To say that our crisis is *moral* means two things. First, it means that it is rooted in the necessity of choosing between right and wrong. Second, it means that conflicts result either from choosing wrong, or else from trying to do right in a world where others are doing wrong. Some might prefer the term "ethics" here, but the main thing is whether a choice is right or wrong, and that the desirability of the results is a secondary consideration.

To say that our crisis is *spiritual* means that our moral choices have a significance beyond social convention. We humans are not absurd, self-aware bugs abiding in the moral void of an impersonal universe that is indifferent to our choices. Quite to the contrary, our lives are "naked and open before the eyes of Him with whom we have to do."[1] The Bible affirms that the ultimate responsibility for social order is personal and individual—that everyone must carry his own load. Moreover, we will all give an account to a personal God for the motives, deeds, and effects of our lives.

In addition, to say that our crisis is spiritual affirms the foundational truth that we are created in the image of God and possess a spiritual nature. Morality, therefore, is not merely a hormonal dialectic between our brains and our gonads. We are not mere biological machines which, by an accident of evolution, acquired self-consciousness and have been tormented by it ever since. Right and wrong, good and evil, truth and falsehood are more than socially useful constructs with no real meaning in themselves. They are terms that define the nature of reality—a reality founded in a real Creator and Judge of all.

In line with these fundamental truths, the Bible searches out the manifold problems of society and identifies the root cause of as a *crisis of character*. This concern for character is a universal one, and the morality that defines character is absolute. It is based upon the principle that one God is the Creator, Sustainer, and

Sovereign over the whole world. "For dominion belongs to the LORD, and he rules over the nations."[2]

The apostle Paul used this moral argument for monotheism as the common ground on which he approached the pluralistic philosophers of Athens:

> And he made from one blood every nation of men to dwell upon the whole face of the earth, having determined prearranged times and the boundaries of their dwelling, for them to seek the Lord. For perhaps they might grope for him and might find him—though indeed he is not far from each of us. For 'in him we live and move and exist,' as even some of the poets among you have said: 'For we are indeed his offspring.'[3]

For this reason, character is not merely a private consideration, a "deeply personal matter" as the cliché goes. Our society has become so divided culturally that, as the landmarks of the old moral consensus have fallen, we have made morality a matter of feelings to be guarded against the encroachment of social tyranny. But we err if we make character development an issue of individualism vs. collectivism. Yes, character is a matter of the responsibility of the individual, but it is more than that. The goodness and strength of any society, anywhere at any time, is defined by its collective moral character.

> Righteousness exalts a nation,
> but sin is a reproach to any people.[4]

Righteousness is a word that has not seen much use outside of church in the last several decades (indeed, it has fallen into disuse within many churches!), but it is one that is crucial to our discussion here. Any nation is elevated by righteousness, and any society is debased by the failure of its people to live righteously. Therefore, from the Bible's point of view, all well-meaning people should be concerned with the moral development of its population. Even in a pluralistic society with many differing religious beliefs (or the lack of beliefs), the moral health of the people is a concern common to all.

There are those who suggest that Christians should not be concerned with moral development—that we are above it all. Don't we believe that salvation comes not from good works and keeping the moral law, but by faith in the Savior, Jesus Christ? Besides misconstruing what we are trying to say, such an argument both misunderstands and misapplies the doctrine of salvation by faith. (I will take up the relationship between salvation by faith and moral character in the concluding chapter.) More to the point in this context, we Christians also have a vested interest in the strengthening of the moral fabric of our society. It is "that we may live peaceful and quiet lives in all godliness and dignity."[5] When a society's character is in crisis, we all suffer the effects together.

On September 11, 2001, the world lurched abruptly into a new era. The peace of that clear, sunny morning was exploded by an unprecedented attack on the free world with the destruction of the World Trade Center and the devastation of the Pentagon. Suddenly, the Western nations, and the United States in particular, were required to summon all their resources of moral character to stand up to a determined but elusive foe. In the shock of the moment, all America—and indeed, the world—responded and rallied to a president who, with grim resolution, pledged a patient and protracted campaign to eliminate the mortal threat of terrorism. Before long, however, both honest differences of philosophy and cynical political pandering began to erode support for—and even a sense of the reality of—the war on terror. At this writing, that war has gone through several phases, and despite promises by political leaders, there appears to be no end in sight. Meanwhile, an aggressive, transnational Islamist movement threatens both Judeo-Christian culture and Western secular humanism. It remains to be seen whether the West will have the stomach or stamina to sustain a long-term campaign against such an enemy.

One thing that must be noted about these self-described enemies of ours is this: What they most despise about America and the West is what they see as moral degeneracy and weakness of character. They see modernity as an inevitably corrupting influence to which the West has succumbed. They are determined to turn back that influence and seek first to drive the United States—the Great Satan—out of the Middle East forever. In so doing, they have imposed upon the current generation the most critical test of our national character it has yet seen. It is a test that will set the course of the future history of the world. Moral character will make the difference in this crisis and conflict. Its failure at this moment, it is no exaggeration to say, may mean the downfall of our civilization. No less than at any other momentous time in history, we face a character crisis of epic proportions.

Character Deficiency Syndrome

The sharpest description and diagnosis of such a crisis of character ever given is found in the wisdom literature of the Bible, which comprises the books of Job, Ecclesiastes, some of the Psalms, and especially the book of Proverbs. This literature teaches that moral character is grounded in reverence for God and constitutes wisdom. It calls the failure of character "folly." The sages who wrote these books, Solomon being chief among them, presented their observations with unsurpassed poetic virtuosity. Their true genius, however, is the method by which they made their observations. These ancient writers were the original behavioral profilers.

The art and science of criminal profiling has become a celebrated subject of motion pictures and television series. Though presaged to some extent by the Sherlock Holmes stories, it actually is a relatively recent development in the study of abnormal human behavior and as a crime-fighting tool. John Douglas is one investigator who helped develop the FBI's elite behavioral science unit, applying inductive methods toward construct-

ing profiles of serial killers with uncanny accuracy. In the book
Mind Hunter, Douglas writes that he always instructs his classes
that whoever wants to understand Picasso has to study his art.
Likewise, whoever desires to understand the criminal personality
has to study his crime. He specifies the difference between his
method and a psychiatrist's:

> The mental-health professionals start with the personality
> and infer behavior from that perspective. My people and I
> start with the behavior and infer the personality from that
> perspective.[6]

The similarity between Douglas's methods and Solomon's
cannot be missed. The same approach is taken throughout
the wisdom literature of the Old Testament. It is a mistake to
regard Proverbs only as a book of moralistic maxims. In fact, it
collects into a single volume hundreds of concise masterpieces
of inductive observation. It describes what people *do* in order to
show what they *are*—or, as Jesus put it, how one may know a
tree by its fruit. Gathering these diverse observations together by
subject matter enables the reader to construct behavioral profiles
that are often startlingly complete.

The challenge is to collect and collate all these observations in
a way that the fuller picture can be constructed. The proverbs that
preserve these observations are dispersed so unsystematically that
they give the appearance of being disconnected and haphazard.
There is purpose in the seeming randomness of lessons. It is to
make the reader work, to think:

> To understand a proverb and the interpretation,
> the words of the wise and their riddles.[7]

The search is part of the fun. First, one must gather the
bits of information on a theme, follow the threads that lead to
other themes, and analyze the relationships between issues. Our
common theme in this book is the fool and his folly.

The words "fool" and "folly" in the English Bible translate several Hebrew words used widely in the Old Testament for individuals who are deficient in character. Don't be *fooled* by our contemporary uses of the word "fool." The fool we're talking about is not necessarily unintelligent. He is *unwise*. This is not someone who is silly or ridiculous, but someone who has never learned that "the fear of the LORD is the beginning of knowledge."[8]

I mentioned that there are *several* Hebrew words. In this book, we are going to look specifically at six terms. They are not interchangeable synonyms, but each one has a distinct shade of meaning which illuminates our central theme. Together they indicate at least four progressive stages or degrees of descent into moral and spiritual depravity. I call this pattern of descent *Character Deficiency Syndrome.*

This is not an attempt to be jazzy or cute. I am not trying to create a New Age cliché here. Every word is deliberate and meaningful. The whole issue is about moral character. Wisdom means knowing the right thing to do and doing it. It is equivalent to the kind of sound and God-fearing character that thinks straight, makes good choices, and does what is right in a complicated world—even when doing right seems to make things even more complicated. "You've got to pay your dues," as the song says, and "it don't come easy."[9] Character willingly pays its dues. Folly amounts to a deficiency of that kind of character. The fool does not want to pay the dues. He wants the good life to "come easy." That is his first mistake. He goes downhill from there—and he *does* go downhill.

Folly does not stay still. It is progressive. Weakness of character is degenerative, and the process of its degeneration has identifiable, integrally connected stages. When we put the biblical clues together, we can see a clear pattern of cause and effect. Hence the term "syndrome."

The first stage, the first degree of folly, signifies the *simple* or *naive* fool, who is unthinking, gullible, and "devoid of understanding." He does not even have a basic comprehension of moral cause and effect. The second degree is the *self-confident* fool. He is known mainly by his stubbornness and by his big mouth. The third degree is the *committed* fool, who has decisively rejected wisdom and instead made a commitment to destructive ideas and behaviors. There are some other interesting—if distressing—dimensions to this stage of the syndrome that we shall talk about when we get to them.

Finally, there is a terminal stage of character deficiency syndrome: the *scornful* fool, a mocker who is openly contemptuous of spiritual truth and moral righteousness. Many fools do not advance to this stage, if for no other reason than that it requires too much effort and commitment. On the other hand, some whom one would never suspect—including many that appear to be upstanding citizens, even clergy—actually descend to this level. They not only harbor a deep hatred for ethical absolutes, they have become evangelists for moral infidelity. They may well have passed a deadline beyond which God will have no mercy for their guilty souls.

This book, then, is about folly in all its inglorious dimensions: its symptoms, its diagnosis, its causes, and—if we may be permitted to borrow for analogy the "disease model" we criticized earlier—its cure.

First, however, we must clarify the context for this teaching—and that context is *wisdom*. It has already been suggested above that wisdom is not a matter of intelligence, but rather moral character. Much more needs to be said. In order to understand folly, we need to grasp what the Bible says about wisdom. Wisdom, we shall see, is not a system of laws and commandments, nor is it an addendum to God's laws. It is rather a worldview, a way of looking at all of life and reality.

The Gist

Four Degrees of Folly in a Nutshell:

1. *The simple fool.* Naive, gullible, willful; doesn't anticipate the consequences of his choices.
2. *The self-confident fool.* Mouthy, annoying, stubborn; knows there are consequences, but doesn't think they'll happen to him—thinks he can "beat the system"
3. *The committed fool.* Angry, egotistical, shameless; disregards consequences, having made a positive commitment to lawlessness
4. *The scornful fool.* Bitter, arrogant, has passed beyond the point of no return; consequences-schmonsequences!

For your consideration

- How is Solomon's basic approach to understanding character similar to that of a modern criminal profiler? How is his different?
- How might the (seemingly) haphazard arrangement of proverbs in the book of Proverbs serve a positive instructional purpose?
- To summarize the biblical teaching on folly the author has coined the term "character deficiency syndrome." What do you think he means by this term? Write out a definition in your own words.

Self-Check:

Which of the following statements would describe your personal response to what you've read so far? (Select all that apply.)

- I'm skeptical; I don't think you can pigeonhole people like that. Everyone is an individual.
- I've already thought of some people who probably match one of these types.

- I'm glad I don't fit into any of those "fool" categories.
- I can actually begin to see myself in what you're talking about...and it worries me a little.
- I'm intrigued. I want to know more.

2

The Worldview of Wisdom

The proverbs of Solomon, the son of David, king of Israel.[1]

When the Greeks contemplated wisdom, they formulated theories through lengthy dialogues, discourses, and debates. When the Hebrews studied wisdom, they condensed it into pithy aphorisms that could be memorized by children and analyzed by almost anyone. The intensely practical bent of these proverbs immediately appeals to our contemporary pragmatism. The proverbs are not, however, alphabet noodles of isolated insights floating in a thin religious soup, able to be transferred intact from one philosophical bowl to another. The biblical concept of wisdom abides in and is defined by a definite worldview within a specific religious context.

This is not to say that the proverbs are entirely unique to the Bible in form or content. In fact, Proverbs bears a literary resemblance to an Egyptian work known as *Instruction of Amenemope*, and even seems to share some of its content. It is probable that

Amenemope was known in Israel during the time of Solomon, and even used as a source for the book of Proverbs (parallels to Amenemope can be found in Proverbs 22:17–23:11). This fact does not at all diminish my point, and even strengthens it. The Egyptian proverbs were not adopted as is, but "circumcised"— i.e., condensed, filtered, and refitted according to the Mosaic worldview—before being written into the inspired text.

The biblical worldview is founded upon the creation of the universe by the infinite-personal God, whose being cannot be identified or defined by any other name than the phrase "I Am." The LORD is righteous and holy, but also a passionate lover of those He created in His spiritual image. He keeps seeking them out when they sin against Him in order to reconcile them to Himself.

To this end, He makes covenants with them—treaties, or deals, as it were—offering them not only conditions of peace, but also bountiful benefits from harmonious fellowship with Him. He also pledges to impose penalties for violating the conditions of the covenant. He calls the conditions "commandments," the benefits "blessings," and the penalties "curses." This truth must not be misunderstood: the Covenant Maker is both generous and merciful beyond description, but He will not be regarded lightly.[2] He is the Creator and the only Sovereign and Judge over all creation and over all people, and there is no neutral ground in His presence.

> Now see that I, I am He, and there is no God besides Me.
> I kill and I make alive, I wound and I heal,
> and there is none who can deliver from My hand.[3]

The commandments God gives are not arbitrary instructions designed to keep people busy with religious activity, burdened with irrational regulations, or chained with restrictive codes. They are presented as reasonable demands that can be rationally understood and applied by anyone.[4] Any intelligent observer can perceive their benefits.

On the other hand, they are not "rational" in the strictly modern or philosophical sense. They do not proceed from empirical criteria for the attainment of human happiness or the fulfillment of humanitarian goals. They are not derived from anthropological investigations, sociological surveys, psychological case studies, or public opinion polls. God's commandments are derived from His own moral character.

> He is the Rock. His word is perfect.
> For all His ways are justice:
> A God of truth and without injustice.
> Righteous and upright is He.[5]

The specific covenant context for our understanding of wisdom is the Torah, the law that God gave through Moses to the nation of Israel. In the book of Deuteronomy, Moses rehearses the demands of the covenant (i.e., the Ten Commandments and all its corollaries). He elaborates on the promised blessings of obedience, spells out in excruciating detail the threatened curses upon disobedience, and finally holds out hope of restoration for those who repent. The climactic words of Moses's sermon rank among the most powerful ever preached in the history of public address:

> See, I have set before you today life and good, death and evil, in that I command you today to love the LORD your God, to walk in His ways and to keep His statutes and His judgments, that you may live and multiply. And the LORD your God will bless you in the land you go to possess.
>
> But if your hearts turn away so that you do not hear, and are drawn away, and worship other gods and serve them, I announce to you today that you shall surely perish...
>
> I call heaven and earth as witnesses today against you, that *I have set before you life and death, blessing and cursing. Therefore choose life,* that both you and your descendants

may live, that you may love the LORD your God, that you may obey His voice, and that you may cling to Him, for He is your life and the length of your days…[6]

The Way of Life

This idea, this image of obedience to God as the Way (or Path) of Life—versus the ways (plural) of death—is crucial to the concept of wisdom.

> To the wise *the way of life* inclines upward,
> to turn away from the grave below.
> There is a way that seems right to a man,
> but its final end—*the ways of death.*
> He who heeds instruction is in *the way of life,*
> but he who refuses correction goes astray.[7]
> For the commandment is a lamp, and the law is light,
> and reproofs of instruction are *the way of life:*[8]

Here is the key premise of Proverbs and of the whole biblical approach to wisdom. Wisdom assumes that living is better than dying. Wisdom takes God at His word when He says that obedience to His law is life, and disobedience is death. Wisdom, then, is fundamentally a matter of morality and faith rather than of intelligence. Thus, "the fear of the Lord is the beginning of wisdom."[9]

It is not that wisdom is completely unrelated to intelligence. On the contrary, the essence of intelligence is to realize the connection between living the life of the good and having a good life.

> Understanding is a wellspring of life to him who has it,
> but the instruction of fools is folly.
> [Wisdom] is a tree of life to those who lay hold of her,
> and happy is everyone who retains her.
> The law of the wise is a fountain of life,
> to depart from the snares of death.

> The fear of the LORD is a fountain of life,
> to depart from the snares of death.[10]

Notice the parallels in these verses between wisdom, the "law of the wise," "the fear of the LORD," and "understanding." Look also at the word pictures that describe them: "tree of life," "fountain of life," "wellspring of life."

Wisdom offers the same benefits and blessings of the covenant that Moses extolled in Deuteronomy: a long life, riches, honor, happiness, peace.[11] This is not by coincidence, nor is it by competition. Wisdom is not another way of life distinct from the law of God. Neither is it another layer of religion carpeting the law. Wisdom neither adds to nor replaces God's law. Wisdom simply understands what it means to live in full agreement with that law—that it is a matter of good sense and self-interest to cooperate with God rather than to strive with Him.

At the same time, wisdom is not exactly coextensive with the covenant. The covenant of law was made specifically with Israel, and its commandments and promises apply particularly to that nation. The laws of the covenant are not arbitrary, however. They are good; they are predicated on God's own moral nature, and they define what God expects not only from His chosen people, but from all mankind.

Wisdom perceives that the good life is good for anyone who lives it and that wickedness brings evil to all its practitioners. Therefore, "Righteousness elevates a nation," whatever its race or creed, "but sin is a reproach to any people."[12] Morality has no racial, ethnic, or religious prejudice. All who live morally will benefit, and those who do not will suffer the consequences of their failure. This is doubtless why Solomon became an international celebrity, attracting the rich and powerful of the world to hear him. Operating within the worldview of wisdom, Solomon was able to demonstrate the bottom-line benefits of an upright life—that it is shrewd to be good—and people were amazed at his insights.[13]

What made Solomon's wisdom so compelling to his contemporaries? Here is a theory: The polytheism that dominated the ancient world offered a veritable buffet of gods and goddesses, each serving a particular interest (generally localized, so that worship of a particular deity was essentially a civic duty), and each carrying its own self-centered ethical emphases. Within this kind of worldview, right and wrong becomes a pragmatic matter of serving selected goals, and morality is relativized to an absurd degree. To people steeped in polytheism, the ethical monotheism of the Hebrews must have seemed like a terrible moral tyranny, even as it does to so many in our own day. Solomon, his international profile being raised through his wealth, became an effective apologist for the God of Israel and the law of Moses. He ably demonstrated to the surprise of his guests that the principles they had previously dismissed as servitude to a strange tribal god were universal ones that could make them as successful as Solomon.

Righteousness goes hand in hand with wisdom. Like wisdom, it is called the way of life.[14] Wisdom, in a manner of speaking, is the instrument for attaining righteousness.

> For the LORD gives wisdom.
> From His mouth come knowledge and understanding.
> Then you will understand righteousness, justice,
> and equity,
> and every good path.[15]

Wisdom, personified as a woman, speaks for herself:

> All the words of my mouth are in righteousness.
> There is nothing crooked or perverse in them.
> I lead in the way of righteousness,
> in the midst of the paths of judgment,
> that I may cause those who love me to inherit wealth,
> that I may fill their treasuries.[16]

Righteousness is the source of profound benefit beyond material riches to the one who practices it—especially if one considers life itself to be a benefit.

> Treasures of wickedness profit nothing,
> but righteousness delivers from death.
> Riches profit nothing in the day of wrath,
> but righteousness delivers from death.
> The righteousness of the blameless will direct his way,
> but the wicked shall fall by his own wickedness.
> The righteousness of the upright will deliver them,
> but hypocrites will be taken captive in their own iniquity.
> The wicked receives a deceitful wage,
> but he who sows righteousness reaps a true reward.[17]
> As righteousness leads to life,
> so he who pursues evil pursues it to his own death.
> Righteousness protects him whose way is upright,
> but wickedness overthrows the sinner.[18]

Even if there were no material benefit at all, righteousness is worth having because its very presence improves the intangible quality of life, regardless of that life's material conditions. *Righteousness is a benefit to be sought for its own sake.*

> Better is a little with righteousness
> than large profits without justice.
> He who follows after righteousness and mercy
> finds life, righteousness, and honor.[19]

These verses carry a tacit recognition that there is such a thing as material prosperity without righteousness. Likewise, there can be righteousness without material prosperity. "What shall it profit a man," said Jesus, "if he shall gain the whole world, and lose his own soul?" (Mark 8:36)

Considering the close connection between wisdom and righteousness, it is almost surprising to discover that the Hebrew word for wisdom has no linguistic relationship with righteousness.[20]

In fact, it carries no connotation of moral virtue at all. Its root meaning has more to do with cleverness and skill than anything else—whether of craftsmanship, salesmanship, or statesmanship. It speaks of the facility to do things well, to handle matters successfully. How, then, is this an appropriate word for moral character? It is because wisdom represents the *moral* skills and perceptiveness that a person needs in order to live righteously.

The fact that one of the most important elements of wisdom is prudence confirms this truth. Wisdom, again portrayed as a woman, speaks and says,

> I Wisdom dwell with prudence,
> and arrive at knowledge of well-designed plans.[21]

Only once in the Bible is this noun for "prudence" used, but the adjective form of the word appears six times in Proverbs.[22] The word conveys an image of someone who knows when to speak and when to keep silent—and usually he keeps silent. He is alert and always knows what is going on around him, not taking things at face value, but studying clues beneath the surface. He is cautious but also knows when to be aggressive and go after what he wants.

Another word, also translated "prudent,"[23] refers to a person of understanding. It rounds out the picture and reinforces what has already been said. We might describe such a person as being "sharp" in the best sense of the word. This is someone who is acute, perceptive, canny—able to size up a situation and devise an appropriate plan of action. The Homeric hero Ulysses and his faithful wife Penelope could both be well described this way. Prudence is a practical virtue that makes moral virtue effective.

The most sublime insight reached in Proverbs is that God Himself is the source for this practical wisdom. It is not merely something He recommends in order to help people get along better in this world. It is His own possession as well. Wisdom speaks again:

The LORD possessed me in the beginning of His way,
before His works of old.
I was set up from everlasting, from the beginning,
before the earth ever was…
When He prepared the heavens, I was there…
When He appointed the foundations of the earth,
Then I was by Him as a master craftsman,
And I was daily His delight, rejoicing always before Him,
Rejoicing in the habitable part of the earth,
And my delight was with the sons of men.[24]

There are two clear worldview implications in this passage. The first is that God built the world by wisdom, and therefore *wisdom is built into the fabric of the world.* "Wisdom" is shorthand for the way things really are. Wisdom is about reality, about the way things work, and therefore about the way to live a happy and successful life.

The second worldview implication is that *wisdom is one, even as God is one.* In other words, spiritual wisdom, moral wisdom, philosophical wisdom, and practical wisdom are all the same. Unlike the worldview of our own contemporary culture that tends toward fragmentation, the worldview of wisdom is unifying. There is not one kind of wisdom for one field of endeavor and another kind for another field that can and will lead to opposite and contradictory conclusions. There is not a lower story of facts that contradicts an upper story of meaning. There is no dichotomy between being a good person and living the good life. It may not always be easy to grasp the connections, however, and part of the purpose of Proverbs is to illuminate those connections.

A Commitment to Truth

Ultimately, wisdom is a commitment to truth, and the walk of wisdom is a walk of integrity. Thus truth and integrity are urged upon the reader of Proverbs with the same language, the same fervency, as is wisdom. Indeed, truth and wisdom are inseparable.

Buy the truth, and do not sell it—
wisdom, and instruction, and understanding.
The integrity of the upright shall guide them,
but the slipperiness of hypocrites shall destroy them.[25]

Underscoring the relation between wisdom and integrity, Proverbs contrasts the path of the upright with the way of darkness.

Discretion shall preserve you,
understanding shall keep you,
to deliver you from the way of the evil influence,
from men who speak perverse things;
who leave the paths of uprightness,
to walk in the ways of darkness.[26]
The way of the LORD is strength to the upright:
but destruction shall be to the workers of iniquity.
The integrity of the upright shall guide them,
but the slipperiness of hypocrites shall destroy them.
The righteousness of the upright shall deliver them,
but hypocrites shall be caught in their own downfall.
Righteousness guards whoever is upright in the Way,
but wickedness overthrows the sinner.[27]

Along with the commitment to live by the truth, wisdom entails a commitment to speak truth as well.

Better is the poor one who walks in his integrity,
than he who is deceitful in his lips,
and is a self-confident fool.
He who speaks truth shows forth righteousness,
but a false witness, deceit.
The lips of truth shall be established forever,
but a lying tongue is but for a moment.
"For," [says Wisdom,] "my mouth shall speak truth,
and wickedness is an abomination to my lips."[28]

This is not a reckless, ruthless honesty that swings a large blade and doesn't care who gets in the way. To be wise is to embrace the twin values of truth and compassion. Mercy and truth must always go together:

> Let not mercy and truth forsake you:
> Bind them about your neck.
> Write them upon the tablet of your heart.
> Do they not err that devise evil?
> But mercy and truth shall be to those who devise good.
> By mercy and truth iniquity is purged,
> and by the fear of the LORD men depart from evil.
> Mercy and truth preserve the king,
> and his throne is upheld by mercy.[29]

The strong identification between wisdom and truth—in all its dimensions—provides a vital key to understanding folly. Folly means a disconnection from truth and reality. It is one point at which our English word "fool" does fit the various kinds of folly we will encounter as we proceed. In our language, to fool someone is to trick him, and to be fooled is to be deceived. This is also the picture in the proverbs.

The common thread through all the degrees of character deficiency syndrome is self-deception. The truth is not always easy, comfortable, or delightful. Sometimes the truth is hard, both to accept and to live out. When we depart from the truth, we are fooled into thinking that there is a better way than the one God has designed and thus become willing partners in our own destruction. The essence of all folly is this self-deception that leads to self-destruction.

Here is the dilemma: If you were deceived, how would you know it? Even worse, if you should deceive yourself, how will you be delivered from your trap?

It does not have to be that way. Wisdom is what prevents deception and preserves from destruction. Wisdom knows to check itself against the objective truth of God's Word. It is trained to do so and disciplined to do so.

Divine Obsession

Whoever would benefit from wisdom, however, must acquire it. Wisdom is inherent in the nature of God, but not in man. We are not born wise—quite the opposite, in fact, as we shall see. The attainment of wisdom is a struggle and requires commitment and determination. It is a virtue to seek virtue, and therefore *it requires character in order to gain character.*

Proverbs in particular is a book that can be read and studied with profit by anyone of any age, but it is specifically written to "the young man."[30] Twenty-three times the reader is addressed as "my son." It is not a child, however, but that individual who is in the process of deciding what values will motivate his life. Solomon addresses this young person in the earliest stages of adult maturation in the language of profit and promotion:

> Get wisdom! Get understanding!
> Do not forget it, nor turn away from the words of my mouth.
> Do not forsake her, and she will preserve you.
> Love her, and she will keep you.
> Wisdom is the principal thing:
> Therefore, get wisdom!
> And with all your getting, get understanding.
> Exalt her, and she will promote you.
> She will bring you to honor when you embrace her.[31]

Solomon also uses the language of romance, as if he were urging his son to pursue the woman of his dreams, marry her, and live happily ever after. This is no ordinary woman—it is wisdom! Let her become your obsession. Do not rest until you have claimed her for your own.

Happy is the man who finds wisdom,
and the man who gets understanding.
For her profit is better than the profit of silver,
and the increase of it than fine gold.
She is more precious than rubies,
and all the things you can desire
are not to be compared to her.[32]

Why such fervent urgings? Because wisdom is not easy to get. Wisdom's suitors must work hard to gain her affection. Many are those who find her desirable but fail to attain her because they seek her casually, half-heartedly, and not with serious intent. Moreover in this world, wisdom's true value is not always apparent. Her beauty, though deep and abiding, is not dazzling like that of sex or money. It takes a certain measure of good moral character in order to want to build moral character. It is the parents' job to provide that foundation of moral training—up to a point.[33] All too soon, however, the parents' job is done, and it is up to the grown-up child to take up the wisdom quest for himself or herself. To do so is to make the first right choice, to choose life.

To fail to make a positive choice to pursue upright moral character is to choose folly by default. As we have seen, there is one Way of Life, but the ways of death are legion. So long as the individual is on the way, there is always the possibility for a change of direction, not just taking a different route, but setting out for a new destination. May it please God that someone who reads this book will see that the path he or she is on is one that leads to death and will turn to choose life. May it please Him that you, dear reader, will be encouraged to build wisdom into your own life and know its happiness.

Danger!

Before we go any further into this subject, I must issue a warning about the danger that is inherent in a study like this. God's Word is a sharp instrument, and as such must be applied carefully, not recklessly. Rightly used, this study on character deficiency syndrome can be a useful tool for self-examination, social criticism, and even for handling issues in one's own family and other kinds of relationships. For those who take the message to heart, it can steer them away from trouble or help them extricate themselves from it. It can assist them to raise their children and enable them to give good counsel to others. It can direct them toward wholesome friendships and protect them from toxic ones.

We must use these teachings to gain insight into how to live our lives, into our times, and into the ways of God. We must *not* try to become self-appointed judges of character, who render a critical diagnosis of every irritating person we come in contact with. "Judge not," Jesus said, "lest you be judged. For with what judgment you judge, you shall be judged; and with what measure you measure, it shall be measured back to you."[34] We will gain no favor from either God or man by setting ourselves up as the arbiter over our neighbor's character, behavior, and disputes. There is no virtue in being a busybody.

At the same time, it must be said that this book is all about exercising judgment. Any time one speaks concerning right and wrong, one renders a judgment. To call any deed, word, or attitude good or bad is to judge it. Not all kinds of judging are scripturally incorrect.

There is a peculiar contemporary context for these caveats, called political correctness. Oddly enough, the same proponents of "PC" who have rejected most of the teachings of Christianity have embraced the premise of nonjudgmentalism. Of course, they have done so for completely disingenuous reasons. The most heinous sin anyone can commit in our present day is the sin of "intolerance." How dare we point a finger of judgment at anyone, as though we are better than they and our morals are better than theirs! Intolerance, of course, is essentially defined as presuming that absolutes in general, and biblical standards of right and wrong in particular, are appropriate and right for society as a whole.

Morality has become a strictly personal issue in our time, on the same level with choosing a hairstyle or a new automobile or a restaurant for a weekend dinner date—essentially a matter of individual taste and preference. Anyone who dares question the moral decisions of another becomes subject to the kind of harangue that used to be reserved for the most egregious moral offenders in society. Christians in particular have had the "judge not" saying of Jesus flung in our faces so many times that we've begun to fling it at one another.

This must be made clear: The same Jesus who said "judge not," followed those very words with the directive not to cast pearls before swine, nor give what is holy to the dogs.[35] Obedience to these latter commands entails a judgment, does it not?

The Bible (both Testaments) distinguishes between the unrighteous censure of others that proceeds from pride and a righteous discernment between right and wrong. The very commandment to love our neighbor as ourselves is bracketed in the context of distinguishing between proper and improper judgments. If one reads it in its context (in Leviticus 19:15–20), one will see that it even includes a command to rebuke our neighbor when he gets out of line. In other words, *there comes a time when God's commandment to love our neighbor requires us to exercise judgment and issue rebuke.*

Before we can proceed further toward understanding those things that need rebuke, we must first spend some time clarifying those things that are to be commended—especially within the perspective of Proverbs. The fear of the Lord is the beginning of wisdom, thus the departure from it must be the beginning of folly. It is fitting, therefore, that we look a little more closely at the kind of virtuous character the fool has no desire to attain.

The Gist

There is a living God who makes covenants with people.

- "Commandments" = conditions; "blessings" = benefits; "curses" = penalties
- God's commandments: not "rational," "pragmatic," or arbitrary either; but moral, derived from his own character.

Keeping God's commandments is called the Way of Life.

- Wisdom takes God at his word, that obedience to His law is life, and disobedience is death.
- Wisdom perceives that the good life is good for anyone who live it and that wickedness brings evil to all its practitioners.
- Moral wisdom is built into the fabric of the world; i.e., "wisdom" is another word for the way things were made to work.
- Wisdom is one, even as God is one, therefore morality and success are inherently linked.

Living in the Way of Life requires a commitment to Truth.

- The common thread through all the degrees of character deficiency syndrome is self-deception.

For your consideration

- What primary truth is the foundation for the biblical worldview?
- Why do you think the leaders of polytheistic nations found the wisdom of King Solomon so compelling? Why is this important in our present day?
- Against what danger is it necessary to guard as we carry out this study of character profiles?

3

The Beginning of Wisdom

Surely I am more stupid than anyone,
and have not a man's understanding.
I have neither learned wisdom,
nor do I have knowledge of the Holy One.
Who has gone up into heaven and come down?
Who has gathered the wind in his fists?
Who has bound the waters in his garment?
Who has established all the ends of the earth?
What is his name, and what is his son's name?
Surely you know!
Every word of God is tested.
He is a shield for those who take refuge in Him.
Add not to His words,
Lest He reprove you, and you be found a liar.[1]

Perhaps against our expectation, the wisdom literature of the
Bible does not engage in a great deal of theological reflection, at

least in the sense of explicit discussion about the nature of God. Even Job, the most theological of the wisdom books, discusses the *ways* of God at length, but simply assumes His existence and His divine nature. The grand climax of the book, God's own reply to Job, makes a direct assertion of divine prerogatives but provides no explanation to satisfy the questions of the human mind.

This does not mean, as some may infer, that the biblical view of wisdom squelches the tendency of the mind to question everything. Far from it. But neither does wisdom consist in attaining fully satisfying answers to all our questions. Wisdom is rather about the development of a character and a life conformable to the will of God and the way He runs the world, and the first principle of wisdom is the fear of the LORD.

The verses above are attributed to a sage otherwise unknown to us as Agur ben Yakeh. His self-deprecating words notwithstanding, Agur's short collection shows him to be a shrewd observer of human nature who, like his Greek counterpart Socrates, was more inclined to ask questions than to offer answers. It also shows that, despite his self-deprecating confession, he is not without knowledge of the Holy One. Indeed, the words that immediately follow demonstrate that Agur knows much more than he is telling. What is then the point of his introductory statement? It is to affirm that there are boundaries to human wisdom and understanding. It is implicit advice to those who seek wisdom to avoid those teachers, first, who claim to have arrived at perfect understanding, and second, who find their source of authority outside of God's Word. At the same time, Agur also counsels against the arrogance of those who would try to manipulate God's Word to make it say what they wish it would say.

As a young pastor fresh out of seminary and soon to be fresh out of ideas, I began to learn theology from a widow who was a member of my church. Joy Lytle lived alone in a tired, nineteenth century two-story farmhouse at the end of a long gravel road. She was diabetic, nearly blind, often in poor health, and did not get to attend services with any regularity. But once I finally learned where she lived, I called on her with some frequency. It was not, I confess, so much to minister to her as to be ministered to. This elect lady who truly lived up to her name, "Joy," continued a ministry that she and her late husband had begun a generation before, of showing hospitality to young preachers, of refreshing their souls. I would sit at her table for hours, drinking iced tea and talking about the Lord. My wife says that whenever I was late coming in from making afternoon calls, if she needed to reach me she could call Mrs. Lytle and would find me there without fail.

And as I said, I learned theology from this woman whose education was mainly from the Bible. One day she looked at me across the table with her characteristic squint and said, "Maybe you can help me with a question that has bothered me for a long time. It's something I've really never understood." I perked up, of course. I love a knowledge challenge, and I was sure I could answer any doctrinal question she would put forward. "It's that scripture that says, 'He changeth not.' I've never really understood that." Well, I launched into an exposition of the passage in Malachi where the words appear. She interrupted me—and her interruptions never came across as rude—"Yes, I know that. But how is it so, 'He changeth not'?" I backed up and tried again with a discourse on the immutability of God, again to no avail. Obviously, I was missing the point. I did not even understand the question. I had always thought "He changeth not" to be an affirmation, not a problem.

But this precious woman, whose effectual prayers I valued far above my own, owned a vital faith forged in sickness and suffering that I had little understanding of. To her, the concept of God's unchanging nature was a wonderful perplexity, a delicious paradox, the thing that she could not see but in which she believed. Like Elisha, who struck the river with the prophet's mantle, crying out, "Where is the God of Elijah," Joy Lytle did not ask her question out of disengaged curiosity on a point of doctrine, but out of the fight of faith in which she warred every day of her life. I don't know if I ever really "got it"—I am still working on her question—but I think I started to. She passed away after a terrible battle with cancer. My choice of texts for the sermon at her funeral was Mark 14:4, a question, "Why this waste?"—how the blessing and honor of Jesus abides on the life that is poured out in love without self-regard, even though the rest of the world and even fellow believers may not understand.

There are questions and problems to which there are no easy answers, and to which even the most sound and correct intellectual answers provide no satisfaction for the soul. Agur reminds us of that point, not to dissuade us from asking the hard questions, but rather to anchor our minds as well as our hearts in the fear of God.

The First Point of All Theology

The starting place, the first axiom of all sound theology and indeed of all sound thinking is this: *God is God, and we are not.* The fear of the LORD is the beginning of wisdom, and the understanding and acceptance of this axiom is the beginning of the fear of the LORD. Though the discussion in Proverbs on the doctrine of God is not extensive, fully developed, or well rounded, the one point that is explicitly and forthrightly addressed is this first point— specifically as it refers to the divine prerogatives.

> The LORD has made everything for its own end,
> even the wicked for the day of evil.
> There is no wisdom, nor understanding,
> nor counsel against the LORD.[2]
> A man's goings are of the LORD.
> How then can man understand his way?
> The lot is cast into the lap,
> but the decision is all from the LORD.
> The horse is trained for the day of battle,

but victory is from the LORD.
Many seek the ruler's favor,
but a man's judgment comes from the LORD.
The king's heart is in the hand of the LORD as the rivers:
He turns it wherever He will.[3]
The plans of the heart belong to man,
but the answer of the tongue is from the LORD.
A man's heart plans his way,
but the LORD directs his steps.
There are many plans in a man's heart,
but it is the counsel of the LORD that will stand.[4]

The life of wisdom is built on the foundation of confidence in the sovereignty of God. The proverbs do not try to explain His sovereignty, either as to its rationale or as to its mechanics. Neither do the proverbs mitigate the force of this doctrine in any way. Because God is God, he has both the power and the right to behave in a godlike way. What God wants to do, He does. What He wants for the final outcome will be. He can overturn the judgments of man, but man cannot overturn His judgments. Nothing happens at random, nothing is a chance occurrence; everything has a purpose, even the things that seem to be at variance with His purpose.

All of this is offered without any consciousness of a tension between the sovereignty of God and the free will of man, despite the fact that, apart from these few verses, virtually all the rest of the book is addressed directly to the mind and will of man. Humanistic philosophy may be driven to perplexity trying to reconcile the coexistence of these two issues, divine sovereignty and human free will, but covenant wisdom does not even frame the matter in those terms. God is seen exercising His rightful, righteous rule. Man is seen as a being of responsibility, called to live a life of purposeful righteousness for which he is accountable to his Maker. It is an accountability that he cannot escape.

> The hearing ear, and the seeing eye,
> the Lord has made them both.
> The eyes of the Lord are in every place,
> keeping watch over the evil and the good.
> *Sheol* and *Abaddon* are before the Lord,
> how much more the hearts of the children of men!
> All the ways of a man are clean in his own eyes,
> but the Lord weighs the spirits.
> Every way of a man is right in his own eyes,
> but the Lord weighs the hearts.[5]

Sheol and *Abaddon* are personifications of the grave and the destruction and oblivion of death, similar in expression to the personification of Death and Hades in Revelation 20:14. God beholds all things in the realm of the dead, so that even those who die do not escape His scrutiny. If God knows these things, how much more does He know the secret things of human intentions? Men justify themselves and excuse their faults, but God is the final arbiter and judge of all, and nothing escapes His sight. He knows the truth. After all, God is God.

Moreover, God, being God, determines for Himself what He will reward and what He will punish. There is no standard outside of Himself that rules over Him, but right and wrong are determined by His own character. Yet when He announces what He abhors in contrast to what He favors, His covenant character comes into clear focus:

> There are six things which The Lord hates—
> seven that are an abomination to Him:
> haughty eyes, a lying tongue,
> and hands that shed innocent blood,
> a heart that devises wicked purposes,
> feet swift in running toward evil,
> a false witness that utters lies,
> and he who sows discord among brethren.[6]
> Everyone who is proud in heart
> is an abomination to the Lord.

Depend on it: he shall not be unpunished.
For the perverse is an abomination to the LORD,
but His friendship is with the upright.
The curse of the LORD is in the house of the wicked,
but He blesses the dwelling of the righteous.[7]
Blessings are upon the head of the righteous,
but violence covers the mouth of the wicked.
The memory of the righteous is blessed,
but the name of the wicked will rot.
The mouth of the righteous is a fountain of life,
but violence covers the mouth of the wicked.[8]

God is God, but His rule is neither arbitrary nor tyrannical. He is good, and His standard of righteousness is benevolent toward man. The expression "six things…seven…" is a poetic convention, a metaphor for a list that is not exhaustive, but is complete with regard to the point it is making. And the point is not that these seven things are the *only* things God hates, but that the state of affairs described is an offense to God in its every movement.

That state of affairs consists of the issues that comprise human conflict. See how the things he hates are the very things that bring destruction in human relationships: deceit, injustice, malice, the application of human mind and energy toward evil purposes, the bearing of false witness, and the stirring up of trouble between people who should dwell together in fellowship. In other words, God is not concerned solely with religious matters or our "deeply personal beliefs." He is concerned as well with the way we live our lives and with the social relationships between people.

At the same time, He most certainly is concerned with what truly are the most deeply personal things about our lives. He understands and judges *our motives*. The latter three proverbs contrast three unrighteous things with the righteous ones of whom God approves: the proud in heart, the perverse, and the wicked. Concerning the proud in heart, it does not matter how self-assured he is that he will get away with whatever it is he is plotting, the proverb gives us assurance. (The literal expression is "hand to hand," an idiomatic phrase, like "let's shake on it," meaning "I promise; you can take my word.") that he will get his comeuppance. The perverse person is one, as we shall see later, who goes his own way to the disregard of God's commandments; God abhors him, whereas He shows the loyalty of a friend to those who seek to live within His will. Summarizing the whole matter, the wicked abide under God's curse, and the righteous under His blessing. There is no moral neutrality. One is either righteous or wicked, and his life is either blessed or cursed.

It's Moral Reciprocity…Not Karma

As modern western man has rejected his biblical roots and denied the authority of absolute moral standards as declared in divine revelation and grounded in the character of God, other ideas have come in to fill the void. Many people, especially those who lead our public institutions, seem receptive to the Marxist-derived alternative of political correctness. From the East, however, the concept of *karma* has filtered into much of our moral discussion, especially within the popular culture. Karma is the "belief (in Eastern religions) that every act produces an effect on the soul. Good works "clean" the soul. Evil works add "weight" to the soul. Thus karma is the moral law of cause and effect."[9] The word has entered the functional vocabulary of Americans, and the younger they are, the more likely they are to use the term in discussions of right and wrong, whether casual or serious—even if they are not necessarily adherents of New Age doctrines in general.

Like an immigrant neighbor who retains the customs of his homeland, the word seems to coexist alongside western thought with its own culture, friendly enough but not quite assimilated and not truly well understood. The concept of karma has a parallel in Judeo-Christian morality, which is often expressed as the law of sowing and reaping. Many in our culture would seem to think the two principles are the same thing, but they are not, any more than the Brahman of Hinduism is the same as the Yahweh of the Bible. Like the Hindu deity, Karma is a blind, impersonal, inscrutable principle, indifferent to whom it helps or harms. Strictly speaking, it does not even operate in the present life but affects the soul as it returns for another cycle. Not so the law of sowing and reaping, which is the rational extension of the moral rule of a personal God who tirelessly observes the thoughts and deeds of all men, and who is diligent to keep His promises—especially to those who are under His covenants.

In a universe so superintended by a moral God, there is a principle, not of blind karma, but of *moral reciprocity* always at work. The perspective of wisdom is that one will ignore this principle at one's own peril, but may also put it to work in one's own favor.

> Whoever diligently seeks good seeks favor,
> but if he searches after evil, it shall come to him.
> If the righteous shall be paid back in the earth,
> how much more the wicked and the sinner![10]
> Whoever digs a pit will fall in it,
> and whoever rolls a stone, it shall roll back on him.
> Whoever causes the upright to go astray in an evil way
> shall fall into his own pit,
> but the perfect shall inherit good.[11]

The second verse above ("If the righteous..." Proverbs 11:31) is worth an extra look. The most straightforward understanding of it sees the righteous being paid back for his righteousness and the sinner being paid back for his sin, both "in the earth," that is, in this present life. I would make three observations before going on. First, though reward in this present life is in view (as it is throughout proverbs), there seems to be at least a tacit nod toward an afterlife. Otherwise, what would be the point of the phrase "in the earth?" In the earth as opposed to what? (The phrase could be translated "in the land," but doing so does not overturn the observation here, it only muddies the meaning of the proverb.) If there is no existence after death, what else is there to compare it with? Second, Christians are often accused of an outlook that is "pie in the sky by and by," and to be sure, the New Testament teachings on moral payback do stress the age to come. Yet even in the Gospels, Jesus promises his disciples that those who leave all to follow him will receive reward in the present life, as well as eternal life.[12]

Third, when this scripture was translated into Greek (the Septuagint, the version commonly quoted in the New Testament), those ancient interpreters read the word translated here as "pay back"[13] in its negative sense of retribution. In that version it emphasizes that even the righteous are paid back for wrongdoing—thus how much more the wicked! This is the translation quoted in 1 Peter 4:18. There, the idea is that no one is innocent, and that if God does not let the righteous get away with sin, certainly the prospects of the unrepentant must be terribly bleak.

> Whoever despises the word brings destruction on himself,
> but he who fears the commandment shall be rewarded.
> Evil pursues sinners,
> but the righteous shall be paid back with good.
> Whoever walks uprightly shall be delivered,
> but he who is perverse in his ways shall fall at once.
> Happy is the man that fears always,
> but he who hardens his heart shall fall into calamity.[14]

Thus far the rule of moral reciprocity seems as impersonal (at least in its source) as karma. Other words of wisdom, however, make it clear that there is one personal, divine Operator of the system of recompense.

> Do not say, "I will pay back evil."
> Wait for the LORD, and he will save you.[15]
> The eyes of the LORD preserve the one who has knowledge,

but he overthrows the words of the hypocrite.[16]
Whoever rewards evil for good,
evil shall not depart from his house.
Whoever mocks the poor reproaches his Maker;
and whoever is glad at calamity shall not go unpunished.[17]
Rejoice not when your enemy falls,
and let not your heart be glad when he is overthrown,
lest the LORD see it, and it displease Him,
and He should turn away his wrath from Him.[18]
If your enemy be hungry, give him bread to eat,
and if he be thirsty, give him water to drink:
for you will heap coals of fire upon his head,
and the LORD will reward you.[19]

This theology of moral cause and effect lays the foundation for the teachings of Jesus concerning non-retaliation and forgiveness. We do not need to seek personal retribution for offenses committed against ourselves, because a just God will not permit the guilty to escape judgment. The apostle Paul even quotes from these proverbs as he instructs Christians to follow the Lord's teachings in a hostile world.[20]

Contours of Character: Moral Sense

The fear of the LORD, then, begins with the acknowledgment that God is there, with all the powers and prerogatives of deity at His disposal, and that He is not loath to use them. Neither is He an indifferent, absentee landlord, but a righteous King who vitally interested in the prosperity and happiness of His people and in their deportment and relationships. He sees, He cares, and He rewards—in His own time. It is this awareness, not just mentally as a doctrine but experientially as an essential point of personal faith, that the fear of the LORD germinates beyond a mere dread that one might be caught doing something wrong and into a full-blown moral sensibility.

Where there is no vision, the people cast off restraint,
but he who keeps the law, happy is he.
Evil men do not understand justice,
but those who seek the LORD understand all things.
An unjust man is an abomination to the righteous,
while one who is upright in the way is an
abomination to the wicked.
As a troubled fountain, and a corrupted spring,
so is a righteous man who gives way before the wicked.
Those who forsake the law praise the wicked,
but those who keep the law contend with them.
By the blessing of the upright the city is raised up,
but it is overthrown by the mouth of the wicked.
When it goes well with the righteous, the city rejoices,
and when the wicked perish, there is jubilation.[21]

Proverbs 29:18a is often quoted (from the King James Version) in both religious and secular contexts for motivational purposes: "Where there is no vision, the people perish." Invariably, it is to support the point that people need to get a vision—whether it be it a shared vision or an individual one—so as to mobilize resources and achieve it. Of course, "vision" is supposed to mean a goal or objective, a desired future state of being. This verse has been used as the core of so many great speeches and sermons that it almost grieves me to point out that the "vision" of 29:18a has nothing whatsoever to do with human achievement or possibility thinking or any other such thing at all. It is a *revelatory* vision, one that brings an oracle or prophecy such as Abraham received in Genesis 15:1. It is God revealing His will, His commandments, His promises.

Where this is lacking, the people do not "perish" in the sense we usually use the word.[22] It actually means "to throw off," or "to let loose." A clearer translation would be "the people are left naked, defenseless," or else "the people run loose." The selected rendering above, I think, combines well both connotations of the verb. The people throw off self-restraint and become unruly.

This principle can be observed not only on an individual level, but especially on social and cultural levels. We have seen this principle progressively at work in the Western world as nations, including America, have rejected the biblical revelation on which they were founded. The source of the depredations of modern morality must be found at this point: that our society does not any longer consider divine revelation to have any authority over our lives.

So powerfully expressed is the thought of 18a that we almost forget to notice the promise of 18b. Make note of the contrast between the two lines. The regretful observation of 18a is about "people," society, but the promise of 18b is to "he," the individual. "*He* who keeps the law, happy is *he*." It would be folly to deny the power of social and cultural pressures to distort the pattern of virtue or the impact those pressures have on any individual. Yet *here is an affirmation that it is possible to live righteously in an unrighteous environment.* Though the rest of society may forsake its revelatory vision and proceed to cast off all restraint, the individual does not have to do so.

What difference can one person of righteousness make in such an environment? Much, as the following verses in this set show. The health of society is dependent upon those who stand for morality, righteousness, and justice when the standards are falling all around. All that is needed for evil to triumph is for good men to do nothing—an observation made by the English statesman Edmund Burke, but by Solomon in different words (Proverbs 25:26) two and a half millennia before him. Yet if a godly remnant rises up and asserts the claims of righteousness, there may indeed be a fierce battle for hearts and minds, but there is also hope of recovery. This is because to forsake the law of God does damage to society, while a return to righteousness restores it to health.

It is absolutely necessary, however, that moral restoration be seen by a change in life and ethics, and not merely in religious words and practices.

> To do righteousness and justice
> is more acceptable to the LORD than sacrifice.
> Whoever turns away his ear from hearing the law,
> even his prayer is an abomination.
> Happy is the man who always fears,
> but the one who hardens his heart shall fall into wrongdoing.
> Whoever covers his transgressions shall not prosper.
> but whoever confesses and forsakes them will receive mercy.[23]

A revival of religious faith in a nation will bring no real restoration if it is a matter of appealing to people's religious feelings without a corresponding alteration in their moral behavior and lifestyle. To obey is better than sacrifice,[24] and religious behavior that does not issue in repentance is no more acceptable to God than irreligious behavior.

The Wellspring of Character: The Heart

It is not that Solomon is a legalist or even a moralist. Deeds do not in themselves constitute spirituality, nor do they take the place of spirituality. Everything of moral and spiritual significance— every thought, attitude, decision, and action—proceeds from the inner life of the individual, that is, from the heart.

> Keep your heart with all diligence,
> for out of it are the issues of life.[25]

In our language and culture, when we talk about the heart we usually are referring to the emotions and affections. The Hebrew concept corresponds to ours to a certain extent. There are a number of proverbs that paint a richly textured picture of the heart as the seat of the emotional life.[26] But the heart is much deeper, much more complex than that. It comprehends the whole inner life, not just the emotions but the deepest motives, deliberations, and decisions as well. Indeed, the heart is the person, and the person is made up of whatever is in his heart.

Thus a wise person consults with his heart before he opens his mouth. The thoughts of the heart are deep thoughts, and only a counselor with understanding can draw them out. Deep though it may be, the heart of man is untrustworthy, and it is folly for a person to follow his heart. Indeed, if his heart is twisted—bent in any way against God's righteous laws—he will end in disaster.[27]

In fact, Proverbs is as realistically skeptical about the human heart as any of the prophets. Though it holds great respect for the heart as the seat of all our motivations, it reminds us that we do not know ourselves—let alone control ourselves—as well as we may think. Only God knows the heart, and He is the only competent Judge of it.

> Who can say, I have made my heart clean,
> I am pure from my sin?
> The spirit of man is the lamp of the LORD,
> searching all his innermost parts.
> The refining pot is for silver, and the furnace for gold,
> but the LORD tests the hearts.[28]

In Proverbs, the heart and the spirit are virtual synonyms. God has a high regard for the lowly heart/spirit and a corresponding low regard for the uppity.

> Before destruction the heart of man is haughty,
> but before honor comes humility.
> Pride goes before destruction,
> and a haughty spirit before a fall.
> It is better to be of a lowly spirit with the poor,
> than to divide profits with the proud.
> A high look and a proud heart,
> the very light of the wicked, is sin.
> A man's pride shall bring him low,

but one who has a lowly spirit shall obtain honor.
Pride comes, shame follows,
but with the lowly is wisdom.
By pride comes only contention,
but with those who take advice is wisdom.
The LORD will uproot the house of the proud,
but he will establish the border of the widow.
The reward of humility and the fear of the LORD
is riches, and honor, and life.[29]

In this cluster of sayings, humility is credited with numerous benefits, while pride is blamed as the reason why promising projects end in failure. There are several practical reasons why pride goes before destruction: it prevents one from taking advice, it leads to flawed plans, and it produces flawed goals. Above all, however, there is the issue of divine superintendence over the affairs of mankind. God Himself is the opponent of those who exalt themselves above their fellow man, and God Himself takes up the cause of the lowly ones who cannot defend themselves. Humility is a corollary of the fear of the LORD and an essential element of sound character.

The Muscle of Character: Faith

Trust in the LORD with all your heart,
and lean not upon your own understanding:
In all your ways acknowledge Him,
and He will direct your paths.[30]

The above words are among the best known, best loved, and most quoted in all the Bible—and deservedly so. It is at the same time a commandment, a promise, and a capsule commentary on what God requires of us all. It summarizes in a few words what our lives are (or ought to be) all about. It is the epitome of wisdom, of character, of practical spirituality. Like the rest of the words of Proverbs, it is applicable in innumerable ways, but it cannot be lifted out of the context of the Torah and all the blessings and curses of the law covenant without doing violence to it.

The primary point of the matter is that wisdom is embedded in faith—not as mere belief in doctrines or in submission to traditions, but in personal, heart-given trust in the person of the LORD. To trust in Him is to trust in the principles of His Word, but also to trust in His divine superintendence over one's own life. As we are commanded to *love* the LORD our God with all our hearts,[31] so are we to *trust* Him with all our hearts. We must resist the constant temptation to lean on our own understanding. That does not mean we must not *use* our own understanding. We are continually admonished throughout Proverbs and the other wisdom literature to seek, find, and engage to understand what is going on around us and to use our understanding to full benefit. To "lean" means to put our weight on it, to be dependent on it, to give our own understanding credit for being able to direct our lives rightly. We can know and understand much, and that is a large part of human dignity. Humility requires that we realize and acknowledge that the best of our knowledge and understanding are limited. Only God is all-knowing, all-wise.

To acknowledge Him in all our ways must be more than a friendly wave or a formal salute. Verse 6 literally says, "In all your ways, *know* Him." The Hebrew word is *yada* (yah-DAH), a word for intimate knowledge, for personal relationship. To acknowledge God, to know God in all our ways, at the very least means to look at God's will and direction in everything. Or as one author puts it, "Consider no circumstances so clear you do not need His direction."[32] This wisdom hymn continues with admonitions and promises:

> Be not wise in your own eyes:
> Fear the LORD, and depart from evil.
> It will be health to your body
> and marrow to your bones.
> Honor the LORD with your substance,

and with the first-fruits of all your increase.
So shall your barns be filled with plenty,
and your vats shall overflow with new wine.
My son, do not reject the chastening of the LORD
nor become perturbed by His reproof,
for whom the LORD loves He reproves;
even as a father the son in whom he delights.[33]

"Wise in your own eyes" is one of those quintessential biblical expressions that has so much impact one would think it must show up everywhere in the Scriptures. It does not. It actually is comparatively rare, but it powerfully portrays an attitude with such clarity that it needs little explanation. To be wise in your own eyes is to have a deceptive self-esteem, to think yourself to be smarter and more capable than is true. In the present context, however, it specifically refers to the pride of one who thinks he can direct his own life and affairs and come to a true conclusion about the ultimate realities and values of life. It is set in contrast to the covenant-endorsed approach to a happy, healthy, successful life—namely, to fear the LORD and depart from evil. Moreover, trusting in the LORD also means looking for His hand of instruction and correction as expressed in the difficulties, pains, and losses common to life. Such suffering does not mean divine neglect, and certainly not hostility. It is the mark of the Fatherly love of God toward His own, the mark that He truly does regard you as His child.

It is thus clear that the blessings promised to the wise do not come to them unmixed with adversity. At least part of the reason for that, according to the above words of Solomon, is that all of life is a school for wisdom in which we are always being taught and must always remain teachable. None of us gets it completely right, and thus we are all always subject to corrective discipline. We must not become disgusted, disillusioned, or (as we translated it above) perturbed. Our comfort is that there is a rational, loving hand behind it who knows how to turn it to our good. Old

Agur testified that he was not quite ready to call wisdom the accomplishment of his life. Excellent character is a process, not an achievement. In a world so filled with temptation to leave the straight and narrow, it is naive to think that wisdom is easy.

It is in the naive or simple soul where folly takes root. It is here that our analysis of character deficiency syndrome begins.

The Gist

Key Idea: In the Bible, wisdom seldom refers to intelligence. It primarily has to do with the character and a life conformed to the will of God and the way He runs the world. *Therefore, the first principle of wisdom is the fear of the* LORD.

God is God, and we are not. The life of wisdom is built on the foundation of confidence in the sovereignty of God.

The nature of God's law. God's law and His character are one and the same.

The heart of God's law. God is concerned with the way we live our lives in relationship with other people.

Moral reciprocity. The biblical concept of moral reciprocity ("sowing and reaping") is different from the Eastern idea of karma. Karma is impersonal. In the Bible, moral consequences and rewards are personal—between the soul and God.

The primacy of the heart. Every thought, attitude, decision, and action proceeds from the inner life of the individual, i.e., from the heart.

For your consideration

- How does the wisdom literature portray the sovereignty of God? How does the same literature portray human free will? Why doesn't one cancel out the other?

- When the Bible says "heart," how is that different from the modern use of the word? Why is that significant in the study of wisdom vs. folly?
- Proverbs 29:18a (KJV) says, "Where there is no vision, the people perish." Motivational speakers often quote this verse to admonish us to "get a vision." What does the verse really mean?

4

Without a Clue

Suppose you found in your mailbox today a letter on an impressive, official-looking stationary from some office of a West African nation, say Nigeria. It is legitimately postmarked from that location. The text of the letter explains that a foreign contract overpayment has created a fiscal emergency in that country's banking system, and that tens of millions of dollars must be quickly moved out of Nigeria into foreign banks. If you will make your bank account available to hold some of these funds, they will let you keep thousands of those dollars for yourself. There is no risk involved—except that they do ask that you disclose enough of your financial information to make sure you are trustworthy. They also want you to send an "advance fee" to pay for transfer costs. How do you respond?

If you decide to keep your own money in your bank account and your sensitive financial information to yourself, you may consider it profit. The many who have generously opened their accounts to this windfall have received nothing in return for their generosity but a sizeable debit in their bank accounts and a compromise of their personal security.

This is not a hypothetical situation, but an actual scam that has been around since the 1980s and continues to hoodwink thousands of victims out of millions of dollars every year. The Nigerian letter, known by law enforcement authorities as a "4-1-9" or "advance fee" fraud, is a new and sophisticated version of an ancient swindle. In the 1920s, it spawned a variation known as "The Spanish Prisoner" con. The Internet has facilitated an explosion of frauds like this. In one six-month period, I received fourteen different e-mail solicitations to get rich very quickly just by letting these folks use my bank account for awhile.

I have received scores of such solicitations over the years, some of them with a religious or charitable theme, and not just from West Africa, but from Asia and the Middle East as well. I have treated them all as the first, which I immediately deposited (wistfully, I admit) in the household trash. I could only wish that I had always shown that kind of good sense and self-control in the face of the offer too good to be true. Unfortunately, I have on other (happily rare) occasions also suffered the same embarrassment and loss that comes to all who share the lapse of character we shall define in this chapter.

The first, or latent stage of character deficiency syndrome is to be "simple," and the Bible provides a thorough description of the *simple fool*. The Hebrew word is *pethi* (pe-THEE), from the root *pata* (pa-tah), which means open, spacious, or wide. It is tempting to call this fellow an "airhead," but that would be missing the point. Remember, in the Bible, neither wisdom nor folly is a matter of intellect or even personality. Both are moral issues, and both are a choice.

The simple one is empty, rather, in the sense of being naive, immature, lacking judgment and discernment. The phrase most often associated with this word is "one who lacks understanding."

There is a kind of simplicity that is a virtue. This is not it. This is not simplicity but *simpleness*, the front door to folly, which is the way of destruction. The word denotes someone, as we will see, who is gullible and easily enticed. He is usually contrasted with the "prudent" person, who has learned or is learning how to make choices based on moral convictions rather than feelings. Prudence is the normal (i.e., God-intended), healthy human condition— but *simpleness* is the prevailing one, the universal default pattern of human behavior.

Moral Carelessness

In August 2007, a missing child alert e-mail went viral, seeking information and prayers for a fifteen-year-old named Evan Trembley. Hundreds of thousands saw it on the Internet and responded.

It was a hoax. There really was such a lad, but he never really was missing.

The kicker in this story is that the hoax originated with—Evan Trembley! For a template he borrowed an e-mail hoax that was already in circulation. He changed the name and wrote himself into it, including a personal photo, and made it seem more real by including a (fake) police officer contact. He then sent it as a joke to a few friends, who apparently also forwarded to a few friends, and so on, and so on....

When Evan's family started getting phone calls, it was bad enough, but when the police in his home city began receiving calls and e-mails to a nonexistent detective, they got involved and things got a bit more serious.

This is a beautiful illustration of the kind of trouble the simple get into. Doubtless young Evan intended no harm, and certainly, it never occurred to him that something like this could get out of hand. Exactly. It never occurred to him! Simple![1]

The chief characteristic of the simple one is credulity, gullibility, dullness. One might think that the simple one needs only to become sophisticated through education and experience. His situation is not that, well—simple. Remember, the key issue is moral character, not intellect, or personality, or even common sense. This sort of naivety is not merely the product of innocent trust. The simple fool chooses to trust those who are liable to mislead him, while at the same time he remains skeptical of those who would instruct and advise him about right and wrong. He may see himself as wise and understanding.

Moral character proceeds from choices that are freely made. The simple person, however, does not see his choices as being morally loaded. For him, it comes down to a matter of what he wants. Notice how Solomon diagnoses his problem:

> The simple believes every word,
> but the prudent watches well where he steps.[2]

In other words, the simple one trusts people without weighing either the wisdom of their words or the goodness of their motives. The only thing that matters is that someone is telling him what he wants to hear and to believe. This soul cannot—or rather, will not—tell the difference between someone who is telling the truth and someone who is feeding him a very clever line. It is a relatively mild form of character deficiency, but one that makes him easy prey for those who would take advantage of him or lead him astray into virtually any kind of vice. In his mind, exercising discernment might short-circuit a good time or cut off a "once in a lifetime" opportunity. The simple one is a fish ready to bite the hook.

This habitual gullibility leads to a pattern of behavior that can only be described as careless and foolhardy.

> A prudent person foresees the evil and hides himself;
> but the simple pass on, and are punished.[3]

He simply does not calculate consequences. It is not that he is overconfident. He just does not think ahead because that would be too much trouble. Neither does he consider that there are moral causes and effects. Moral thinking might interfere with what he wants to do. He may even regard prudent planning to be pessimistic. To him, optimism is to plunge ahead and assume luck will favor him.

At first glance, the proverb above presents the picture of two responses to an impending disaster. A hurricane approaches the coast. The prudent board up their homes and businesses and take their families to a safer place further inland until the storm is passed. The simple assume that the storm will probably pass by as usual and do nothing. The fun-loving among them take their surfboards out to catch the best waves that have ever hit the beach and play until the storm overtakes them and it is too late to escape.

There is more to be found in this proverb, however. It lies in the contrast between the attitudes of the prudent and of the simple. These attitudes not only control how the two react differently to a set of circumstances. They also control how each one actually *creates* his own set of circumstances. *The prudent individual acts with foresight, while the simple individual just acts.*

Prudent foresight is not anything like psychic clairvoyance. No one knows the future but God. No one can truly calculate or comprehend all the compound effects of any single deed or word. It is only reasonable, however, to anticipate the direct consequences a given choice may produce. It is not hard to understand that doing right is good and that wrongdoing creates havoc. It is true that sometimes doing the right thing is difficult, or that the goodness of the moral choice may be obscured by the pressing needs of the moment. It is also true that evil often wears the cloak of expediency. Doing right often must be done by faith. This is why we have the wisdom literature in the Bible—to show us the advantages of the right choice and the disasters of the wrong.

Watch Your Tongue

Proverbs is filled, for example, with admonitions that one should think before one speaks. On the positive side, cautious speech rewards the speaker in at least three ways.

It preserves him.

> Whoever guards his mouth and his tongue
> guards his soul from troubles.[4]

It blesses those who are looking for and need to hear a truthful, straightforward, thoughtful response.

> Whoever gives a right answer kisses the lips.[5]

It brings esteem to the speaker of the good word, adorns the moment in which it is spoken, and adds enduring value worth keeping.

> A word fitly spoken
> is like apples of gold in settings of silver.[6]

By the same token, thoughtless speech brings all kinds of dismay and disaster. It may simply result in sheer annoyance that antagonizes others.

> He who blesses his friend with a loud voice,
> rising early in the morning,
> it shall be counted a curse to him.[7]

More seriously it can cause hurt feelings and resentment.

> Like one who takes away a garment in cold weather,
> like vinegar on soda,
>
> so is he who sings songs to a heavy heart.[8]

And what appear to be careless words may be a mask for true malice.

> The words of a talebearer are like tasty morsels,
> and they go deep into the [hearer's] heart.[9]

> Like a madman hurling firebrands, arrows, and death,
> so is the man who deceives his neighbor and says,
> "Was I not joking?"[10]

> As the churning of milk brings butter
> and the wringing of the nose brings blood,
> so the forcing of anger brings strife.[11]

All of these sayings illustrate the potential that words have for doing good and for doing ill. This is but one of the categories of human experience in which the principles of wisdom apply.

Prudence is a matter of anticipating—with goodwill and a moral conscience—the consequences of words and actions. It comes with the recognition that not only will one's actions affect others, they will inevitably come back to affect the actor, as we have already seen:

> Whoever digs a pit shall fall into it,
> and if he rolls a stone, it will roll back on him.[12]

Consider once again, then, the essential description of the simple fool. It is one of a few proverbs that appears twice in the book. Commentaries have various explanations for this duplication, and I do not want to make too much out of it—but surely if a teacher repeats himself, there may be something worth noting about what he's repeating:

> A prudent person foresees the evil and hides himself,
> but the simple pass on, and are punished.

The assumption underlying this proverb is that much (if not most) of the trouble we experience in our lives is preventable.

Who would walk knowingly into a catastrophe? The folly of the simple one is not that he has evil intentions, but that he will not pay attention to the warning signs. There is no better illustration of this than to examine how people fall prey to a fraud, the subject with which we opened this chapter.

The Sting

He who puts up security for a stranger will suffer for it,
while he who hates going surety is secure.[13]

The above proverb is not an attempt to deter generosity, but an alarm about the dangers of exposing one's own assets to cover someone else's liabilities. Specifically, it is an emphatic warning about "going surety" (literally "striking" as in clasping hands over a deal), providing security for someone else's debt, not as an investment but as a shield for their high probability of failure. To "hate" it, in this context, means going to any lengths to avoid it. There is here also a warning to steer clear from any opportunity that places one's assets—including good name and reputation as well as finances—into the hands of another. The sense of urgency is almost frantic. Note in these verses the interplay of hand and mouth, and how the mouth of the one puts him in the hands— i.e., at the mercy—of another.

My son, if you put up security for your neighbor,
have struck hands with a stranger,
If you are trapped by the words of your mouth,
are captured by the words of your mouth,
Do this now, my son, and get free,
for you have fallen into your neighbor's hand:
Go, humble yourself, and plead with your neighbor.
Do not permit your eyes to sleep or your eyelids to slumber.
Free yourself, like a gazelle from the hand [of the trapper],
like a bird from the hand of the fowler.[14]

Solomon is saying that whoever has entered this kind of contract is in a trap, whether he realizes it or not. It is urgent not to wait for the trap to close, but to do whatever one has to do to get out of it. If necessary one should take a loss, but escape while it is possible before all is lost. Some would argue that this attitude is overly cautious, even paranoid, but there is no question that whoever possesses it is less likely to be defrauded than one who does not.

Frauds have been around as long as there has been human commerce. The range of schemes is as wide as the range of human need and desire, from quack cures to investment mirages, from get-out-of-debt offers to fraudulent home repairs. In an age of technology in which anything seems to be possible, the most improbable inventions can be plausibly represented for purchase or investment. Pyramid schemes, from simple chain letters to sophisticated offerings of "securities" or unorthodox forms of "insurance," are enduringly popular and claim new victims every day. The Internet, offering the instantaneous digital transfer of information and funds, provides swindlers a new and efficient tool for exploiting the simple.

Every kind of hoax and confidence game has been described and analyzed by law enforcement, legislatures, and consumer protection groups. Most of those that are currently being run have been tracked and documented, and no one need fall prey to them. Anyone who is willing to put forth a reasonable effort can find out (from the Federal Trade Commission, the Federal Bureau of Investigation, the Better Business Bureau and other sources) whether the "opportunity of a lifetime" is bona fide or fraudulent.

One particular scam that has been propagated over the Internet and through e-mail in recent years provides us with a way of examining how *any* fraud works. It offers membership in something called the World Currency Cartel.[15]

This "cartel" purports to have uncovered the "secret flaw" in the world currency exchange, and claims to be able to convert small amounts of money to huge amounts by passing it through the exchange markets. It only takes minutes for a transaction. Working at your computer for only a few hours a day, you can become a "MILLIONAIRE," the e-mail announcement screams. For a one-time membership fee, these people pledge to conduct the first transaction for you and also send you complete information on how to carry on doing it yourself. You can then go on to multiply your money as much as you wish "every day, every week, every month. All very LEGAL [*sic*] and effortlessly!" (I presume the breathlessly capitalized words are supposed to give us assurance, as though they represent some kind of oath.) Floaters of this scam eventually began to request their victims to fax their checks rather than send them through the mail, apparently hoping (falsely) that they can avoid the jurisdiction of US Postal Inspectors.

Despite their loud protests that this offer is completely "legal," the ethics of such an offer are readily impeachable, even if one takes it at face value. A currency exchange does not manufacture products or create wealth, but only trades money. The extraordinary profit these entrepreneurs are offering would have to come at someone's loss. Assuming that there *is* such a thing as a "secret flaw" in the system, there is no way such transactions could make one party a 400–500 percent profit without another party being robbed. Anyone who joined this club would be throwing in with a den of thieves, yet there is no doubt that many who consider themselves decent, honest, hardworking people have "invested" in this opportunity. Unhappily for them, their good faith investments get them nothing of value. They themselves are the ones who are robbed.

How can this swindle—or any swindle—ever be successful? How is it that people can be deceived by what an impartial observer would easily see through? On one level, the success of the scam depends on the persuasiveness of the sales pitch. Swindlers always present themselves as people of lofty motives.

> We at the World Currency Cartel would like to see a
> uniform global currency backed by gold. But, until then, we
> will allow a LIMITED number of individuals worldwide
> to share in the UNLIMITED PROFITS provided for by
> world currency differentials. [*sic*]

Every successful pitch has to have some statement of truth ("the hook") on which to hang the offer. In this case, the true statement is that exchange rates are in constant flux and that the manner in which one currency is exchanged for another is enormously complex. The fact that the whole process is a mystery to most people only aids the con artists. They do not have to be specific. By allusions (without explanations), they imply that they regard the recipient of the offer to be savvy, which of course, strokes the ego and keeps the "pigeon" from asking too many questions.

A vital part of the setup is the presentation of testimonials ("the plant") to assure the victim that "this is for real" and these are people who can be trusted. Some scams use "satisfied customer" testimonials. The "World Currency Cartel" hoax cites "editorial excerpts" from reliable sources such as the *New York Times*, *NBC Nightly News*, *Wall Street Journal*, etc. None of these excerpts are documented for ready reference, and grammatical inaccuracies alone make them suspicious. Sometimes those who use this technique take their citations from paid advertisements written like news stories that they themselves placed. Sometimes the news story of reference is genuine, but may not say what the fraud implies that it says, but one would have to check up on the documentation in order to find that out.

In order to keep the mark from becoming too inquisitive, there is, of course, an urgent need to reply *now* ("the bite"). The offer is limited to a certain number of respondents. Moreover, there is a limited-time special offer so that those who act now do not have to pay the full membership fee, but only a much lower "administrative fee," plus shipping and handling costs for the documents they will send.

All the persuasive aspects of the pitch still do not explain why otherwise decent people will involve themselves in something that they should know is wrong, and thus allow themselves to be taken by these crooks. Some victims stay on the hook for a long time or keep coming back for more. Why?

The answer is that every con man knows that there is a kink in human nature. He knows that we all want something for nothing and are willing to believe that there can be gain without effort. The bait for the hook is the appeal to our secret desires: whether for pleasure, for wealth and possessions, or for self-exaltation and personal esteem. (Or in the words of 1 John 2:16, "the lust of the flesh, the lust of the eyes, and the pride of life.") Whatever it is you want most, the con man has something to offer you—a shortcut. The simple will ignore the warning signs and go for the once-in-a-lifetime opportunity to get it all in one swoop. Beguiled by the promise of easy gain, he becomes willing to do something illicit. The confidence artist ensnares him through cords of his own greed and guilt.

The Heritage of the Simple

There are indeed consequences to every choice according to whether the deed is good or evil. It is possible that the simple one may learn from those consequences, but too often he is shielded from the unpleasant results of his choice by others who truly may be well intentioned. Their help is misguided. If the simple one does not experience pain from his mistakes and misjudgments, he is doomed to repeat them—and worse.

> The simple inherit folly,
> but the prudent are crowned with knowledge.[16]

As we look at the total description of the simple one, it is hard to avoid the similarities between this aspect of character deficiency and the foolishness associated with youth. Indeed, much of the book of Proverbs seems to be aimed toward the adolescent. We must not make too much of the comparison between the naive fool and the teenager because folly has no respect for age or class. Nevertheless, the comparison is there to be made. The simple one is, in some respects, someone who has a lot of growing up to do.

The goal of the maturing process is to gain the practical moral knowledge that will make one "prudent." *Prudence consists of making the wise choices that enable a person to be successful in life—and possessing enough self-discipline to live by those choices.* Those who do live this way accumulate that precious commodity, wisdom. Thus, "the prudent are crowned with knowledge." They get more of it, and it rewards them—in addition to the fact that the knowledge is its own reward.

On the other hand, folly is not a plateau but a slippery slope. In the fourth century AD. St. Augustine observed that the wages of sin is—*more sin!* The path of the naive fool will lead him into more serious and destructive forms of folly. If the simple one will not turn toward wisdom, and if nothing interrupts his course, he will eventually develop into a fool in the fullest sense of the word. The word "folly" in Proverbs 14:18 above, is *'ivveleth* (ih-ve-LETH), usually translated folly or foolishness. It speaks of an advanced stage of moral perversity specifically associated with the third degree of character deficiency syndrome. It represents the bankruptcy of moral character, the willful determination to take the wrong path. We shall consider it in detail in later chapters. For now, it is worthwhile to note that it is the inheritance of the simple one, i.e., it is what he has coming to him if he does not seek wisdom. There are only two ways to take: the way of truth, light, and life, or that of falsehood, darkness, and death.

The Obstacle to Wisdom

One obstacle that blocks the simple one's path to wisdom is his acute susceptibility to peer pressure. Solomon must have the simple one in mind when he warns,

> My son, if sinners entice you, do not consent.
> If they say, "Come with us!
> Let us lie in wait to shed blood.
> Let us ambush the innocent without cause.
> Let us swallow them up alive like *Sheol*
> and whole, like those that go down into the pit.
> We shall find all kinds of precious wealth.
> We shall fill our houses with loot.
> Throw in your lot with us.
> We shall all have one purse"—
> My son, do not walk in the way with them.
> Keep your feet from their path.[17]

This is not just a father commanding his son not to join a violent act of larceny. It is a plea to a young man to stay away from lawless influences altogether. It is an extreme example of why young people should be careful of their choice of friends and role models.

The bloodthirstiness of the outlaws' invitation is shocking. Why would anyone raised under any standard of decency, especially a king's son, enter into such an outrageous act as described above? He would do it in order to be accepted by a group. It is not a far-fetched scenario. In the Bible, one only has to go back as far as David's sons to see examples of how youths raised under high privileges and low controls can gravitate toward unwholesome friendships.[18]

The pledge of a share in "one purse" is more than a promise of money. It is an invitation into a fellowship, albeit the fellowship of a criminal gang. People will do many things, even illegal and immoral things, in order to keep from being alone or feeling alone. Peer approval is a powerful motivation, peer suggestion is an amazing persuader, and peer pressure can be an overwhelming force for anyone—especially for the simple one.

Add the love of money to the desire for acceptance, and the simple one may indeed find himself involved with gangsters to plot violence against innocent victims. Like Oliver Twist, who believed that the thief Fagin had his best interest at heart, so the simple one will tend to believe those who offer to let him in on "the deal of a lifetime." Easy pickings mean easy wealth. Callous souls will argue that anyone who can be easily robbed deserves to be robbed and that it is his own fault for being weak and vulnerable. Who is going to be open to such a vicious philosophy? The willing, gullible, simple fool—particularly the one who has not experienced the influence of a strong father figure in his life.[19] This latter point is a topic in itself, and we'll consider it in a later chapter.

Before we get there, however, we must see how the emptiness of the simple one's conscience leaves him vulnerable to the biggest, perhaps the deadliest, fraud of all.

The Gist

The chief characteristics of the simple fool are *gullibility, credulity,* and *moral dullness.*

Easy to fall. The basic difference of attitude between a simple person and a prudent one is *alertness.* Prudence looks ahead—with goodwill and a moral conscience—to the consequences of one's words and actions. The simple fool doesn't look, but plunges ahead and assumes luck will favor him.

Easy to scam. Every fraud or con exploits the weaknesses of the simple fool that are inherent in all of us.

Easy to manipulate. The simple one, because of underdeveloped and fluid moral convictions, is highly susceptible to *peer pressure.*

The road to folly. If the simple one does not turn toward wisdom, and if nothing interrupts his course, he will eventually develop into a fool in the fullest sense of the word.

For your consideration

- Why are frauds so successful at exploiting people who do not think of themselves as being gullible?
- Why is escaping from the consequences of a wrong moral choice the worst thing that can happen to the simple fool?

5

The Seduction of the Simple

The simple one is ruled by his urges. Of all the urges we experience, sex is one of the most powerful and primal. One of the good things God created, it holds profound possibilities both for creation and destruction. Its sinful misuse harbors some of the deadliest dangers known to the individual and to society. Yet the logic of sexual sin is deceptively compelling: How can something that feels so good, both physically and emotionally, ever be truly bad? Thus, sexual temptation is the epitome of the irresistible bait.

The naive fool's lack of judgment, together with his reluctance to curb his passions, makes him especially vulnerable to the snare of sexual immorality. The seventh and ninth chapters of Proverbs contain lengthy descriptions of the temptation and seduction of the simple one. Some might say that the story is rendered in stereotypes. I propose that these are *archetypes*. This is not about the battle of the sexes but about the war with sexual lust. In a larger sense, it is not even merely about sex, any more than the story of the Fall in Genesis 3 is about stealing fruit. *It is all about the allure of lawlessness and the danger of living according to passion rather than principle.*

Consider the nature of this play. If this were supposed to be a story about social realities, the sexual predator would be male and the victim female. Certainly, that is by far the more common scenario in any society. Why, then, does Proverbs put the focus on a far less common situation, the temptation of a young man by a seductress? No, it has nothing to do with sexism or sexual oppression. It is because the story is not about *social* realities, but it is about *moral* ones. Solomon takes a classic and timeless male sexual fantasy—perhaps using an actual case study of a young man whose fantasies were apparently fulfilled—and as we shall see, plays up all its luscious elements. His graphic poetry is not for prurient purposes, but in order to show the simple fool vividly that if his secret dreams were to come true, they would be a nightmare.

The simple one, in his typically naive pursuit of pleasure, starts out with the itch that must be scratched. When I say naive, it is in the context of moral character. Our fool is probably not naive about the *facts* of sex and the possibilities it holds for pleasurable experience. Neither is he naive in the sense of innocent ignorance of godly moral standards. He knows the commandments, and he has been taught that sex outside of marriage is wrong. This kind of naivety is rather a refusal to look ahead and foresee the consequences of breaking God's commandments.

The Harlot

As we dissect the seduction of a simple fool, first have a look at a description of the harlot, the panderer to lust. It is perhaps a sign of our time and our disconnection from our historic moral moorings that a number of synonyms for whore, including the tersely vulgar "ho," have become common street slang for females in general. The archaic euphemism "harlot" seems quaint, almost genteel alongside any of these vulgarisms. Nevertheless, it is the term we prefer in this context in order to remind us that we are dealing with an *archetype* capable of innumerable variations. Indeed, the harlot in the story would not be recognized on the street for what she is. She is a prostitute not by occupation, but by character. Her character is known not by her social status, but by her behavior.

> A woman of folly is brazen.
> She is simple and knows nothing.
> For she sits at the door of her house
> on a seat in the high places of the city,
> to call to those who pass by,
> who are going straight on their way.[1]

The harlot is identified in Proverbs 9:13 as "a woman of folly" (literal Hebrew phrase). She is called *a foolish woman* in the KJV, but this passage is not merely about a streetwalker. The ESV and NIV interpret the phrase as a personification: "The woman Folly." That comes closer to the mark. The woman described here is not merely a prostitute for hire. She's not even a particular female individual at all, and she's certainly *not* a symbol for women in general. She is rather a *type* of a certain kind of social influence that tempts the simple. The reason we know that she is a type and not a specific individual is that she is portrayed in direct contrast to Wisdom (9:1–12), which is also depicted as a woman. The "woman of folly" here is a figure representing *all* persons and entities that seek to lure the simple into immoral sexual involvement. *She represents every social influence that panders to lust.*

It doesn't particularly matter at this point whether the motive is pleasure, profit, or politics. The harlot here *could* represent prostitution, which appears in every age and culture; or she could represent the multibillion-dollar pornography industry, which has exploded in our information era to an extent unprecedented in history. She may represent the total commercialization of sex that has grown to dominate our whole culture, or she could simply represent that large segment of an affluent society that thinks the purpose of life is to "party."

Notice what this passage says about her so far:

She is "of folly."[2] The word here is different from the ones we've seen so far in our discussion. It speaks of the *self-confident* kind of folly associated with the second degree fool, whose character we will describe in later chapters. In this case, the word refers to her casual attitude about sex and her lack of concern for the immorality of extramarital sex.

She is "brazen." The KJV uses the word *clamorous* (not to be confused with glamorous). The NAS offers the adjective "boisterous," the NET calls her "brash," while the ESV and NIV simply says she's "loud." The point is that she makes a noisy scene. She is not subtle at all in her approach, at least in the sense of being understated. She does not care if polite society finds her offensive, so long as she is noticed. Subtlety may lure the *wise* away from wisdom, but it would be wasted on the *simple*. The object is to get his attention, and the tactic is successful. Internet surfers know that certain words typed into a search engine will bring up, along with the index of web sites, banner advertisements with some of the crudest sexual images imaginable. They are designed to catch the attention of the simple—the male in particular—arouse his curiosity, and entice him to lust. Salacious billboards and garish neon signs advertising "XXX Video" and "Foxy Ladies" mar the vistas of our highways because there are so many simple fools who are drawn in by such crude stuff. It would not be there if it did not work.

She has business savvy. Notice how she positions herself "in the high places of the city," at a place of high visibility, easy access, and low accountability. She is maximizing her ability to attract a clientele. This proves that folly is not a result of inferior intellect. The harlot is morally foolish, but not lacking intelligence. If there is a profit in it, this person knows how to make it. Her very position in the marketplace seems to give her an aura of legitimacy. After all, if she were that bad, "they" wouldn't let her set up business in such a prominent place, would they? There is actually a marketing strategy at work to increase the social acceptability of immorality. The more people see something displayed in public, the less shocking it becomes, and the more used to it they become. Eventually, they expect it to be there. Even if they do not personally partake of these products and services, they begin to regard those who want to remove them as priggish agitators. What happens, for example, when a mainstream magazine displays a sensationally indecent cover that transgresses even the lax boundaries of bad taste to which we have already become accustomed? There is liable to be a greater public outcry against the store that removes the magazine from its front rack than there will be against the magazine with the salacious cover. What happens when a motion picture that shocks its audience with debased humor, depraved violence, or defiled sex proves popular and makes money—or even if it loses money but gains publicity? It is admired for breaking long-standing taboos.

She herself is "simple." Isn't that ironic? Streetwise as she is, she is just as unthinking, gullible, and morally naive as her "mark"— especially in that she is unaware that there will come a day of reckoning for her deeds, her sin. There is pathos in the statement, "she is simple." The harlot is not purely and simply a villain here. There is a sense in which she is as much victimized by the lust-monger's misdeeds as he is by hers. Exploitative businesses damn their own proprietors as much as their customers. They seem unaware of what their traffic in immorality is doing to themselves. Do the students who pay their way through school by by selling sex videos on the Internet think they can sell their sexual identity so cheaply without consequence?

We must dissect the harlot's seductive pitch and see what is her appeal. There is much more here than what appears on the surface.

"Whoever is simple, let him turn in here,"
And as for him who lacks understanding, she says to him,
"Stolen waters are sweet,
and bread eaten in secret is pleasant."
But he knows not that the dead are there,
and that her guests are in the depths of *Sheol*.[3]

First, notice that the advertising here is directed to the lowest common denominator, the itch that must be scratched. There are plenty of these simple fools around to be customers, playmates, and marks. It is too much trouble to try to seduce the morally upright unless one enjoys the thrill of the chase (but that is another level of folly). Why spend time and effort tearing away at a set of tough-minded moral convictions? There is no profit in that. Go for the one who lacks understanding.

Ah, the lure of forbidden fruit. "When it's bad, it's better." It always has been hard to resist, even for the wise. For the simple, the temptation is virtually unbearable. "But he knows not that the dead are there," because the dark consequences of immorality are concealed, whether by ignorance, or by indifference, or by the malicious intent to seduce.

Turning back now to Proverbs 7—it is like watching a nature film. Here is the sequence where the predator entraps the prey and pounces upon it. The simple fool is enticed into making *three deadly decisions*. Each one is a step that leads him further into the trap. Each one makes it more difficult for him to change his mind, until finally it is virtually impossible for him to back out of the situation, even if he wants to.

Flirting with Temptation

Years ago, I heard it called the Principle of Propinquity, well-expressed in the line from *Finian's Rainbow*, "If I can't be near the girl I love, I love a girl I'm near." It sounds simplistic and humorous. In real life, it is neither. It has been the terrible downfall of many upright men and women who never imagined that they would lose their hearts to someone they should not have. They sacrificed their marriages and families, turned their backs on their own morals, and trashed their reputations. They never thought it would happen to them, but they were only fooling themselves. They should have known that spending unguarded time with someone of the opposite sex creates attractions and nurtures affections that could have been avoided from the beginning.

The first deadly decision is to take the path of temptation in the first place.

> For at the window of my house,
> through my lattice I looked out.
> And I watched among the simple,
> I perceived among the youths
> a young man without understanding,
> passing through the street near her corner.
> And he went the way to her house,
> in the twilight,
> in the evening,
> in the black night,
> in the darkness.[4]

"And he went the way to her house," knowingly, yet unthinkingly, as though he wants to only to be amused and titillated, thinking he can handle the pressure of temptation. There are several revealing details. He is alone, apparently with time on his hands. This tells us that he doesn't normally keep company with a group which prowls around looking for illicit excitement. Therefore, either this is something new for him that he knows nothing about, or else he has come out deliberately looking for a sinful thrill. His general behavior seems to indicate the former. It is erratic, as though he is feeling his way through, uncertain as to where he is going or what he is going to find.

Why, then, is he out here? Curiosity perhaps. Perhaps the harlot has already been flirting with him and giving him some kind of invitation, and he has come out to see what might happen next. Remember, he does not think ahead, and he has not made any of the moral decisions a young man of character must make before he's ever in a morally challenging situation. This kind of fool thinks he has to be placed under temptation before he can make a moral decision.

A note, then, to parents and spiritual leaders: It is not only desirable, but urgent to lead young people to make key moral decisions for themselves as early as possible—preferably in preadolescence and early adolescence. It is not enough to tell them about right and wrong or even to get them to agree to your standards. They must be persuaded to make up their own minds and to determine in advance that they will never violate their own chosen standards. The time to make a decision about premarital sex is not in the midst of a clinch on the couch while the parents are away. The time to make a decision about alcohol or drug use is not at a party surrounded by a raucous group of peers. Those who make their moral decisions early are not invulnerable, but they will not yield as easily to temptation. Those who wait until they are tempted are sitting ducks.

It is interesting how consistent human behavior is across time and culture when it comes to flirtation. The setting of this story may be Israel in the ninth century bc, but the situation is recognizable in any contemporary gathering place. Males try to be cool and females try to be coy. The whole point is to get the other party to commit first so one will not make a false move and be humiliated by a rejection. So the young fool is out on the street thinking that he is being cool. It is exciting just to be out here, and he is not doing anything wrong or illegal—yet. He deceives only himself.

Here is the simple fool, then, aimlessly loitering in the neighborhood. What is the young man doing out on the streets after sunset? Why is he still out so late into the night? Even a casual observer would know that he must be scouting for mischief, but he still seems to be trying to hide his own motives from himself.

There is also in the poem a sense of the passing of time. He arrives early in the evening, at the twilight. Then he dawdles in the area until it is late, until the darkness of night. This is all the more striking in the context of the ancient society in which the drama is played. This may require a little effort of historical imagination, for even though we are only a few generations away from a similarly agrarian culture, we can scarcely conceive a world where *no one* goes out at night for any wholesome purpose. Moreover, the contemporary reader must consciously remember the obvious fact that we are reading about a world without electrical power. The young man in Solomon's poem is strolling through narrow city streets where there are *no lights at all.* We moderns can hardly imagine the darkness.

The darkness is an important element in this scene. Sin, especially sexual sin, likes dark environments. Darkness alleviates inhibitions. Darkness creates anonymity. Darkness fosters the illusion that sex is purely a physical act in which the soul is not involved. Darkness prevents the simple one from seeing the obvious flaws in the argument that there can be "safe sex" outside of marriage. If the simple one persists in his quest for the ultimate sexual experience, there will probably come a time when he is sufficiently desensitized to his conscience so that daylight will be as good as darkness. Until then, however, the darkness has always provided a sense of safety and security for the practice of immorality. This, too, is a lie.

Sniffing the Bait

> And there, a woman comes to meet him,
> dressed like a harlot, crafty of heart.
> She is loud and defiant—
> her feet never remain at home.[5]

He is now in deep trouble. Unfortunately, he does not know it, *because his second deadly decision is to make contact with the harlot.* He engages the woman in conversation—or, to be more accurate, is engaged by her, for as you see she does not wait for him to make the first move.

> Now in the streets, now in the commons,
> Near every corner she sets her ambush.
> So she catches him and kisses him.
> With a shameless face she says to him:
> "I have peace offerings with me—
> Today I have paid my vows.
> So I came out to meet you,
> to seek your face,
> and I have found you."[6]

Her aggressiveness is breathtaking—especially considering the ancient Near Eastern culture that provides the setting for this story. Society would have frowned severely on this kind of forwardness. The picture is of a presumably devout Hebrew housewife acting more scandalously than a Canaanite cult prostitute. She obviously is more than confident that the young man is going to be receptive to her pitch. Her boldness catches him completely off guard! The simple young man is overwhelmed and taken captive by influences he is not prepared to resist.

It starts with a dazzling appeal to the male's visual sense through the "attire of a harlot." The clothes she wears (and does not wear) accentuate her sensual features, expose at least enough of her to arouse his desire, yet conceal enough to be tantalizing. In that ancient society, such a woman would so dress in order to distinguish herself from other women. It is another mark of our time that girls and young women wear sensuous clothing in order *not* to stand apart from their peers. Social mores may change, but the game remains the same.

Once she has captured his eyes, she makes an outlandish physical play for him. She grabs him and kisses him. Men commonly fantasize about being irresistible to a woman who cannot keep her hands off him. For our simple young friend, this kind of sexual overstimulation short-circuits his rational decision-making process. For any alert and thinking person, the warning flags would go up immediately. This should be the cue to run away, an alarm screaming that he must escape while he still can, just as young Joseph did (Genesis 39:12).

The simple one, however, overlooks the obvious and reacts according to his feelings and desires. From this point, his hormones are making his decisions for him. He is too busy enjoying his fantasy come true to comprehend what is happening or about to happen.

Observe next her remark about "peace offerings." What does it mean, and what is the point? It is a brilliant tactic. With this one oblique sentence, she makes the young fool perk up his ears and sets his lustful mind in motion, while disarming whatever religion-inspired scruples he may have.

First, she is inviting him to a sumptuous dinner. The peace offerings were hunks of meat from an animal offered as a sacrifice. One share went on the altar, one share went to the priests, and another share went home with the worshiper who brought the offering. It was an ample portion, and usually it was shared with family and friends in a large feast. The lady is home alone, however. With a pretense of innocence, even piety, she has an excuse to invite the simple fool to her home. She needs a man to come help her eat all this food, because it is unlawful and unholy to save any of it.[7] It would be a shame to let it go to waste.

The priority of values is turned completely upside down. She is talking about observing minute regulations regarding minor religious ordinances and using them as an opportunity to violate the seventh commandment of God's law. There is almost a suggestion that the sacrifice would sanctify the sin and make it the right thing to do! Like the Pharisees whom Jesus denounced with scalding words for "choking on gnats yet swallowing camels,"[8] many in the present day believe a show of piety or even mere civility absolves them of gross immoralities. It is an ancient and still contemptible form of hypocrisy.

There is more. She has just "been to church," so to speak. She presents herself as a devout worshiper of the LORD. Who would suspect any wrongdoing? If anyone should suggest aloud at this point that there is something improper about the relationship between these two, such a person would be coldly rebuffed and probably be accused of having a dirty mind for imagining such a thing. Thus religion provides a cover for immorality. Once again, the ancient Scripture uncovers a contemporary scandal.

Among ministers alone, the problem is alarming. A number of surveys suggest that up to 30 percent of male ministers in Protestant denominations have had sexual relations with women other than their wives.[9] These surveys only refer to the clergy. We shall not now inquire how many men and women have committed adultery within the fellowship of the church, or how many young people have lost their purity with other teens in their own youth group. We shall only acknowledge, grieving, that it happens and that many persuade themselves that God has permitted and even approved their liaisons.

There is yet one more sensual implication in her innocent-sounding announcement that, "I have peace offerings with me—today I have paid my vows," and it is explosive. The young man would not fail to recognize it, and it would bring hot blood to his cheeks. In order to offer her sacrifices and pay her vows, she had to be ceremonially clean. This was a polite and "innocent" way of telling him that she was finished with her menstrual period. In other words, without saying anything lewd or off color, she is telling him that she is ready for sex and wants it. One must give her credit: she is good at this—very good. Virtually without effort, she has effectively disabled what moral defenses the gullible young fool may have had, at the same time raising his level of lust still higher, and all she has done is invite him to dinner—a sacred dinner at that.

The harlot's most dangerous asset, it is clear, is not her physical attractiveness but her "crafty heart." Yes, we did observe earlier that she was brazen and lacked subtlety, but this is something different. The word "crafty" or "subtle" here is the same word used to describe the serpent who tempted Eve[10]—who was nothing if not successful. The harlot goes on to tell him,

> I have spread my bed with tapestry,
> colored sheets of Egyptian linen.
> I have perfumed my bed with myrrh,
> aloes, and cinnamon.
> Come, let us take our fill of love until morning,
> let us delight ourselves with love.[11]
> For my husband is not at home—
> He has gone on a long journey.
> He has taken a bag of money with him.
> He'll be away for two weeks.[12]

Wait a minute: this is *subtle*? Actually, when it says she is "subtle" or "crafty of heart," it means that she intuitively knows what it takes to seduce her fool. First, she engages his lustful imagination with a lush description of her bed and how she's prepared it. Her choice of words is exquisite. The verb "spread" is unexpectedly evocative, isn't it? (The Hebrew expression literally is "with spreads I have spread my bed.") "Let us take our fill of love," the language of feasting blended with that of affection, covering over the stark ugliness of lust with a facade of romantic beauty.

The romanticizing of sin is something that draws many women into immorality, deadening the conscience with an appeal to love—the good that counterbalances the evil. It is a time-honored theme in literature, from *Anna Karenina* to *Madame Bovary*, from *The Great Gatsby* to *The French Lieutenant's Woman*, because it rings true to human experience. (A more postmodern trend is represented by the bestselling *Fifty Shades of Grey*, written by a woman for a female market, which seemingly finds a way to romanticize even sadomasochistic sex.) The subtext of many a magazine article directed toward women and teenage girls is that if she will give her guy great sex, he will give her deep love. The romantic appeal is not lost altogether on the typical lusty male, however. One of the things that makes a woman appealing to a man is her romantic outlook and her need for affection. *Vive la différence!* It is something that God created and, when used as God intended, is a righteous and good thing. Here, however, we see it exploited in a most unrighteous way.

Having filled the simple one's ears with words sweet and fragrant, the harlot abruptly switches her approach. I think the very tone of her voice here changes from melodious and cooing to flat and businesslike. In blunt contrast to her lyrical proposition, she refutes the only rational objection the simple fool has left in his head, namely that they might get caught. No, no, she assures him. The "old man" is gone on a business trip and won't be back for at least two weeks! Subtlety does not consist only of unspoken implications. Any good salesman knows when to be indirect, and when to be direct and press for the sale. Meanwhile, the simple one is prone to take every word, every promise, and every implication at face value.

> With her enticing speech she makes him yield.
> With her flattering lips she seduces him.[13]

The script is not the main thing here. What is happening is that she is reeling him in with sweet talk. "She makes him yield," she compels him, almost forces him into bed. The magnetism of lust cannot be overestimated.

Consider male psychology for a moment. What man thinks he is susceptible to flattery? Most men have been conditioned to think that women are the ones who can be seduced by smooth words. They may acknowledge that other men may be suckers, but most believe that they themselves are immune to flattery. A wise man, however, knows that no one is immune. Whoever thinks he cannot be cajoled into doing something he knows he ought not do is the very man who is in the most danger.

The story told in this passage is so vivid that we must remember: it is not primarily about a literal situation in which a promiscuous female entices a gullible male into bed with her. There is a larger point being made. This is a study of *moral psychology*, a personification of sexual temptation. It is also a study of *moral sociology*, portraying the way a whole industry—indeed a whole culture—has learned how to manipulate illicit lust for fun and profit. Through this story, we may observe how the prime target for this kind of manipulation is the simple fool, the soul with the underdeveloped character. We would like to make sure none of us joins him because his fate is not a happy one.

So far we have seen only two of the fatal decisions of the simple one. The third, which closes the trap, is yet to come.

The Gist

The sex trap.

- "The naive fool's lack of judgment, together with his reluctance to curb his passions, makes him especially vulnerable to the snare of sexual immorality."
- Three prolonged passages in Proverbs (in chapters 5, 7, and 9) describe the dangers of living according to passion rather than principle.
- Just as wisdom is personified as a woman, so also is folly—but folly is a harlot, who represents every social influence that panders to lust.
- The simple fool makes three decisions that lead to his destruction:

    1. Willingly to take the path of temptation.
    2. Willingly to engage in behavior that stirs lust.
    3. [*See the next chapter.*]

For your consideration

The scenario depicted by Solomon is not really the most common occurrence—and it was not so in Bible times either. Why then do you suppose Solomon uses it? What is his point?

Darkness

From the most ancient times, darkness has provided a literary image associated with ignorance, superstition, evil, a cover for nefarious activity, and even a personification of the ultimate enemy. Darkness, both literal and figurative, is also a major theme in this chapter as an influence on behavior—not for the better. But is there something behind it more than a primitive fear of the unknown? A study carried out at the University of Toronto and detailed in an article in the journal Psychological Science (March 1, 2010) shows that people are more likely to cheat in a dimly lit room than in a bright one; and even wearing shades increases the likelihood of dishonesty.

- Why do you think physical darkness has this kind of effect on behavior?
- Has the presence of darkness ever influenced you do to do something that you would not have considered doing in the light? If you followed through, how did you feel about it afterward? If you did not, what caused you to turn away?

6

The Trap Closes

The story of the simple fool and his seduction continues. He has been the target of a smoothly executed enticement into illicit sex. Remember that the vivid picture of temptation presented in Proverbs does more than illustrate the dangers of sexual immorality. It also provides a paradigm of every kind of temptation and the ultimate downfall of those who yield to it. So far we can draw at least three general conclusions.

Forbidden fruit is never wholesome. It can be beautiful, tasty, and often compelling. It wouldn't be tempting if it looked poisonous, but poisonous it is. Immorality will not become less toxic just because it is legal, offered in the open market, and consumed by millions of others. An appealing appearance cannot change a vice to a virtue.

Tempters are never innocent. Jesus said, "Woe to the world because of the things that cause people to sin! Such things must come, but woe to the man through whom they come."[1] Why should anyone be trusted who is trying to get his neighbor to violate God's commandments? The motives of those who would draw others into doing wrong may vary, but they are never pure. For certain it is not because they love their neighbor as themselves. No matter what they say, they do not have the best interest either of the customer or the community in mind. Beyond the issue of motive, God will not hold anyone innocent who transgresses His law and will double the judgment on those who draw others into the vortex of their own damnation.

No one falls into sin accidentally. Not only do we ignore the warnings, we actively choose the path of our own destruction. It is a pathway paved with little compromises which may not be sinful in themselves, but which lead us gradually into the shadows where we do engage in acts that violate God's commandments. "If we say that we have fellowship with [God], and yet walk in darkness, we lie, and do not practice the truth."[2] The simple one is trapped in a delusion, having convinced himself that his pursuit of temptation is innocent and harmless. The first step of the simple toward wisdom is to stop lying to himself about the path he is on.

It is worth pausing at this point to explain what I mean by the term "sexual immorality," or what used to be called simply "fornication." Sex is not immoral, but neither is it morally neutral. There are rather both moral and immoral uses of sex—and almost everyone thinks so. It is a common but mistaken belief that the sexual revolution brought in a philosophy that anything may be done and everything is permitted.

There are those who express that philosophy; however, they usually only do so for a limited period in their lives, but then by their own admission they "grow up." Even people who cheat do not want to be cheated on. The sexual revolution did not do away with morality, but shifted its center of gravity from God to the self. This is all well and good so long as the self is cooperating (intentionally or not) with the wisdom God has embedded in his creation (see chapter 2). The self, however, is not a stable platform for morality. The boundaries of self-oriented morality are indefinite, subjective, and tend to shift frequently. Wisdom, therefore, will seek to understand *why* God in his commandments blesses some kinds of sexual activity and prohibits others.

The guiding principle of sexual morality is not, as some might think, the seventh commandment: "Thou shalt not commit adultery." There is a more elemental principle involved. Jesus clarified it when he was asked about the issue of divorce. He directed his questioners not to a commandment, but to God's purposes in creation: "From the beginning of the creation God made them male and female. For this cause shall a man leave his father and mother, and be united to his wife; and they two shall be one flesh." (Mark 10:6–8. See also Matthew 19:4, 5.)

The last of all beings to be created, humans were made in the biological likeness of animals, yet also in the very image and likeness of God (Genesis 1:26, 27). At the very least that means that biology is not the whole story of our lives. We were given the ability to choose how to direct our biological drives—whether for better or for worse. Moreover according to Jesus, God decreed marriage as the primal institution of humanity. There is deliberation, choice, and commitment: "For this cause shall a man leave…and be united to his wife." Thus the pairing of a man and a woman is not merely a mating, even a mating for life. It is much more than that: "They two shall be one flesh."

The marriage bond is the foundation of every other relationship and all social order. Out of it grow relationships between parents and children, brothers and sisters, relatives and neighbors, and so on. Sex is only a part of the marriage bond but it is a crucial part, and also one that is possibly the most vulnerable because of the volatile nature of sexual desire. At its core, then, sexual immorality is an attack on the marriage bond: whether to weaken it before the marriage even begins; or to break it after a marriage has been made; or to discredit and devalue marriage as a social institution.

The young man in our story has put all these concerns aside, for as we have seen he is not looking for gratification of his lusts with a single woman, nor with a prostitute, either of which would constitute the lesser sin of fornication. He is about to commit adultery with a married woman. Let it be emphasized again, the point of this story is not to say that men are naïve and women are evil. It is rather to draw our attention to just how much trouble a simple fool can get into despite the fact that he does not mean to.

It is time now to return to the tragic story in Proverbs 7 and see it to its bitter conclusion. We will see that for all its hapless, humorous dimensions, simple folly is no laughing matter, but is the cause of great hurt and heartbreak.

The Third and Fatal Decision

Thus far in this story/paradigm, the simple fool—depicted here as a young male—has made two fateful, deadly decisions. First, he decides to take the path that puts him on a collision course with full-frontal temptation. Second, he directly engages that temptation in a ridiculous test of his own willpower. There is no contest! He now makes his third and most disastrous decision. Up until now, he could have walked away—perhaps not completely clean, but at least not thoroughly soiled. But *now he willingly surrenders to the temptation.* He follows her home for a night of pleasure, unaware of the ultimately disastrous consequences.

> Immediately he goes after her,
> as an ox goes to the slaughter,
> or as a criminal in chains is led to punishment,
> till an arrow strikes his liver;
> as a bird rushes into the snare,
> because he does not know it will cost his life.[3]

Though he goes with her of his own choice, the picture here is of a man being *led* away—stupidly, forcibly, and tragically. He is led away *stupidly*, like an animal to the slaughter, with no inkling of the fate that awaits him. He is led *forcibly*, like a felon being led away in handcuffs to jail, because he will not be able to avoid the consequences and will not like them when they descend on him. He would resist or escape if he could, but there will be no escape from judgment. He is led away *tragically*, as a bird flying into a snare, about to be shot through by the hunter's arrow. Like the bird, he might have eluded the trap if he had flown away from it. Instead he eagerly rushes in for the bait, and he will pay with his life—probably figuratively, but perhaps literally.

So an exotic and mysterious story has a chilling end, but it does not have to be this way. Elsewhere it is told how *wisdom* will protect the young person from the Harlot,

> [whose] lips drip like a honeycomb,
> and her mouth is smoother than oil,
> but at the end she is bitter as wormwood,
> sharp as a two-edged sword.
> Her feet go down to death,
> her steps lay hold on *Sheol*.[4]
> She does not consider the path of her life.
> Her ways are unstable, and she does not know it.[5]

> Remove your way far from her,
> do not go near the door of her house,
> lest you give your honor unto others,
> and your years unto the cruel,
> lest strangers be filled with your wealth,
> and your labors go to the house of an outsider,
> and you mourn at the last,
> when your flesh and your body are consumed.[6]

Interestingly, there is no direct mention of legal consequences, despite the fact that under the law of Moses adultery was a capital offense, and there were criminal and civil penalties attached to less heinous kinds of fornication. This may indicate that in the days of Solomon such laws were rarely enforced. Or it may simply reflect the focus of the wisdom literature on practical consequences rather than formal ones. Either way, what is depicted is the contrast with what wisdom offers. It is the opposite of longevity, honor, wealth, health, and life (see Proverbs 3).

A wasted life, poverty, depression, sickness, and death. Really? Is this not just moralistic hyperbole, the exaggeration of do-gooders trying to frighten young people away from essentially harmless fun, the most natural form of recreation there is?

In the first place, there are some old-fashioned social consequences of sexual immorality: the failure of trust, the loss of honor, and the provocation of anger, jealousy, hatred, and vengeance.[7] Our popular culture seems to believe these issues are no longer relevant in a liberated era, but jealousy is as stubborn and unyielding a vice as lust. It is a factor that those who are simple do not consider but the prudent person observes: people will be hurt and offended by an immoral deed, and they will take it personally. Some of them will want revenge. People still commit jealous murder when they cannot otherwise cope with the anger of betrayal.

The loss of wealth is another consequence that almost no one in our society today considers, but it is real. In the first place, shameful practices can themselves become expensive habits. Millions of dollars are spent in our nation every week on prostitutes, pornography, phone sex, strip clubs, and the like. These are dollars which are lost for family necessities, education, investment, charity, purchase of durable goods, wholesome recreation, or any edifying purpose at all. This does not include the countless man-hours that are squandered for all productive purposes, which can never be regained for the glory of God or the betterment of human life.

Fornication can also be costly if it is the bait that lures the simple into a swindle. Perhaps sex is employed to distract the victim from the trap, or perhaps the sex is itself the trap designed to extort money from the victim. There are also social costs.

Adultery still breaks up marriages, and ruined marriages are always costly, not only in money but also in emotional and social costs, many of which have been masked but not eliminated by no-fault divorce laws. There is no greater possibility for loss of wealth, however, than that which goes along with the loss of *health*, when "you mourn at the last, when your flesh and your body are consumed."

In Solomon's day, people were familiar with the scourge of gonorrhea and possibly also some syphilis-like disease—afflictions that are hideous, devastating, and life-shortening. Early symptoms of gonorrhea include painful urination and pus-like discharges. The infection expands throughout the reproductive tract of both male and female, causing sterility. Carried by the bloodstream, it can also infect other parts of the body, crippling the patient for life. It is particularly devastating to a woman because it can spread through the uterus into her abdominal cavity, producing life-threatening peritonitis.

Additionally, an infected mother can infect her baby as it passes through her birth canal. The gonococci invade the infant's eyes and within a few days create a horrible, pus-ridden infection that causes blindness. This disease has been known since ancient times as the leading cause of infantile blindness. Jesus's disciples may have had this fact in mind when, confronted with a man born blind, asked, "Who sinned, this man or his parents, that he was born blind?"[8] A common sight to this day in many Third World nations is the blind beggar along the roadside, whose plight most likely *is* the result of the sin of one or both of his parents. The problem is less severe in modernized societies, not because gonorrhea is no longer a threat, but because it is now routine medical practice to anoint the eyes of *all* newborns with antiseptic drops as a prophylactic measure.

Syphilis, a comparatively modern disease of mysterious origins, is even more insidious, appearing in stages that cause acute symptoms that then disappear making it look as if the disease is healed. It is not. It may lie dormant for years, but eventually it comes roaring back to ravage the body with symptoms ranging from heart disease to paralysis, from crippling pain to insanity.

In the 1940s, medical science thought that first sulfa drugs, then penicillin would eradicate these afflictions. In the 1960s and '70s there came, along with the much-heralded "sexual revolution," an explosion of sexual plagues with new varieties and multiplied numbers of patients. Since many felt that the familiar term "venereal disease" implied a Victorian moral judgment on liberated behavior, a new nonjudgmental but descriptive term was coined—sexually transmitted diseases, or STDs. It seems that in every era, a new euphemism is coined that makes people feel better about a problem caused by sinful behavior.

Society probably needed a more expansive umbrella term anyway. So far medical science has identified some *twenty-five* diseases that are transmitted exclusively or almost exclusively through sexual contact. Some are humiliating, irritating, and acutely inconvenient—words that describe the milder manifestations of genital herpes. (In the freewheeling 1970s, we began hearing a lot about "the heartbreak of herpes," an expression that seems quaint today.) Some STDs are painful and scarring. Some are crippling. A few are fatal—AIDS having become the most notorious. Meanwhile, we still have the "big two"—although like yesterday's rock stars, they no longer grab the headlines. The old scourges have produced new strains that are increasingly resistant even to the most powerful antibiotics.

Who is carrying these diseases? The Center for Disease Control estimates that one in five Americans between the ages of fifteen and fifty-five are currently infected with one or more *viral* STD. They also estimate that twelve million Americans are newly infected each year and that sixty-three percent of them are under the age of twenty-five. This does not include *bacterial* infections, including a plague now rampant among young women: Chlamydia, the bacteria most often responsible for pelvic inflammatory disease (PID), which can result not only in life-long chronic pain but also permanent infertility.

No doubt that the scariest of all is the HIV virus, cause of acquired immune deficiency syndrome, or AIDS. First noted in 1981, by 1993 it had killed over 160,000 victims. In the western world, it initially afflicted—overwhelmingly—the male homosexual population (for a little while in the early 1980s, it was called "gay plague") and intravenous drug users. The virus did not discriminate between immoral behaviors, however, and also spread into the heterosexual population through sexual contact and also infected many innocents through tainted blood supplies. Although the life expectancy of those who carry the virus has lengthened considerably through advances in medication, there remains no cure, but a virtual sentence of death upon those infected by it.

If the proliferation of happiness-ruining, life-shortening STDs were not disturbing enough, scientific evidence is mounting to confirm a fact Solomon clearly knew—that teenagers are the most vulnerable and have the most to lose. For one thing, adolescence is a time of risk-taking and experimentation. When teens feel the freedom to take risks and experiment with sex, the results can be disastrous. The actions of one hormonally charged moment can affect a young life forever. Physiological factors involved in maturation also increase both susceptibility to and debilitating effects of STDs. Even for mature adults, the idea of "safe sex" is an oxymoron. For teenagers, it is a dangerous lie.

We should not be surprised. Sex has always had the power to give life through procreation. It also has always had the power to take it away, being an efficient vehicle for the transmission of disease. A man and a woman who marry as virgins and remain faithful to one another need never worry about its dangers, but sex outside the marriage covenant has always been a risky and sometimes deadly affair. There was no AIDS in the tenth century BC, but there was enough manifest danger to provoke Solomon to write this eerie warning of a deathbed scene, when "you mourn at the last, when your flesh and your body are consumed."

The sage is not finished. He relentlessly, passionately pleads with his simple son to listen and obey his warnings to stay away from…

> …the evil woman,
> from the flattering tongue of the immoral woman.
> Lust not after her beauty in your heart,
> neither let her take you with her eyelids.
> For by means of a harlot a man is reduced to a crust of bread,
> and the adulteress will prey on his precious life.
> Can a man take fire in his bosom,
> and his clothes not be burned?
> Can one go upon hot coals,
> and his feet not be scorched?
> So is he who goes in to his neighbor's wife.
> Whoever touches her shall not be innocent.
> People do not despise a thief
> if he steals to satisfy his soul when he is hungry,
> but if he be found he shall restore sevenfold,
> he shall give all the substance of his house.
> But whoever commits adultery with a woman
> lacks understanding.
> He who does it destroys his own soul.[9]

Suppose our simple friend enters the deceitful world of sexual freedom and still manages to dodge the AIDS bullet and every other STD out there. His chances are not good, but it is possible. Suppose that he does *not* contract a horrible disease. Suppose that he does *not* lose his livelihood or his fortune. Suppose he does what God says is wrong, and nothing terrible happens to him. Is he free?

> Can a man take fire in his bosom, and his clothes not be burned?

Can one go upon hot coals, and his feet not be scorched?

No, and neither is there any such thing as sin that does not have effects, but those effects may not be immediate or visible.

The Most Terrible Consequence

There is one awful consequence of sexual sin that we have not yet mentioned: guilt—*not merely guilt feelings, but real moral guilt.*

> Whoever commits adultery with a woman
> lacks understanding.
> He who does it destroys his own soul.

We might not think of the great King David as an example of the simple fool, but that is surely what he became when he took to bed the wife of one of his most loyal officers. It was a one-night tryst, an exercise in passion-as-analgesic for his boredom and her loneliness. It was not supposed to be a long-term relationship, but she became pregnant. Abortion—taking the life of the most innocent party in the affair, the easy way out for modern America—was not an option at all. Neither was an open, celebratory display of the affair, followed by a Hollywood-style divorce and remarriage. This was a society that still believed adultery was morally wrong and that marriages were sacred before both God and man. There would have to be a cover-up. King David set up the situation so that his faithful soldier could get some "R&R" at home, and so the pregnancy could be credited to the woman's husband.

The plan would have worked, too, except for one unpredicted flaw: the career soldier was a man of honor and character, whose own sexual self-control when drunk exceeded that of his boss's when sober. The cover-up having been dismally botched, the king decided that the only solution to his dilemma, the only way to preserve his public honor, would be if this man of true honor were to become a casualty of war—quickly, before the pregnancy began to show. He therefore plotted the battlefield death of the soldier, a murder by enemy, so that he could lawfully marry the widow who was already pregnant with his son.

Astonishingly, he pulled it off, and it seemed as though he would get away with it. There was no evidence, no "smoking gun." On the contrary, what the nation of Israel saw was the valiant death of a hero, richly honored posthumously. They saw their king show his honor for the hero by marrying his childless widow, considering it an act of generosity since the king already had several wives and obviously did not need another one. And they saw God's apparent blessing on their union with an early announcement of a new royal child on the way. Everything the public saw brought applause to a king whom the people viewed as compassionate (and potent). No one outside of a small, tight-lipped circle—probably no more than two or three people including the king—knew anything about the real story.

But God knew.

The issue lay hidden for about a year. A baby was born to the king's newest wife, and celebrations were held in honor of the new prince. Then God revealed everything to a prophet and sent him on a career-busting mission to confront the king: "You are the man."[10]

> Can a man take fire in his bosom,
> and his clothes not be burned?
> Can one go upon hot coals, and his feet not be scorched?

At this point, something remarkable happened, and it is something that separates David from other sinners whose stories are told in the pages of Scripture. The first response most people have when confronted with their sin is to justify themselves. David was a man in power. He could have flown into a rage, mocked the prophet's declaration, and demanded that proof be brought forward. Of course, the prophet had nothing but God's word. David could have arrested the prophet, charged him with slander against the king, and have him executed.

David did no such thing. Instead, when confronted with his guilt, he collapsed in grief over his sin. Though there was not a shred of evidence of sin or crime that would hold any weight in a court of law, the guilt weighing on David's heart had already crushed him. The prophet's revelation and condemnation of David's terrible secret came to David as a painful liberation from his inward agony, like the lancing of a boil. Psalm 32 reflects his experience:

> While I kept silent, my bones grew old
> as I groaned all day long.
> For day and night Your hand was heavy upon me—
> my moisture was turned to the drought of summer.[11]

He cries out to God for mercy, pleading with God,

> Let me hear joy and gladness,
> that the bones which You have broken may rejoice.
> Hide Your face from my sins,
> and blot out all my iniquities[12]

David truly did have a heart for God. What was so devastating to him was not the prospect that he might lose his family, wealth, health, or kingdom. It was that the guilt of his sin came between him and his God. For him, nothing was equal to the horror of that.

The subsequent history of King David demonstrates the lie that one can escape sexual sin without evil consequences. It is true that, although adultery was not only a sin but also a capital crime in ancient Israel, David was not required to forfeit his life. Some object that David should have stood trial, and the fact that he did not is evidence of a double standard—"It's good to be the king!" There is even the suggestion that God is impeachable for favoritism, or that His grace is cheap, providing an excuse for gross wrongdoing. The truth is that, political considerations notwithstanding, there was insufficient evidence to indict David, let alone convict him. The law required a minimum of two witnesses (Numbers 35:30, Deuteronomy 17:6, 19:15), and no one was compelled to testify against himself. The declaration of a prophet was not evidence in a court of law. David had covered his tracks extremely well. The probability that any witness with certain knowledge of his crimes could be found (other than the parties directly involved) would have been close to zero. Why, then, did God did not personally take David's life? That is consistent with God's usual forbearance with man's misdeeds. It is not God's way to exact temporal penalties for a felony. His judgments take a higher track, as is demonstrated in this story.

God indeed forgave David this great sin. Nevertheless, the repercussions from his adulterous choice shattered his family and ripped his kingdom apart. He was placed in dire peril, and many had to lay their own lives on the line in order to save his life and his throne. He endured the betrayal of his closest friends, an excruciating emotional ordeal in itself. He suffered a succession of wrenching tragedies that culminated in the violent death of his beloved but rebellious son, who nearly succeeded in a ruthless attempt to overthrow him.[13]

Even so, David considered himself blessed because God forgave his sin and he escaped with his soul.[14] Do not look for cheap grace if you dabble in sexual sin.

It's Not About Abstinence

What, then, should the passionate young man or young woman do with the sex drive that is destroying many a simple fool? The answer is found in the marriage bed. When we address young people on this subject, it is a great mistake, I believe, to stress mainly that sex is a dangerous activity from which to abstain. Far better is the biblical approach, which teaches that *sex is a precious gift that is worth the wait.* It is something to anticipate, not as a thing in itself, but as a wholesome part of a lifelong love relationship. On the other hand, sex is inherently an adult activity. Despite the sexually overheated messages constantly delivered throughout our culture, there is no harm and much benefit in delaying sexual experience to adulthood. For this purpose, marriage is biblically understood as an essential rite of passage.

> Drink waters out of your own cistern,
> and running waters out of your own well.
> Should your fountains be dispersed abroad,
> streams of water in the streets?
> Let them be only your own,
> and not for strangers among you.
> Let your fountain be blessed,
> and rejoice with the wife of your youth.
> As a loving deer and a graceful doe,
> let her breasts satisfy you at all times,
> and be seduced always with her love.
> And why will you, my son,
> be seduced by a forbidden woman,
> and embrace an outsider's bosom?[15]

This is a wonderfully voluptuous poem, sensuous and evocative without a hint of lewdness. Again we see that Lady Wisdom is no prude, and that righteous living does not require ascetic renunciation of pleasure. It is entirely possible to enjoy a full, active, joyful sex life without transgressing the law of God. The world defines safe sex as reduction of the risk of pregnancy and disease. The Bible defines safe sex as fidelity within a monogamous marriage. It is entirely protected from sexually transmitted disease and provides a protective and nurturing environment for the babies who will be born into it. The world seeks a kind of sexual freedom that has no boundaries, only license. The Bible extols the sexual freedom that can be played out within the protective boundaries of a lifelong covenant between a man and a woman.

There is nothing wrong with sexual license, so long as it is the marriage license.

The opening image in this proverb is that of a needless waste of water, of emptying the household storage tank (cistern) on to the city streets, or of bringing up water from the well just to let it run out. No one in his right mind would do such a thing. Water is a precious commodity in Bible lands, an arid region where droughts are common. Wisdom urges the simple one to think of sex, with all its pleasures and powers, as a precious thing, something to be savored, managed, and used wisely, not squandered aimlessly. This is one thing that it is right to be selfish and stingy about.

"Rejoice with the wife of your youth...let her breasts satisfy you at all times." There is certainly no prudery, no Victorian blush within these lines. It is the language of feasting. "Let her breasts satisfy you" is a vivid, deliciously physical figure of speech. The main point is not about a mammary fixation. "Her breasts" is a metonymy that refers to a wife's sexuality. The emphasis is on *her*, "*her* breasts" and not another's, with a focus on sexual exclusivity, on monogamy.

Still, the blessing on the sex itself is unambiguous. "Let her breasts *satisfy* you." There is nothing wrong with seeking and find-ing sexual satisfaction. There is no scolding tone, no depreciation of sex as a moral weakness or an unworthy issue that ought to be minimized in marriage. There is instead an invitation to "eat, drink, and be drunk with love,"[16] to indulge freely, happily, and without inhibition. There is no moral purpose served by a hus-band and a wife concealing their sexual needs and desires from one another. Through love, rather, let them serve one another.[17] There is such a thing as sexual freedom that has God's blessing, and it is within a marriage between one man and one woman.

The phrase "at all times" carries multiple meanings. It means *whenever*. There may be times, seasons, and circumstances in mar-riage that require one or both partners to suppress their desire, but that is not the norm. The sex drive is good, and sexual desire is meant to be fulfilled. It means *continually*, for God has granted great freedom of sexual expression to husband and wife, with no biblical restrictions on how many times they may make love in a week or a day. It means *only*, for marriage is an exclusive relationship. It also means *lifelong*, because God's manifest intention in the marriage bond is for a husband and wife to grow together in oneness of spirit, soul, and body.

In the Song of Solomon also the woman's breasts provide one of the memorable sensual images, but not by any means the only one. This astonishing love song weaves a lush variety of vivid imagery into its erotic tapestry: the lover's kiss on the lips; the graceful gazelle and the vigorous stag; the garden of luscious fruits and the vineyard of fine wine; the sensuousness and power of chariots and horses; and the evocative symbolism of the wall and the door. It is easy to see why this book is not read aloud in church very much. Even so, its place in the canon of Jewish and Christian scriptures is secure, even if interpreters and commentators do not always know how to deal with it.

Whatever else the book is, it is clearly a song that celebrates the marriage of a woman with a man in unmistakably erotic terms. The very presence of this book among the inspired books of the Bible demonstrates the divine blessing upon the act of love, a blessing present from the creation of the first man and woman (Genesis 1:28, 2:18–24). Significantly, the book is written from the feminine point of view. Thus we see also the divine favor upon a woman's enjoyment of pleasure as much as the man's, and (contrary to the way many modern feminists portray the biblical worldview) a wholehearted embrace of female sexuality.

Even so, the focus in the Song of Solomon is not on sex *per se*, but on the bond of love between a wife and her husband. It is about the process of letting go of the restrictions of youthful chastity, and the learning of trust between two souls who have made a full, unconditional commitment of love to one another—with sex being the physical expression of that love.[18]

Although it is not usually considered part of the wisdom literature, the Song of Solomon reinforces the message of wisdom within its celebration of marital love, and adds to it. The true secret of sexual satisfaction, the Song shows us, is not found in unbridled self-expression or self-indulgence. Neither is it found by trying to make sex into a mystical religious experience within itself. It is rather in purposeful self-control, and in awaiting the protection of a loving, covenant relationship. Three times the bride admonishes her maiden friends—evoking passion itself in her oath ("I adjure you by the gazelles and by the young does of the field")—telling them, "Do not stir up or awaken love until it pleases."[19] There is a right time, a right person, and a right set of circumstances for the expression of passion, and it is worth waiting for.

Finally, the above proverb addresses not only the young, but also those who may be tempted in their middle or later years to stray from their marriage vows. In this case, "rejoice with the wife of your youth" means to go back and rekindle the flame. The years of facing life's joys, challenges, and heartaches together need not diminish the physical and emotional enjoyment between husband and wife. On the contrary, the sweetness and satisfaction of erotic love in marriage can and should increase along with the sharing of experiences and memories.

To depart from this wisdom is to forsake the good life.

The Gist

Morality. Sexual morality is rooted, not in the prohibition of adultery, but more fundamentally in God's purpose in creating us in his own image.

Consequences. The consequences of sexual sin may be relational, social, economic, psychological, or physical. The most devastating consequence, however, is real moral guilt.

Preparation. Moral training of the young should not focus primarily on abstinence from sex as a dangerous activity, but putting sex in its proper place and waiting for its fulfillment as a precious gift.

For your consideration

- Why is it important that the biblical view of sex is rooted first of all not in the Commandments but in Creation?
- If sex is such a positive thing in the Bible, why is there so much said about its dangers?
- In the Song of Solomon, what is the significance of the refrain, "Do stir up or awaken love until it please"? How does that relate to the question of sexual satisfaction?

7

Better Wise Up

Once a person commits himself to an immoral deed, he will indeed have to bear the consequences of it. If, however, we can reach him before that happens, he can be delivered from these terrible effects. There is hope for the simple one.

Hope for the Simple

First we must get to the heart of the simple fool's problem. Appropriately enough, it is simply stated: He has a wayward will.

How long, O simple ones, will you love simplicity?[1]

He does love his carefree approach to life. Remember the song from the Disney movie *The Lion King*, "Hakuna Matata,"—no worries? That is the theme of the simple fool. He loves what he thinks is an uncomplicated lifestyle, and he is turned off by discipline. In his carelessness, he is caught in a trap from which he cannot escape. Listen to his lament:

> How I have hated instruction,
> and my heart despised reproof!
> And I have not obeyed the voice of my teachers,
> nor inclined my ear to those who instructed me.[2]

He had hated instruction and despised reproof because discipline means bridling one's appetites. He would have had to deny himself some of the pleasures he desired. In his immaturity, the idea of delayed gratification was beyond him. Why did he not listen to his teachers or pay attention to people who were trying to instruct him? It is as simple as this: he did not want to be told he was wrong.

Therefore, since he prefers blissful ignorance to uncomfortable truth, he can't understand the danger he is in until it is too late.

> The turning away of the simple [from wisdom] shall slay them.[3]

He is drawn, for example, to illicit sex (as represented by the harlot) not because he is in open defiance of the moral law, but because,

> He knows not that the dead are there,
> and that her guests are in the depths of *Sheol*.[4]

He does not understand that his actions will have such dire effects. It never occurs to him, and that is the depth of his tragedy.

Nevertheless, there is hope for him—if we can get his attention. That is why in Proverbs, wisdom, like lust, is also depicted as a woman in the marketplace trying to gain the notice of the simple.

> Wisdom shouts in the street!
> She lifts her voice in the marketplace.
> She cries out at the busy intersections.

At the entrances of the city gates she speaks her words.[5]

What a wonderful and unexpected word picture! Wisdom is no stuffy, prudish snob. She is right out there in the marketplace, competing on the street level, elbow to elbow amidst all the illicit and sleazy temptations, working just as hard as they are to get the attention of those who need her services. The point is that wisdom is not hidden, camouflaged, or mysterious. On the contrary, wisdom is out in public, in plain view and available to anyone who will look and listen.

Becoming wise is not about abiding in ivory towers, peering through stained glass, or wearing sackcloth robes. One need not enroll in an expensive school, attend an intense seminar, join some cloistered order, or survive a grueling obstacle course to attain it. The simple one is often deterred by thinking that wisdom—specifically, moral discipline—is too lofty, too complicated, and too difficult for an ordinary person to attain. Therefore, he is willing to lower his standards and never even ask whether he could live a better life. The simple fool assumes that being good is an impossible dream, so he'll settle for just being "okay" if he can. Wisdom is there, however, and if she can get the simple one's attention, half the battle for his soul has been won.

The Education of the Simple

We need a reminder here. We all start from the point of simpleness. We are all naive. None of us by nature is either wise or prudent. These things must be learned. Moreover, we need the help of teachers. Here's the progression:

God is the Source for our wisdom.

> For the LORD gives wisdom:
> From His mouth come knowledge and understanding.[6]

We already saw in a previous chapter the intimate relationship between God and wisdom.[7] The important point here is that God does not hide wisdom or make it obscure. The phrase "from His mouth" indicates the importance of the Scriptures, specifically the law (Torah) as the source of God's gift of wisdom. The psalmist confirms this truth when he testifies that meditation on the laws and commandments of God have made him wiser and more understanding than his enemies, his teachers, and even the ancients.[8]

> Your word is a lamp to my feet and a light to my path.[9]
> How can a young man cleanse his way?
> By taking heed according to Your word.
> Your word have I hidden in my heart,
> that I might not sin against You.[10]

The individual must be motivated to acquire wisdom.

> Get wisdom! Get understanding!
> Forget it not, nor turn away from the words of my mouth.
> Forsake her not, and she shall protect you.
> Love her, and she shall watch over you.
> The first thing of wisdom is: Get wisdom,
> And with all your getting, get understanding.
> Exalt her, and she shall promote you.
> She will bring you honor when you embrace her.[11]

Wisdom is something that can be gained, and it is worth having for its own sake. Wisdom will bless the one who has it, but the blessings will only come after wisdom has been obtained, and that takes will and effort. To win a championship, an athlete must embrace training. The first thing of wisdom is not to gain the benefits *from* wisdom, but to seek the benefit *of* wisdom.

Parents are the most important channels of wisdom.

> Hear, my children, the instruction of a father,
> and give attention that you may gain understanding,

for I give you good doctrine.
Do not forsake my law.
For I was my father's son,
tender and the only son in the eyes of my mother.
He taught me also, and said to me:
"Let your heart hold fast to my words.
Keep my commands, and live."[12]

My son, keep your father's commandment,
and do not forsake the law of your mother.
Bind them continually upon your heart,
and tie them around your neck.
When you go, it will lead you.
When you sleep, it will protect you.
And when you awake, it will talk to you.[13]

Notice how in the latter stanza the parents assume the role of lawgiver, and their commandments are compared to the divine commandments. This is a solemn responsibility passed on from generation to generation, marking the parents—especially the fathers—as the primary educators of their children. Consider the far-reaching implications of this familiar yet not well-understood proverb:

Train up a child in the way he should go,
and when he is old he will not depart from it.[14]

Many a parent has looked to Proverbs 22:6 as a promise and clung to it for hope that their children would eventually turn out all right—especially if they have departed from the faith and morals in which they were raised. I would not at all criticize that motive or diminish that hope. Still, I am not am not saying anything that careful scholars have not been saying for a long time when I point out that this is not quite what the verse is saying.

First of all, it is not really a promise to frustrated parents so much as it is a verifiable observation about character education. The verb the KJV translates as "train"[15] has not so much to do with ongoing instruction or training as it does inauguration and dedication. It is related to the word *channukah*, which is used of the dedication of Solomon's temple and of the restored temple,[16] as well as the Jewish celebration that commemorates the temple's rededication under the Maccabees. The remainder of the first line, literally, is "according to his way," but let us not understand this subjectively. Remember that in Proverbs, any way but the Way of Life is a way of death. We have seen how when the simple one chooses his own way the results can be catastrophic.

What, then, does the verse mean? I do not propose something radically different from the conventional, traditional interpretation, but I believe the emphasis is somewhat different.

> *Dedicate* a child in the way he should go,
> and when he is old he will not depart from it.

We are using the word "dedicate," not in a ceremonial way to highlight some ritual, but in a much fuller and broader sense. The verse is not really about providing instructions so much as it is about instilling purpose. Every individual has a purpose for life, a destiny to fulfill in his life. It is something that should be instilled in children at an early age. Godly parents need to dedicate their children to Him and proceed to raise them up within that godly purpose.

Yes, every child should be brought up in obedience and respect for rightful authority, with respect for the rights of others, with due knowledge and obedience to the divine commandments, and with sure knowledge and understanding of their parents' faith. But it will all be of no avail if they are not imbued with a deeper sense of a purpose of God for their lives. On the other hand, if that is imparted to them when they are young, they will never get away from it—though some in a flight of rebellion may try.

But there is another proverb pertinent to this subject, not nearly so well known as the former, but no less important a principle.

> A righteous man who walks in his integrity,
> blessed are his children after him.[17]

The most effective training in wisdom, i.e., strong moral character, is given by a parent who lives it out in front of his children. Nothing is more effective than that, and nothing is more ineffectual than verbal teaching without living example. In this verse, though, the negative does not even come up. Only the positive is presented, and it is both an observation and a promise.

It is easy, perhaps, to miss the implications of this verse for character development. At first glance, it appears to be saying that a man of integrity acquires blessings that he can leave to his posterity. To some extent that is the case, but that is not really the perspective of wisdom. It certainly does not mean that his life of integrity ensures his children of blessing regardless of their own way of life. No, a righteous man's children are blessed after him because they emulate him. He has modeled for them how life ought to be lived, and that life of righteousness and integrity blesses them *because it becomes their own*. He will pass away, but the power of his life will continue in and through his children as they live the way he showed them by his own example.

It is vital that parents understand their biblical role in training their children for life. Fads in child rearing throughout the modern era have ranged from the "omnipotent parent" to the "powerless parent." More recently our society is trending toward extremes, with some parents being obsessively involved in their children's lives (the "helicopter mom" phenomenon) perhaps as a reaction to so many other parents being simply absent from them.

Several years ago there, a brief but stormy controversy was stirred over a book that claimed parents come in third behind heredity and peers in shaping their children's destinies.[18] Regardless of how many people actually read the book at that time (or since), millions who never even saw its cover or read its arguments were influenced at the moment by sensational headlines in the media that announced authoritatively (as headlines do), "Peers, not parents, mold child's character." A *simple* public is often swayed both from biblical truth and common sense by little more than this kind of common propaganda. It dovetails with a willingness of parents to abdicate parental responsibility for the pursuit of individual interests.

It must be repeated and emphasized, against social trends if necessary, that *parents are the primary educators of their children* and that they must not relinquish their role to anyone, be it the state (the old liberalism), or peers (the new liberalism), or heredity (*laissez-faire* libertarianism). They must not think they can delegate their responsibility to schools, let alone to daycare centers. We live in a society that talks incessantly about our commitment to children, but with apparently little substance to that commitment beyond emotion and guilt. Many in our society want the government to take a heavier responsibility for rearing our children so that we who have them can have greater freedom to pursue our own happiness. There is a need for a revival of parenthood and a restoration of the moral commitment of fathers and mothers to their own children.

The following statement should be self-evident, even absurdly obvious, but I feel compelled to make it nonetheless: Children are not qualified to rear themselves. Parents must not abdicate their responsibility to bring up their own children. They must instead deny themselves for their children's sake. Parenting is not a pastime; it is a life's calling. Moreover, parents have God-given authority to direct the upbringing of their children—an authority that must be exercised with the same wisdom that the children are expected to learn, and an authority that should be taken over by society only when something has gone dreadfully, criminally wrong at home.

It is also time to reconsider an age-old truth—that fathers are indispensable for the moral and spiritual development of the next generation. The whole concept of fatherhood has suffered in recent decades under a social crusade that purports to bring equality to the sexes. The "equality" to which the politically correct reformers aspire looks a great deal like androgyny. Author David Blankenhorn observes, "Today's expert story of fatherhood largely assumes that fatherhood is superfluous." This assumption, grounded in "the most expressive individualism that a society can imagine," fosters the fallacy that "human completion is a solo act." Blankenhorn's thesis is that if the interest of children is put ahead of the adult's quest for self-actualization, a starkly different "cultural script" emerges. We must conclude instead that rearing children requires "mutual dependency, grounded in the realities of gender complementarity."[19]

In other words, parenting is by design—*God's* design—a two-party enterprise, with the mother and the father each bringing unique strengths to the task. There are some things dads do that moms cannot do as well. Unisex parenting is an emergency situation, sometimes unavoidable, and single parents certainly should receive help and support from a close community. It is, however, not God's primary intention and not a laudable personal choice. It is no trivial matter to insure that a generation of children be raised by fathers as well as mothers. To proceed otherwise is to add chaos to the lives of our children, and thus to raise hazards to the future of society.

Such a warning is no exaggeration. Our age is one that likes to proceed on the basis of what "studies have shown." The studies are in, and they document the effects that the widespread erosion of fatherhood has already had on our society. They demonstrate a strong correlation between father absence and poverty, child abuse, juvenile delinquency, violent crime, and adult criminality. The same correlation extends to low achievement in school, school disciplinary problems, and dropout rates. It is also connected to abuse of drugs, alcohol and tobacco, to suicide and a variety of psychiatric problems among youth, to teenage sexual activity, and to other related social problems.[20]

Children who live absent their biological fathers are, on average, at least two to three times more likely to be poor, to use drugs, to experience educational, health, emotional and behavioral problems, to be victims of child abuse, and to engage in criminal behavior than their peers who live with their married, biological (or adoptive) parents.[21]

At the same time, "studies have shown" an impressive number of positive effects that can be demonstrated from the presence of an involved father in the home. Positive father involvement is linked to educational achievement and economic and physical well-being. It is also linked to emotional and social health issues, including the child's development of empathy, pro-social behavior, and healthy self-esteem.[22] The point here is not that fatherhood is the panacea for all our social ills. It is, rather, that fathers have a unique and indispensable role in the communication of moral wisdom from one generation to the next. It is time once again for us to shoulder it.

The Salvation of the Simple

Returning to the simple fool, if he is to be reached—to be *saved*, if you will—wisdom must get his attention. The question is how do we get him to start making the choices that will make him a better person rather than those that simply feel good at the moment?

For one thing, he can be "scared straight," so to speak.

Strike a scorner, and the simple will beware.
When a scorner is punished, the simple one is made wise.[23]

The "scorner" in these verses is someone we shall consider in greater detail later on. He is the fool in a very advanced stage of rebellion. He is a scoffer, a mocker who holds truth and moral righteousness in contempt. He is at the end of the line that the simple fool is only at the beginning of.

Remember that the simple fool has no real conception that wrongdoing has consequences. He needs to see it to believe it, or even to understand it. He particularly needs to see his mischief-making role models come to a bad end. The point here is that those in authority—whether they are parents, school administrators, employers, or law enforcement and the judicial system—must see that lawlessness and rebellion is punished swiftly and decisively. "When the scorner is punished, the simple one is made wise." We call this deterrence. The Bible calls it a kind of education. That is the negative part, and it is necessary, but there also has to be something positive to attract the simple fool.

Let the simple one be enticed by wisdom. Indeed, wisdom has its own "sex appeal." Understanding brings pleasure, and discipline carries its own joys. This fact needs to be paraded before the eyes of our naive friend. "O you simple ones, understand wisdom!"[24]

Wisdom, like lust, is also personified in Proverbs as an attractive woman who is working hard to gain the attention of the simple. Unlike lust, however, this lady has class! She has it all—beauty, wealth, dignity, respect.

> Wisdom has built her house,
> she has hewn out her seven pillars.
> She has butchered her meat,
> she has mixed her wine,
> and she has set her table.
> She has sent out her maidens;
> she cries out from the highest places of the city.[25]

You might think that a lady like this would be aloof, remote, and hard to reach. The opposite is the case. Listen to her call out:

> *"Whoever is simple, let him turn in here!"*
> As for him who lacks understanding, she says to him,
> *"Come, eat of my bread,*
> *and drink of the wine which I have mixed.*
> *Forsake naivety and live,*
> *and go in the way of understanding."*[26]

She openly seeks a relationship with the simple one and offers both nourishment and sublime pleasures—if only he will stop looking for the good life in all the wrong places and instead "go in the way of understanding."

In one sense gaining wisdom—sound moral character—is a quest, a challenge. It isn't always easy, and discipline isn't always pleasant. If it were always easy and pleasant, why would we even *need* discipline? At the same time, it must be clear that goodness is neither complicated nor out of reach. Does the simple one, empty as he or she is, have what it takes to understand what wisdom and character is all about? Certainly, *just do right*. "Oh, but it can't be as easy as that." No one said it was easy, only that it is not complicated. Just do right. The whole point of the book of Proverbs, and all the wisdom literature in the Bible, is that simply to do right is the way of the good life.

But how do you know what is right? *This is where God's Word comes in as the salvation of the simple.*

> The law of the Lord is perfect, converting the soul.
> The testimony of the Lord is sure, making wise the simple.[27]
> The entrance of Your words gives light:
> It gives understanding to the simple.[28]

Wisdom, understanding, and a change of heart all come through the Scriptures—*all* the Scriptures. "All Scripture is God-breathed, and is profitable for doctrine, for reproof, for correction, for instruction in righteousness."[29]

The proverbs in particular are useful to develop prudence, knowledge, and discretion—which happen to be the key deficiencies of the simple. This is why it says in Proverbs 1:4 that the purpose of the book is

> To impart prudence to the simple,
> to the young man knowledge and discretion.

Finally, it must be pointed out that the gospel of Jesus Christ is especially addressed to the simple. The apostle Paul says of his own urgency to preach that gospel, "I am debtor...both to the wise and to the unwise."[30] In one sense he is speaking of the class structure of his day, the educated and literate versus the uneducated and illiterate. However, the word translated "unwise" here literally means "an unthinking person," someone who does not have understanding, who does not apply the mind.[31] In this context, it certainly seems to apply to the simple.

Moreover, we have all at some time been in the same boat with the simple one. Titus 3:3–7 clearly refers to our character deficiency and moral fallibility when it says,

> For we ourselves also were sometimes *foolish* [unthinking], disobedient, deceived, serving assorted lusts and pleasures, living in malice and envy, hateful, and hating one another.
>
> But then the kindness and love of God our Savior toward man appeared.
>
> Not by works of righteousness that we have done, but according to His mercy, He saved us by the washing of regeneration and renewing of the Holy Spirit, which He shed on us abundantly through Jesus Christ our Savior, in order that being justified by His grace, we should be made heirs according to the hope of eternal life.

God seems to have a special place in His heart for the simple. We are assured this by the psalmist, whose personal testimony ought to encourage all of us to look to the Lord when we don't have the answers:

> The LORD preserves the simple;
> I was brought low, and he helped me.[32]

Amen.

The Gist

Not easy, but not complicated. Wisdom for the simple is not mysterious or hard to find; it is open, obvious, and accessible.

Go to the Source. God is the Source of all wisdom, and its precepts are clearly taught in His word.

Find the motivation. The simple one must become motivated to seek wisdom for himself; it will not grow automatically.

Underestimated. Parents are the most important channels of wisdom.

Deterrence. The simple one can be deterred from a bad path and "scared straight" if he starts to go wrong, but it is better instead if he discovers the pleasures of wisdom for himself.

For your consideration

- If wisdom is the true way of success, what do you think is the greatest obstacle to achieving it?
- What does it mean that parents are the primary educators of their children?
- Why is it so important to instill a sense of purpose in children?
- What crucial role does the Bible as God's word play in the bringing of the simple to wisdom?

8

The Master of Swagger

As we expand our discussion of folly to the next level, remember that to be a fool is not to be silly or ignorant. Folly is the biblical word for a self-destructive lifestyle. I use the term character deficiency syndrome because the problem of folly is about moral, not intellectual feebleness and because it consists of degenerative and aggravated stages, in a definite sequence, with identifiable symptoms.

We noted in our discussion of the simple or naïve fool that if his tendency to follow his passions goes unchecked, he will descend to a deeper level of character deficiency. This is the *self-confident fool*. The Bible has more to say about this character than any of the others.

The Soul with No Understanding

The Hebrew word is *kesil* (k^e-seel). Some of the commentaries call this one the "silly fool." This rendering is baffling to me. If it is a pun on the Hebrew ("k^e-silly"?) it misses the point widely. The verses in which this word is used reveal an individual with a number of characteristic faults, but silliness is not one of them. The root verb *kasal* means "to be fat." Related Hebrew words, interestingly, often have a positive meaning. *Kesel* has to do with a fullness of hope, and *kislâ* speaks of confidence. This particular term, however, carries all the negative connotations of fatness. No, we must not stoop to call this one a "fat head"—but he *is* "full of himself."

The *kesil* is the person who, like the simple fool, is inclined to make the wrong moral choices, except that there is a difference. The simple fool might stumble into a disaster, but the self-confident fool will swagger in, convinced that he is the master of the situation. The self-confident fool cannot claim that the inevitable consequences never occurred to him. He proceeds deliberately into his sins with the delusion that he can avoid the consequences ("It will never happen to me!").

Proverbs describes the self-confident fool as a soul with no moral understanding. The key to understanding the self-confident fool is his spiritual blindness.

> LORD, how great are your works,
> and how deep are Your thoughts!
> A stupid man does not know,
> neither does a fool understand this.[1]

In these verses, our friend the *kesil*, the self-confident fool, is paired up with the *ba'ar* (ba-AR), the stupid man. The King James Version says "brutish." This fellow is animal-like—not that he is necessarily violent, but rather that he acts irrationally, on impulse, without the use of reason, spirit, or deliberate choice. Basically, he is, as they say in the South, just plain dumb. It is possible to be a fool yet still be otherwise bright and very clever. Not so the *ba'ar*. On the other hand, it is possible to lack common sense and still be a person of good character. Not so the *ba'ar*. That he is a subcategory of fool is demonstrated by his stiff-necked attitude. In particular he (or she—always keep in mind that folly is not prejudiced by gender) does not appreciate correction.[2] He seems to be a very compatible companion and willing accomplice of the self-confident fool. A number of comedic possibilities come to mind, but we shall pass them by. We really want to get on to talking about the self-confident fool himself.

"Lord, how great are your works, and how deep are your thoughts." Amen. Understanding of the greatness of God's works and the depth of His thoughts leads us to worship. But the self-confident fool has no perception or concern about God's thoughts. His lack of understanding is closely related to his ignorance of sound doctrine and theology. It is probably not possible to know which came first—his ignorance about the things of God, or his lack of understanding of those things. It is safe to say, though, that he has probably never taken the time to really study or think about God or ethics or morality. He really has no interest in it.

> Wisdom is before the face of him who has understanding,
> but the eyes of a [self-confident] fool are on the ends of
> the earth.[3]

His character deficiency is linked to a kind of moral attention deficit disorder. Again, which came first is hard to say. They seem to be inextricably connected. The point is that his attention is given to everything in the world except the things of God and the things of righteousness.

Even if he has studied such things, it has been to obscure the truth rather than to clarify it. In 1 Corinthians 15:35, the apostle Paul refers to those within the church who raise quarrelsome questions about the doctrine of the resurrection and calls them fools. Though he is not writing in Hebrew, the Greek word he uses[4] refers to a mindless, senseless person; someone who lacks understanding or common sense; someone who refuses to think, who refuses to see the truth when it's put before him. It sounds very much, in the present context, like the self-confident kind of fool.

Willful Ignorance

This ignorance of the self-confident fool is neither unintentional nor incidental, a mere consequence of being too occupied with other things to take the time. The self-confident fool is willfully ignorant because he really does not want to understand. He does not want to learn. It is as though he fears that the truth will ruin his life. Listen again to the words of Paul, this time in his letter to the Romans:

> For the wrath of God is revealed from heaven against all ungodliness and unrighteousness of men, who suppress the truth in unrighteousness...Because, when they knew God, they neither glorified Him as God nor were thankful, but became vain in their imaginations, and their *foolish* heart was darkened. Professing themselves to be wise, they became *fools*.[5]

The word "foolish" in this passage means to be without discernment or understanding; unable to bring data together to form a sound conclusion. The word "fools," however, is a different Greek word from the one we saw previously.[6] It describes someone who is dull-witted and stupid, as opposed to someone who is bright and intelligent. It is not the vocabulary that carries the meaning of the passage, however, but the context. The people described here are enormously confident of their ability to direct their own lives without guidance from their Creator. Their foolishness is deliberate—a choice made more or less consciously. Eventually those who suppress the truth because they do not want to hinder their quest for "the good life" become completely incompetent even to recognize the truth, let alone live by it.

The bottom line is that *the self-confident fool does not understand God or His ways.* He has no serious comprehension either of truth in any ultimate sense, or of the moral requisites for life. This lack of understanding results in a proud self-deception because he thinks he does know all these things. Furthermore, the self-confident fool thinks that rebellion against moral authority is something to be valued.

> The wisdom of the prudent is to understand his way,
> but the folly of [self-confident] fools is deceit.[7]

As is the case with most of the Proverbs, there is much more going on in this simple couplet than meets the eye. Part of our problem is that most of us do not read Hebrew. If we did, we would see that the word translated "folly" here is unrelated to the one translated "fools." The *fools* in question are the self-confident, second-degree fools we've been talking about. The *folly* spoken of here, however, pertains to the next step down the ladder toward moral self-destruction. Folly in this verse is the characteristic behavior of what we will describe in this book as the committed fool, the *true* fool, who has passed on to the third degree of character deficiency syndrome.

What is happening here—and we shall see it consistently—is that the *self-confident* fool admires and emulates the moral rebellion of the *committed* fool. He may not yet have reached the point of casting off all restraint, but he is already incorporating a number of rebellious traits—which may range anywhere from irreverence and insolence to criminal mischief—into his value system. At some point along the line, he or she has decided that the best role models for him are those who resist or even attack "the system."

What the self-confident fool does not realize is that he is being deceived. (Of course, if he did realize it he would not be deceived!)

The anti-authority lifestyle does not deliver the happiness and freedom it promises. He truly expects to be rewarded with peace, love, satisfaction, and joy from his vain pursuits. When pain, misery, and the scorn of society arrive instead, he will probably blame others rather than repent of his errors.

A deeper look into the wisdom literature reveals that this lack of understanding in the self-confident fool is profound, comparable to darkness and blindness. The book of Ecclesiastes describes this reality in considerable detail.

> And I turned myself to behold wisdom,
> and madness, and folly.[8]

Throughout the book of Ecclesiastes, the words translated "fool" and "folly"[9] speak of thickheadedness. The root meaning of this particular word, which is "to be stopped up or blocked," highlights a primary characteristic of the *kesil*, namely stubbornness. (*Sikluth* and *sekel* are thus so conceptually close to *kesil* as to make them essentially synonyms, and that is reflected in the contexts of scriptures in which they appear.) We can rightly call him also the *stubborn fool*.

> Then I saw that wisdom excels folly
> as far as light exceeds darkness.
> The wise man's eyes are in his head,
> but the fool walks in darkness.[10]

This observation seems to be obvious and commonplace. Of course, wisdom is better than folly! It is hard to understand who would think otherwise.

The full significance of this affirmation, however, is only revealed by its context. The book of Ecclesiastes is a critical examination of the humanistic worldview, of life "under the sun." The verdict is that if we must assume that this life on earth is all there is, and that if there is no life after death or eternal judgment, reward, and punishment, then life is futile and meaningless. That is why the verses quoted above are framed by this pessimistic conclusion:

> And I myself perceived also that one event [death]
> happens to them all.
> As it happens to the fool, so it happens even to me.[11]

The point is that, even if it is true that both the wise and the foolish share the same ultimate fate, wisdom is still better a better life than folly. The morally upright life is better than the self-centeredness of the *stubborn fool*, the same way that light is better than darkness. The problem is, how do parents and educators convince young people that discipline, morality, and deferred gratification are worth the price if this life is all there is? If life itself is absurd, what is the point of wisdom? A darkened worldview begets children who walk in spiritual darkness.

Darkness is a terrible reality, but the moral darkness in which the fool walks is self-imposed, accepted easily and willingly. To walk in darkness is to live by the fluctuations of feelings and circumstance, bereft of certainty, led mainly by one's own lusts and appetites.

> For what has the wise more than the fool?
> Better is the sight of the eyes than the wandering of the desire.[12]

The self-confident fool is not at all interested in gaining moral and spiritual understanding, nor will he use the resources of wisdom he still has.

> A fool has no delight in understanding,
> but only in revealing his own mind.[13]

Some well-meaning people think they can reach this soul through education. They will enroll him in a self-improvement class or a seminar that promotes a positive mental attitude. The mark of the self-confident fool is that even if he goes to the seminar and submits to the motivational training course and picks up a tip here and there, he is not interested in really learning, let alone changing. Why should he? As far as he is concerned, he does not have a problem—everyone else does.

He will be glad to give his own opinion, however. The trouble, time, and expense of all these educational experiences might even be worth it to him, so long as he is able in the process to impart his own "wisdom and insight" into the proceedings. The value of his input to others is likely to be negligible because,

> A wise man's heart is at his right hand,
> but a fool's heart is at his left.[14]

A moment's thought will make the meaning of this saying clear. Most people are right-handed, and even those who are not still have to live in a right-handed world. The right hand is the "go to" hand. What kinds of things do people set at their right hand when they arrange their desks, or their kitchen, or workstation? They put the things they use most frequently there in the spot that will be easiest to reach. Meanwhile, at their left hand they place things they want out of the way, because they rarely reach for them.

In this proverb, the heart represents the inner self. It includes the faculties of reason, spiritual understanding, moral sensitivity and conscience, as well as affections. If a wise person keeps his heart at his right hand while the stubborn fool relegates it to his left, it underscores that the fool does not want to increase his moral and spiritual understanding, nor does he want to use even what he has.

The self-confident fool, thickheaded as he is, therefore lives a shallow, unreflective life. He absorbs his values from the popular culture and its media and lives reactively to the pleasures and stresses of life. He finds the purpose for his life on the weekend ("Thank God it's Friday") in leisure activities that may range from the refined to the vulgar to the shameful, and he dreads

Mondays, when he must return to work weary and hung over from the pursuits that he thinks make his life worthwhile.

The Song and Sacrifice of Fools

Completely lost on him is the message of Ecclesiastes, which tries to make him face the fact that *his humanistic values are misplaced.*

> It is better go to the house of mourning than to go to the house of feasting; for that is the end of all men, and the living will take it to his heart. Sorrow is better than laughter, for by the sadness of the countenance the heart is made better...The heart of the wise is in the house of mourning, but the heart of fools is in the house of mirth. It is better to hear the rebuke of the wise, than for a man to hear the song of fools.[15]

In other words, the self-confident fool has no real comprehension of the serious side of life, and especially of death and mortality. He labors to shield himself from these realities. Neither does he want to hear any contradiction of his opinions, beliefs, and feelings. He would rather be praised by fools than be corrected by the wise. The song of fools is much easier to listen to than the rebuke of the wise because the song of fools is about escapism and dodging the realities of life. The quintessential song of fools will be a song that "touches his heart" (i.e., makes him happy or sad), but does not actually say anything. It makes him feel as though he has gained insight and character, while in fact he has only been stroked and congratulated in his own self-esteem.

His religious faith (if you can call it faith—if indeed he is religious at all) is likewise shallow. He is irreverent when it comes to the things of God, although he may go through the motions of religion and even be quite vocal about it. His spiritual commitments, lacking strength of heart and force of will, are purely external.

Watch your step when you go to the house of God, and be
more ready to hear than to give the sacrifice of fools; for
they do not realize that they are committing evil.[16]

"The sacrifice of fools"—a vivid expression, but of what? What
is the sacrifice of fools, and what is its hallmark? It is *a mouth that
extends far beyond the heart.*

Be not rash with your mouth,
and let not your heart be hasty to utter anything before
God.
For God is in heaven, and you upon earth,
therefore let your words be few.
For a dream comes through much activity,
and a fool's voice is known by a multitude of words.
When you vow a vow unto God, do not fail to pay it,
for he has no pleasure in fools.
Pay that which you have vowed.
Better that you not vow, than that you vow and not pay.

For in the multitude of dreams and many words,
there is also vanity.
But you, fear God.[17]

The religion of a self-confident fool is filled with boasting
about spiritual experiences and insights. On the strength of a
fleeting emotion or for the purpose of impressing someone else,
he will make a show of religious faith accompanied by hollow
commitments. He does not reckon on the fact that God takes
such things with great seriousness, and that it makes a difference
what God thinks about it.

Consider the nature of a vow, since that is the case in point
in the above passage. A vow is a spiritual movement of profound
gravity. It is the most absolute commitment a finite soul can
make. The terms of a vow may be limited or open-ended, but
are always measurable. One either fulfills the vow or not. A vow
may not be easy to fulfill, however, and must not be made lightly.

Anyone, even a self-confident fool, may be seized by a powerful religious stimulus that might lead him to commit his life to a certain course, but no one can foresee the future. The changeable circumstances of life may make it difficult to follow through even on apparently easy commitments. The temptation to let go may be strong.

In the world of commerce and law, people enter into contracts where there are tangible penalties for a unilateral withdrawal from agreements. Because God is invisible and there are no tangible penalties apparent, the fool thinks that he may revoke with impunity the commitments he makes before God. On the contrary, the self-confident fool may even believe that he has positive merit in God's eyes just because he made a vow in the first place.

Do not charge him with insincerity, for he will insist that he is completely sincere. Sincerity is an emotion in his view. He is sincere if he *feels* sincere. He meant what he said when he said it, but it would be unfair for anyone to hold him to it, even God. God, in fact, should be the first one to forgive and forget (according to the fool's conceit) because He knows that no one is perfect and that circumstances can make our vows immensely impractical. If he feels a certain way, then it seems obvious to him that God must feel the same. This is what the self-confident fool thinks. To him religion consists of external exercises, words and rituals, and personal feelings.

In this belief, the fool is terribly mistaken. This is an error with eternal repercussions. God holds every soul responsible to obey His commandments and to keep their commitments—especially those made in His name under oath. "You shall not take the name of the LORD your God in vain. For the LORD will not hold him guiltless who takes His name in vain."[18] "Do not be deceived— God is not mocked."[19]

The Pharisees, a religious party within Judaism in the days of Jesus, were known for their scrupulous observance of rituals. One of them once accused Jesus (of all people) of compromising God's law because he did not practice ceremonial hand washing before dinner. The ritual was not about hygiene but holiness, the object being to cleanse oneself of contacts with impure people who would make the food unclean by their second-hand touch. Now the law has some regulations regarding ceremonial cleansing, but this was not one of them. It was a rule the Pharisees had made up in order to make sure they did not even come close to violating a ceremonial law.

The response of Jesus was unusually sharp:

> Now you Pharisees make the outside of the cup and dish clean, but your inward part is full of extortion and wickedness. *Fools*, did not he who made the outside make the inside also?[20]

Some people miss the point of wisdom Jesus is making here. The fault was not in their scrupulous observance of paralegal rules. It was that their rules had effectively replaced the law itself. The foolishness of the Pharisees was in thinking that righteousness consists of fulfilling external duties and that once these duties had been carried out they had exhausted their obligations before God.

Duty is not high on the list of fools' virtues in our own time, but the basic analogy holds. We live in an era in which *feelings* often serve as deeds in themselves. The self-confident fool of contemporary times is perhaps more likely to think that he has cleared his account with the Almighty by having the right feelings of love or contrition or awe, regardless of whether he acts righteously or not. He may even congratulate himself when he reads the above passage, thinking that by having appropriate emotions his righteousness exceeds that of the Pharisees.

Jesus warns the one as well as the other that God is not deceived by shows. He is equally unimpressed by the performance of minor external duties and by religious feelings. He who weighs the deeds also weighs the motives of the heart, and He knows the true value of each.

Maker of Mischief

Not only is the self-confident fool shallow, *he has begun to adopt perverse values*, and these will eventually show up in lawless behavior. He thinks it is fun to plan and carry out lawless, perhaps even violent or lewd schemes.

> It is like sport to a [self-confident] fool to do mischief,
> but a man of understanding has wisdom.[21]

The "mischief" referred to here does not refer to childish pranks, such as blanketing a house with toilet paper or breaking a few windows or defacing a wall with obscenities. The Hebrew word[22] can describe a sinister plot or a crooked scheme. It can designate corruption and bribery. In Leviticus, it is translated "wickedness" and possesses a sexual connotation, particularly having to do with incest and sexual abuse within the family.[23]

The self-confident fool is not just toying with some little peccadillo. These are serious misdemeanors that he regards as "sport." So far the fool is just dabbling in mischief, but what is more alarming than the behavior itself is his attraction to it—and the fact that he is building it into his value system. Lacking a clear understanding of right and wrong and being attracted to some wrong things, he begins to blur the distinction between the two. Having willingly subjected himself to lawless influences—whether from unsavory friends, unscrupulous business associates, pornography, or some other—he begins to approve the immoral things he is attracted to.

To put it in the most courteous way, this is not the kind of person, male or female, whom you would like to see your daughter or son bring home for a fiancé or a best friend. All these characteristics are essentially interior to the individual, however.

They identify his character flaw but do not overtly distinguish him from anyone else. How, then, may the self-confident fool be recognized? As we shall see, it really is not difficult. This type of fool is all too willing to make himself known.

The Gist

Blind. The key to the self-confident fool is that he is spiritually blind and has no interest in gaining moral understanding.

Self-deceived. The self-confident fool is proudly self-deceived, because he wrongly thinks he does possess understanding.

The fool's hero. The self-confident fool admires and emulates the moral rebellion of the committed fool, although he has not (yet) committed himself to it.

Perverse values. The self-confident fool has begun to adopt perverse values that inevitably express themselves in destructive, even lawless behaviors.

For your consideration

In one scripture passage, the self-confident fool is paired with the "stupid" person. In another, it is said he would rather "hear the song of fools" than the rebuke of the wise. We know that people in general tend to associate with other people who are likeminded.

- What role do you associations and friendships play in character deficiency syndrome? If fools did not have other fools to reinforce their folly, would they become wise?
- Ecclesiastes 5:1 speaks of "the sacrifice of fools." How does God discriminate between the worship of the wise and that of fools? What do you think motivates the worship of a fool as opposed to someone who has understanding?

9

A Most Difficult Person

The *self-confident fool*, the soul with no moral understanding, proceeds to reveal himself through three outstanding characteristics: obstinacy, verbosity, and unreliability.

The Obstinacy of the Self-confident Fool

First, as I suggested earlier, *he is extraordinarily stubborn*. Jesus said that one of the evil things that proceeds out of the human heart is foolishness[1] (Mark 7:21–23). The second-degree fool seems to have an inbred antipathy toward moral understanding. He may go through the motions of trying to learn moral and spiritual discipline to no avail because he really does not want it.

> Why is there a price in the hand of a fool to get wisdom,
> seeing he has no heart for it?[2]

It is therefore pointless to try to teach him—i.e., to give him straightforward advice, or to counsel him as though he is interested in corrective instruction. The picture here is of someone who pays good money to a counselor to help him solve his problems, then proceeds to resist or ignore everything the counselor offers. There is a homely old saying that comes to mind: "Never try to teach a pig to sing. It only wastes your time, and it annoys the pig."

The self-confident fool resists wisdom because, to put it bluntly, he hates it. He hates moral understanding for the startlingly simple reason that he does not want to be told what do.

> How long...will fools hate knowledge?[3]

This seems like an extreme statement, but there is no other explanation for his behavior. He hates knowledge, and he will hate the well-meaning person who tries to correct him.

> Speak not in the ears of a fool,
> for he will despise the wisdom of your words.[4]

In other words, save your breath. He does not want to hear your advice if it contradicts his plans and desires.

Good sense imparts a healthy fear of evil. The self-confident fool ignores good sense. It gets in his way. He is quite confident that doing wrong will not harm him, and if you try to tell him otherwise he will storm in anger.

> A wise person fears, and departs from evil,
> but the fool rages and is confident.[5]

No one is perfect, and anyone is liable to make a false turn. True friends and brethren will confront their companion who is headed the wrong way before he goes too far. Here is where the clear difference between a person of true moral character and one with character deficiency shows up. Confronted with the fact that what he is doing is wrong, the person of good character is horrified and immediately changes direction. The self-confident fool loses his temper and unleashes it against those who love him enough to broach his anger with a rebuke—and then proceeds to pursue his unethical ends.

One may show him *how* he is wrong, explain the likely results of what he wants to do, and give real life examples. It does not matter. He will neither budge from his opinions nor change his ways.

> The desire accomplished is sweet to the soul,
> but it is an abomination to fools to depart from evil.[6]

Of course, everyone likes to see his own plans succeed and his own desires come to fruition. What makes the self-confident fool what he is, is his determination to see his plans through to the end even if he knows that they are wrong, and even if the consequences are sure to be destructive.

This may seem rather abstract, so we should try to apply this in a personal way. Enter with me, if you will, into an exercise of the imagination. Suppose *you* are the one who is planning mischief, it does not matter what. It may be a shady get-rich-quick scheme, or cheating on your income tax, or an extramarital affair, or plotting a diabolical revenge on someone who has offended you. (This is only a hypothetical situation, of course. I know that you, dear reader, would *never* actually contemplate such a thing!) A friend tries to get you to look at the situation morally, and demands, "How could you do this?" Do you want to hear this question or continue this line of discussion? Of course not. Having been involved on both sides (!) of this kind of conversation, I can testify that it is not a pleasant experience.

Nevertheless, if you are a person of otherwise sound character, the question will provoke soul-searching and (one may hope) repentance.

If you were a self-confident fool, however, you would resent it intensely and end the conversation as soon as possible, but probably not before telling your friend to mind his own (expletive-described) business. "The fool rages and is confident." If you were such a fool, you would press ahead with even greater determination, armed with a self-righteousness that only those who feel persecuted can wield. Sensible discussion may provoke your rage, but it will never shake your confidence. (Again, I only propose this scenario for the sake of illustration. I cannot conceive that the self-confident fool would even have read this far! But if he did, he probably would not recognize himself, either.)

Not only is it futile to reason with the self-confident fool about moral principles, neither is there any use in talking about the consequences of deeds and choices. It is a sad thing to watch the fool's deeds snap back and slap him in the face—the expulsion from school, the lawsuits, the trouble with the IRS, the broken marriage, the rebellious children. To all our amazement, he still probably will not budge, nor will he catch on at all, because

> a reproof enters more into a wise man
> than a hundred stripes into a fool.[7]

The "stripes" it is talking about is a reference to corporal punishment, specifically to being beaten with a rod. The law of Moses permitted corporal punishment for some infractions, but limited the number of stripes (i.e., strokes) administered to a maximum of forty.[8] In Jewish law and custom, this evolved to a limit of thirty-nine, the final blow being withheld as a precaution to make sure the limit would not be exceeded by an accidental miscount.

Once more, for the sake of illustration, please permit a personal question: How many blows from a sturdy, springy rod swung mercilessly and relentlessly by a strong hand would it take to dissuade *you* from an antisocial course of action?

To the wise person, one word of criticism goes straight to his heart and so stings his *conscience* that he needs no more than this. Yet if this proverb were to be taken literally (and I think it is intended rather to be a figure of speech), the fool in question has had at least three and probably more run-ins with the law, considering the number of stripes he's had to endure. A friend of mine who had a propensity for getting into trouble used to call himself a "slow learner." To say that the self-confident fool is a slow learner is an understatement.

The blows administered may not be by the hand of the law, however, so much as by the hand of circumstance. The self-confident fool is, by definition, incautious. He often takes huge risks and is often caught—if not by investigation, then simply by his own blunders. The stripes from which he refuses to learn may come from the disastrous consequences of his choices.

It is possible, however, that something worse than disaster could befall the self-confident fool. He might *succeed*, to his own peril and detriment.

> For the turning away of the simple shall slay them,
> and the prosperity of fools shall destroy them.[9]

Their *prosperity* will destroy them. The worst thing that can happen to the self-confident fool is success. If he fails and experiences some adversity because of his deeds, maybe he will stop and think about the things he doesn't want to think about. If, on the other hand, his plans prosper, will he regard that as being the mercy of God preserving him? Will he even feel lucky to have dodged the bullet? Neither. He will see his success instead as proof that he is a genius and confirmation that all the moralizing that people are trying to "shove down his throat" is bunk. His self-congratulation may take a pious turn if his sees his deliverance as the answer to his superstitious prayers. He may even consider himself blessed, one of God's favorites, or simply lucky.

On the other hand, he may move instead in the direction of infidelity: Who needs God? Who needs the church? Who needs the Ten Commandments? His life is just fine, his plan is perfect, and he is more than ready to tell you all about it—which brings us to the next subject.

Words Are Deeds

The obstinacy of the self-confident fool is only one of his distinguishing characteristics. *Probably the most publicly obvious mark of such a person is his verbosity.*

> A fool's voice is known by multitude of words.[10]

It is possible to know one is talking to a self-confident fool by his words—by both their quality and their quantity. For the self-confident fool, words are deeds. There is something about this fellow that compels him to speak unedifying words out of his unfruitful mind and to keep on speaking, regardless of who is listening or of what the effect of his words might be. The following string of proverbs paints a cumulative picture of the self-confident fool that is emphatic and unmistakable.

> Wisdom rests in the heart of him that has understanding,
> but that which is in the center of fools is made known.
> Every prudent man acts with knowledge,
> but a fool lays open his folly.
> A fool utters all his mind,
> but a wise person keeps it in till afterwards.
> A prudent man conceals knowledge,
> but the heart of fools proclaims foolishness.[11]

We shall look at each of these statements one at a time because there are some nuances to these verses that make them difficult to translate but rewarding to explore.

First is Proverbs 14:33, which the King James Version translates almost literally:

> Wisdom rests in the heart of him that has understanding,
> but that which is in the midst of fools is made known.

To borrow the pet phrase of my high school philosophy teacher, this is all well and good, but what does it *mean*? The first part of the proverb seems fairly straightforward, but the second part is not so easy. This is one of those occasions when patience with the tedium of grammar pays off a dividend of insight. Wisdom is the clear subject of the first clause ("Wisdom…understanding"), but in Hebrew the subject of the second clause ("but that…made known") is not entirely clear. It may be that the subject is still wisdom. If that is so, the proverb may be read in one of two ways.

One way is the way the NIV translates it: "Wisdom *reposes* in the heart of the discerning, and even among fools she lets herself be known." On the other hand, the verse could be read as the *Modern Language Bible* puts it: "In the heart of a man of understanding wisdom *quietly rests*, but she must make herself known to the inner self of fools." Both of these translations bring out the idea that the Hebrew verb "rests" implies being quiet.

It is also possible, however, that the subject for the second clause is implied in its own predicate rather than stated outright. This is often the case in Hebrew poetry. The Amplified Bible follows the King James here, and reads as follows:

> Wisdom rests [silently] in the mind and heart of him who has understanding,
> but that which is in the inward part of fools is made known.

Here is the point: *this proverb shows us the difference of demeanor between the wise person and the self-confident fool and explains the reason for that difference.* There is a clear contrast between the quiet confidence of the wise and the exhibitionistic bravado of the fool. The wise person knows what he knows and is confident about what he can do. He feels no need to display his understanding in a self-serving manner to all who pass by. There is a serenity, an easy self-assurance in his soul—a product of the wisdom itself. He has the poise to sit still and be quiet until the time to speak arrives. The self-confident fool, however, reveals the emptiness of his confidence in his compulsion to make known what is in him. He must voice his opinion, supply his thoughts, and broadcast his "knowledge," yet he evidently carries no sense of propriety regarding time, place, or circumstance.

A biblical case in point is provided by Job's three friends—Eliphaz, Bildad, and Zophar. They watched their friend suffer for a week and sat there silently with him for all those seven days. When Job finally broke his own silence and gave vent to his agony with a bitter lament, they felt compelled to reply. They had no idea what was behind Job's misery, and God had not given them any particular insight to share; but they shared it anyway, and in so doing only added to poor Job's pain. His pathetic pleas did not deter them. They kept piling arguments against him even when it became evident that, whether they were right or not, Job was not going to surrender to their insistence that he was an unjust man. Why did they press him so unrelentingly? Apparently, Job's very refusal to yield spurred them on. It irritates the fool beyond all reason when someone does not agree with him, since in his own mind he does have all the answers.

Moving on, according to Proverbs 13:16, the prudent one—the person of insight—deals with knowledge. He acts with forethought based on the best information he can get about the situation. Again, there is a quiet confidence at work here. He has nothing to prove to anyone; he just takes care of business. The self-confident fool, in contrast, lays open or displays the full-fledged folly to which he aspires. This is much more emphatic than saying that he shows himself to be a fool whenever he acts. *He deliberately exposes and flaunts rebellion.* This includes his use of profanity and obscene language.

Someone has defined profanity as the act of magnifying one's own esteem at the expense of God's glory. One of the moral barometers of any culture will be found in its sense of propriety regarding language. Specifically, an observer can discover what a society regards as holy by listening to what it regards as profane. The purpose of profanity is to shock and offend, and its power is measured by its offensiveness to hearers.

When I was a lad growing up in the Oklahoma "Bible belt," the words "hell" and "damn," used outside of their scriptural and religious context, were mildly shocking profanities that were not used by decent people, and certainly not in mixed company or in public discourse. To tell someone to "go to hell" was an insult over which boys would fight and business partners would part company. To curse in the name of God over a matter of personal displeasure was still regarded by most—at least publicly—as an act of blasphemy, because God was still the locus of things holy, and religious faith was still sacred.

Not only so, but also simple personal dignity, self respect, and respect for others forbade most people from public use of "four-letter" language. General Anthony McAuliffe, the commander of the American airborne division trapped in Bastogne during the Battle of the Bulge in 1944, must have been powerfully tempted to give an obscene reply to the German general who called for his surrender. His historic one word reply did register his strong rejection of the demand, but could also be printed unexpurgated in headlines and grade school textbooks. He said, "Nuts." The extravagantly profane General George Patton is reported to have commended the remark as "eloquent."

Today, only a few decades removed from those times, the use of religious profanity is not even regarded as rude. The name of God is regularly used in vain in television situation comedies during family-hour viewing and on the sports pages of newspapers as a compound curse word that is not even capitalized. Obscenities once thought most abusive now punctuate the conversations of school children—not the bad boys at the back of the playground, but the regular kids in the lunchroom and classroom. Is there anything that our culture regards as profane? It would have to be the crudest possible designations for bodily waste and sexual perversion. If this is so, what does it say about what our society believes to be holy?

The self-confident fool "talks trash" because filthy, insulting, abusive speech is part of his act. It is how he makes his point, how he gets things done. It may be in business negotiations, it may be in the city commissioner's court, or it may be in a family discussion. For him, words are deeds.

Words are also the expression of his passions.

> A fool utters all his mind,
> but a wise person keeps it in till afterwards.[12]

The proverb literally says, "a fool sends forth all his spirit, but the wise person, holding back, quiets it." In this context, "spirit" seems to equate with passion and temper. In other words, *when the self-confident fool gets angry, he explodes in a raging torrent of verbiage.* It doesn't matter who is around, who is in the way, or who may get hurt. Anger is an important factor in the self-confident fool's life. It motivates him to action, and it also serves him as a tool to accomplish his will. It is, however, a beast that, once it gains control, is increasingly hard to put back in its cage. When we look at the third-degree fool, the committed fool, we will see how anger begins to take over his life.

There is still more to say about the self-confident fool and his verbosity. There is one more proverb in this connection that needs to be highlighted.

> A prudent man conceals knowledge,
> but the heart of fools proclaims foolishness.[13]

This verse clarifies the common thread through all these proverbs: Wisdom teaches one when to shut his mouth. *The fool thinks he has to say everything out loud and long.*

It is also worth noting the nature of the thoughts the prudent person keeps to himself versus what the fool blurts out. The word "knowledge" is placed parallel to "foolishness." The prudent person conceals knowledge, while the self-confident fool discloses foolishness. "Knowledge" is *da'ath*, a general term covering knowledge gained either by experience or by thinking. When the prudent person has this knowledge, he knows he has it, but that does not mean he is required at all times to reveal it. He can retain or even conceal it in quiet confidence until the most opportune moment.

It might be helpful information that is brought forth at the right moment for maximum impact and effectiveness or simply because of its appropriateness to the situation. As it says elsewhere, "a word fitly spoken is like apples of gold in settings of silver."[14] On the other hand, it may not be positive knowledge at all, but negative. Consider a situation in which one knows detrimental information about someone that could be broadcast as a juicy piece of gossip. While the simple fool would repeat it carelessly and thoughtlessly, a self-confident fool might use it deliberately to build up his own esteem or maliciously to wreck the reputation of the other person. This would not be knowledge, but foolishness. A prudent person, however, understands that gossip is a two-edged sword. He therefore decides to keep that bit of information to himself, to make it a matter of earnest prayer, and to put himself in a position to be used by God as a help in that person's life.

In his classic commentary on Proverbs, Charles Bridges highlights three applications from this verse: (1) It is not necessarily appropriate to express *every* truth to *every* person at *every* time. (2) Circumstances may sometimes dictate discreet concealment of knowledge. (3) While nothing can justify speaking contrary to truth, we are not always obligated to tell the whole truth in every venue to everyone we meet. Wisdom knows how to distinguish a necessary report of malfeasance from an episode of trivial, self-serving tattling. Prudence understands the difference between insuring justice and merely stirring up trouble. A prudent person possesses, with all integrity, both a love for truth and sound judgment of proper times and procedures.

The self-confident fool possesses neither. What he has is an ego and a need to display himself as an important figure. Whatever he spouts, therefore, is all in the category of foolishness whether it's true or false, factual or fatuous. Once again, the word "foolishness" is not a synonym for that which is silly or frivolous. It is *'ivveleth*, that next step toward moral disintegration where the self-confident fool is heading.

This brings us to the subject matter of the self-confident fool's conversation. It generally pertains to this deeper level of character deficiency to which he seems to aspire.

> The tongue of the wise uses knowledge rightly,
> but the mouth of fools pours out foolishness.
> The heart of him who has understanding seeks knowledge,
> but the mouth of fools feeds on foolishness.[15]

The second proverb above (15:14) is about the preparation for what one is going to say. Notice that the knowledge spoken by the person of understanding is attained by the "heart." As was pointed out in chapter 3, the heart does not signify the emotions or passions: Solomon is not like Obi-Wan Kenobi saying, "Trust your feelings." The heart refers to all the inward resources of mind and spirit we possess because we are made in the image of God.

Now recall an earlier observation to see how it fits here:

> A wise man's heart is at his right hand,
> but a fool's heart at his left.[16]

The self-confident fool has a "heart," but he has no use for it. He prefers to "shoot from the lip." His mouth goes for the quick and the clever retort, the cutting remark, the insult that puts his opponents in their place, the cut-down that makes him look good by making others look ridiculous. He would rather complain than work on solutions. He would rather chatter about mindless trivia than to discuss God's Word or any issue of true importance. He would rather impress the people around by his facility with filth and profanity. Therefore, other than practice at sharpening his tongue, he does not really need any preparation for what he is going to say. Little wonder, then, that his mouth pours forth foolishness. At least it makes him easy to spot. It might even make him momentarily entertaining. It does not make him someone we should want to admire or imitate.

Why, then, do we admire this guy—for we do admire him, don't we? We do because his mouth brings him attention, and like fools, we envy the attention he gets. Say what you like about the self-confident fool, he does get noticed. Surely it would be better to be noticed for words that benefit others, that bless people. This could lead us into a whole other study about the use of the tongue, but permit me just for the time being to refer to a couple of New Testament passages.

In writing to the church in Corinth, Paul demonstrates how a self-confident fool speaks on his own authority and reinforces that sense of authority and self-importance through boasting. Notice the sharp edge of prophetic, surgical sarcasm in these words:

> I say again, let no man think me a fool. But if you do, then receive me as a fool, so that I may boast in myself a little. What I am saying [now], I am saying not according to the Lord, but as if in folly, in this confidence of boasting. Since many are boasting in the flesh, I too will boast. For you suffer fools gladly, seeing you yourselves are "wise." Nevertheless, in whatever thing anyone is bold (I speak in folly), I am bold also...Are they ministers of Christ? (I speak as an irresponsible fool!) I am more—in labors more abundant, in stripes above measure, in prisons more frequently, in deadly situations more often.[17]

Then finally, in exasperation, he writes,

> For though I would desire to boast, I shall not be a fool, for I will tell the truth...I have become a fool in boasting. You have compelled me.[18]

The whole point of Paul's rant is that *only fools establish their words through boasting*—because they are the only ones who have to.

How much better to follow the command in Ephesians 4:29,

> Let no unwholesome word go out of your mouth, but only
> that which is good toward building up what is needed, that
> it may give grace to the hearers.

The self-confident fool's words do tend to be unwholesome. The way he uses his tongue can cause all kinds of damage.

> Better is the poor person who walks in his integrity
> than he who is perverse in his lips, and is a fool.[19]

This "perversity of the lips" is demonstrated in at least two ways. For one thing, the self-confident fool is quick to get angry, and thus he uses his mouth to try to get back at those he thinks has injured him. He uses lies and slander as weapons to even the score.

> Be not hasty in your spirit to be angry,
> for anger rests in the bosom of fools.[20]
> He that hides hatred has lying lips,
> and he who utters a slander is a fool.[21]

The latter verse identifies one of the most significant functions of lying: to conceal hatred. Like Iago in *Othello*, such a person hides his malice not for the sake of civility, but to lay in wait for the opportunity to launch an attack or to spring a trap. Though hatred is distinguishable from the self-confident aspects of character deficiency syndrome, in this verse the two are linked. Perhaps the fool has not yet reached such a depth of hatred that would kill, but he is all too ready to destroy the reputation of someone who angers him.

Beyond these faults, it is his insolent mouth that often gets him into trouble to begin with and will be his undoing somewhere down the line.

> A fool's lips enter into strife,
> and his mouth calls for strokes.
> The words of a wise man's mouth are gracious,
> but a fool's own lips will swallow him.
> A fool's mouth is his destruction,
> and his lips are the snare of his soul.[22]

What really ought to worry us, though, is when this kind of person gets into a position of power through the shrewd use of his tongue. Do not think it can't happen. Scripture affirms that it does happen, and experience confirms that it has happened.

> The words of wise men are heard in quiet
> more than the cry of him who rules among fools.[23]

This could mean that those who rule over fools can scarcely be heard by shouting over the noise made by fools. The phrase is not "him who rules *over* fools," however, but "*in*" or "*among* fools," indicating that he himself is one. Certainly, anyone who listens to fools and governs by their counsel must be a fool himself.

His belligerent attitude and willingness to abuse others with his tongue, along with his general unreliability, make the self-confident fool a disruptive force in any society. That is what we will see in the next chapter.

The Gist

Outstanding characteristics: The self-confident fool reveals himself through three outstanding characteristics. The first two of them are:

1. *Obstinacy*. He does not want to be told what to do and does not accept correction.

2. *Verbosity*. For him, words are deeds, and he is known by both the quantity and the objectionable quality of them.

For your consideration

- Can you identify at least three ways a self-confident fool reveals himself by his speech? How can understanding this be helpful in interpersonal relationships? How can it be helpful to you as a citizen/voter?
- Proverbs 1:32 makes the ironic statement that "the prosperity of [self-confident] fools shall slay them." How so?

10

Beware the Fool

No one who lives among other people will be able to avoid coming in contact with this soul who has no understanding. Even if we should happily avoid becoming one, we must all learn how to deal with this cocky personality, and yet there is no satisfactory way to do this. He (or she) provokes an unhappy response from everyone who has anything to do with him (or her).

Parents have to deal with the heartache caused them by their foolish child. The birth of any child is a celebration in hope. It is a lost hope for those whose child turns to folly.

> He who begets a [self-confident] fool does it to his sorrow...
> A foolish son is a grief to his father,
> and bitterness to her that bore him.[1]

The joyful rewards of parenthood are not known in this household. These are words of deep pain: sorrow, grief, bitterness. The embarrassing behavior of the self-confident fool is not a joke to these people. They may put a brave front before the world, and they do earnestly love their wayward child. All the hope they invested is lost in tears, anxiety, and a profound sense of personal failure. They may have raised other children successfully to become decent, upright, productive people, but that does not take away from their sense of loss over the foolish one. The word "begets" in 12:21 does not suggest that the father is the reason for the folly of his offspring, but neither does it offer any relief from self-doubt. All it provides is the plain, unhappy fact that one he brought into the world is a moral detriment to the community.

Friends end up being taken down along with them.

> He who walks with the wise shall be wise,
> but a companion of fools shall be destroyed.[2]

The focus in this proverb is not the self-confident fool, but on his friends. If they are simple, they will likely be strongly influenced by him and follow his example. Even if they are wise enough to abstain from his negative philosophy, attitude, and behavior, their fellowship with him will place them within the arc of disastrous consequences that will meet up with him sooner or later. Once again, we are confronted with the reality that our choice of friends is crucial to our success in life, spiritually as well as materially.

Anyone who comes in contact with him is in danger.

> Let a bear robbed of her cubs meet a man,
> rather than a fool in his folly.[3]

Across the ages and across the continents, the rage of a mother bear is legendary and proverbial. Whoever encounters her is in the gravest peril. There is little chance of escape, and if one is caught in her clutches, an even smaller hope of survival. Yet, to Solomon, there is a danger far more alarming, more devastating, more horrifying than being mauled: to encounter the self-confident fool "in his folly."

What, is this a joke? Well, maybe. This observation is so far over the top that one might wonder whether there is a sense of humor behind this proverb that we are all missing because it's in the Bible. But even if this proverb is an example of comic hyperbole—gallows humor perhaps—it does not diminish the grim truth in it. It is probable that this proverb is inspired by numerous case studies of people who met with disaster when they became entangled in some way with the self-confident fool. Entangled how?

This last phrase of the proverb is wonderfully (or terribly) vague, inclusive of multiple possibilities. It may mean "in the *state* of his folly," particularly the rage that possesses him when his desires are crossed, so that the danger is to get in the way of his irrational wrath and so suffer harm. But it may also mean "in the *midst* of his folly," while he is in the process of carrying out his foolhardy plans but before they come to fruition. In this case, one danger is to get caught up thoughtlessly in his enthusiasm and join in a partnership that is destined for shipwreck. Or it may mean "in the *fullness* of his folly," indicating that union with the self-confident fool is a thing most to be feared when the consequences begin to fall, for all those in the vicinity will suffer with him. They do not even have to be part of his errant projects. They may simply be victims of collateral damage from being in the same neighborhood when the disaster comes, like those who are killed by a drunk driver (certainly a subcategory of self-confident folly), who himself may walk away from the scene of the wreck unscathed.

Even God "has no pleasure in fools."[4] At the very least, we have a hint here that it will not go well with this soul when he must give an account to his Maker. While the immediate context of this terse statement, as we have already seen, has to do with religious observance and the making of vows, the declaration that "He has no pleasure in fools" is a broader principle, brought into the discussion in order to elevate the seriousness of it. It is a sin indeed to worship God in flippancy and sloth, but the greater sin is to stand before Him with the arrogance of the self-confident fool, supposing that he is doing God a favor even for being there.

The Most Exasperating Individual

How do we handle the loud-mouthed, obstinate behavior of this fool? There is a most unusual passage in one remarkable chapter of Proverbs. Most of the book, from chapters 10 through 29, comprises mostly unconnected two-line proverbs, miscellaneous and jumbled with no particular theme or order tying them together. Proverbs 26, however, has a curious string of almost-consecutive proverbs on the subject of the self-confident fool—a swift succession of twelve parallel couplets that together paint a stunning if unflattering picture of this character-deficient soul. (In the presentation below, Proverbs 19:10 serves as the lead-in for this passage, and verse 2 is passed by so as not to disrupt the rhythm of the "essay.") In every verse below, the "fool" in question is the *kesil*, the self-confident fool. Watch for the barb in the final verse that will give a rather startling twist ending to this "Fool's Essay."

> Luxury is not fitting for a fool,
> much less for a servant to have rule over princes.
> As snow in summer, and as rain in harvest,
> so honor is not fitting for a fool.
> A whip for the horse, a bridle for the ass,
> and a rod for the fool's back.
> Answer not a fool according to his folly,
> lest you also be like him.
> Answer a fool according to his folly,
> lest he be wise in his own conceit.
> He who sends a message by the hand of a fool
> is cutting off his feet and drinking poison.
> As the legs of the lame hang limp,
> so is a proverb in the mouth of fools.

As he who binds a stone in a sling,
so is he who gives honor to a fool.
As a thorn that goes into the hand of a drunkard,
so is a proverb in the mouth of fools.
Like an archer who wounds at random,
is he who hires a fool or any passerby.
As a dog returns to his vomit,
so a fool returns to his folly.
Do you see a man who is wise in his own eyes?
There is more hope for a fool than for him.[5]

I do not know what is more devastating: the individual proverbs themselves, the cumulative effect of massing them all together like this, or the potent little shot at the end.

Once again, we may note that the self-confident, second-degree fool's attitudes, thoughts, words, and behaviors are directed toward third-degree folly, that is, wickedness and rebellion. Perhaps it is not his conscious goal to become a wicked and immoral person, but it certainly looks that way, and it might as well be.

Let's take a closer look at the "Fool's Essay":

Luxury is not fitting for a fool;
much less for a servant to have rule over princes.
As snow in summer, and as rain in harvest,
so honor is not fitting for a fool.
A whip for the horse, a bridle for the ass,
and a rod for the fool's back.

The self-confident fool needs to feel the sting of the consequences of his behavior—and eventually he will. It is just a matter of time. The problem is, people keep trying to help him along, apparently motivated by the theory that he only needs some positive reinforcement to encourage him to straighten up.

With this in mind, they give him praises and privileges. It is a bad plan. What serves to motivate the individual with good character, or even the simple one with underdeveloped character, will not affect the self-confident fool the same way. Honor, privilege, luxury, or a carefree lifestyle are not appropriate for him. He will only abuse it. He will turn the nice room that has been given him into a garbage dump. She will "max out" the credit card she has been loaned. They both will flaunt the recognition that has been afforded them and make their friends sorry they ever allowed their name to be associated with them. Moreover, it will only make them worse, since there will be no incentive for them to repent. The fool will even use the elevated position to harm himself and others. Every attempt to honor the self-confident fool will only backfire on the one who conveys the honor.

At this point, the do-gooders come along and urge those concerned to give him something important to do. All he needs is some added responsibility, they say. He is tired of doing all these little insignificant jobs and really just wants a challenge, they say. They are wrong! This again is a bad move, and it will boomerang on the one who executes it.

> He who sends a message by the hand of a fool
> is cutting off his feet and drinking poison.
> As the legs of the lame hang limp,
> so is a proverb in the mouth of fools.
> As he who binds a stone in a sling,
> so is he who gives honor to a fool.

What happens to a stone when it is bound in a sling? It swings right back around and hits the slinger in the face. That is what is going to happen to anyone who assigns a task of serious responsibility to the fool. No one should ever use this individual as a messenger or agent unless he has a death wish. Might as well go ahead and cut off your own feet now, Solomon says. Might as well swallow that bottle of strychnine, he advises. Not only are you going to hurt yourself, you are going to inflict damage on others as well.

That seems to be where verse 10 fits in, although this verse has a long history of being difficult to translate.

> Like an archer who wounds at random,
> is he who hires a fool or any passerby.

The Hebrew word *rab* (rahv) can mean "master," "much," or "archer." The Geneva Bible, inferring that the subject of the sentence is God, rendered the word as "The Excellent." The King James translators made the inference more explicit.

> The great God that formed all things
> both rewards the fool and rewards transgressors.

In this case, the proverb would mean that God pays the fool the wages he deserves, as suggested by the King James and New King James Versions. *Rab* is not elsewhere used to describe God, however, and it seems too great a stretch to suppose it refers to Him here. To translate it as "the Great One" for God here is misleading, because the greatness implied is not an attribute but an achievement.

Instead, I have incorporated a translation here which interprets *rab* as "archer."[6] In this case, the proverb is not about eternal judgment, but temporal consequences. Not only does it make better sense of the Hebrew, it also fits better within the context of the other proverbs in this sequence.

This proverb compares the person who knowingly hires a self-confident fool (presumably to do a job of some significance) to a shooter who fires indiscriminately into a busy marketplace. The addition of the phrase "or any passerby" warns the prospective employer of hiring someone whose character he does not know for a task of importance. The point of the saying, then, is that it is a downright reckless and even hostile act to give too much responsibility to a self-confident fool or to someone who *may* be a fool and has not been well tested. There is no telling who is going to be hurt. Moreover, *it is not the fool who is accountable here, but the person who empowers him.* This is because the damage a fool can do is (or should be) known, and it is up to those who are in authority of business and government to protect the public from letting the impact of their lives spread too far. If our immediate response to this proverb is that it is extreme and exaggerated, perhaps we should remind ourselves of how many organizations have been brought to scandal and ruin because of the reckless decisions and actions of one irresponsible person in a position of responsibility.

It is a mistake to think that one can inculcate some character into this reckless individual even by the use of ordinary methods of moral instruction. He resists ethical thinking and moral feeling.

> As a thorn that goes into the hand of a drunkard,
> so is a proverb in the mouth of fools.

He is as numb to a proverb as a drunkard is to a thorn in his hand. He can memorize the proverbs and the scriptures and quote them back, but for him there is no more power in them to move his life than in the paralyzed legs of a paraplegic:

> As the legs of the lame hang limp,
> so is a proverb in the mouth of fools.

Words of wisdom are of no use to him. He cannot recognize himself in them, nor can he make applications of them.

There is also the problem of dealing with his uncontrollable mouth. The things he says are frequently offensive, both in style and content. What does one say back to him? Verses 4 and 5 appear to many to be contradictory, even being brought forward (by fools) as an example of supposed contradictions in the Bible:

> Answer not a fool according to his folly,
> lest you also be like him.
> Answer a fool according to his folly,
> lest he be wise in his own conceit.

So what are we supposed to do: decline to answer the fool according to his folly so as not to stoop to his level, or answer the fool according to his folly in order to put him in his place?

Actually *the contradiction is not in the proverbs, it's in the fool!* He is absolutely maddening to deal with. Whenever he opens his mouth, one has to use judgment as to whether to respond directly or indirectly, or just to keep silent. Sometimes one is compelled to reply to his aggravating foolishness, because what he says is so offensive one cannot just let it stand. Yet it is pointless to do so. It is not possible to reason with him, and he is liable to make whoever contests his statements look as much the fool as he is. Regardless of the response, there is a risk of ridicule.

Suppose though for a moment that something actually happens to turn the fool around, and he even begins to be weaned away from his negative behavior. The bad news is that it is only going to be a temporary change.

> As a dog returns to his vomit,
> so a fool returns to his folly.

Here in one of the crudest and most vividly memorable figures of speech in all of literature, we see the character of the self-confident fool compared to the familiar regurgitation instincts of a dog. It isn't a pretty picture, but it is powerfully realistic. The truth is that the behaviors of the fool are only symptoms of his problem, and unless his stubborn will can be changed and his spiritual blindness healed, he will inevitably go back to his former lifestyle—probably with a vengeance.

Yet as bad as his situation is, there is a character more exasperating than he, a situation more hopeless than his:

> Do you see a man who is wise in his own eyes?
> There is more hope for a fool than for him.

On one level, this is perhaps talking about the self-righteous soul who thinks he is wise and who can see everyone else's faults but his own. Another proverb in the same vein says,

> Do you see a man who is *hasty in his words*?
> There is more hope for a fool than for him.[7]

The reference here is to the person who speaks before think-ing, and in particular, to making verbal commitments before eval-uating consequences and possible complications. The "hope" in view is the very practical hope for deliverance from self-imposed difficulties. The former proverb, however, takes the deeper look. Behind all behavior is an attitude, and underlying all motives is a perception, a concept, a belief. Those who trust in their own wis-dom are more likely to be caught in the web of deceit than even the self-confident fool.

It is worth it to pause at this point to realize that we are all sinners and that we must not become smug in our self-congratulation that we are not like the self-confident fool whose transgressions are so apparent. It would be wise if we would accept these words as a pre-emptive rebuke to pride.

On another level more in line with our study, however, we have in verse 12 a preview of a condition of character deprivation more serious even than the one we have been considering. In other words, the good news about the self-confident fool is that he is not yet as bad as he can get. There is a worse kind of fool.

The Destiny of the Self-Confident Fool

What, then, does the future hold for the self-confident fool? In the first place, if he is unrepentant *he will eventually descend into the darker regions of character deficiency syndrome.*

> The crown of the wise is their riches,
> but the foolishness of [self-confident] fools is folly.[8]

"Foolishness" and "folly" here are both *'ivveleth*, rebellion, the folly of the committed fool: literally it says, "the folly of [self-confident] fools is folly." But why the apparent redundancy? The key to understanding the second line is that it stands in contrast to the first. The wise, it says, do not seek first riches, but wisdom; yet wisdom rewards with wealth and abundance those who seek her.[9]

Their riches (which do not have to be monetary or even tangible, for riches may be found in relationships or accomplishments or many other ways) constitute a "crown." Not only are they a reward for his dedication to the Way of Life, they are a witness to the world that here is a person the community should value. This is a generalization, of course, not an absolute. Job was such a man until calamity that he did not deserve was brought into his life. The suffering that is an important aspect of a godly life is not in view in this proverb. Nevertheless, the principle of suffering does not cancel out the principle of a rewarded life, but rather tempers it.

The self-confident fool, however, seeks his own aggrandizement, even if doing so causes him to run afoul of God's moral laws. His unbridled self-centeredness inevitably cuts across God's commandment to love one's neighbor as oneself.[10] In the end, his only real increase and reward is a commitment to rebellion.

In other words, folly is his pursuit, whatever he may call it, and nothing he may do can transform it into something morally right and socially useful. Moreover, we have here an incisive critique of the highest aspirations of the self-confident fool: *his real folly is folly itself.* In other words, it is not merely that he is conceited, but that his path is one of self-destruction. While for the time being he still maintains some degree of restraint upon his appetites and behavior, the direction of his life is ultimately to cut loose from whatever it is that is holding him back—be it religion, society, family, or conscience. If he continues to follow this direction, he will become what he seeks. This is why we are describing the deficiency of character as a *syndrome*: it is not a static condition, and it does not stand still. It is a descent.

The self-confident fool will not only descend morally, *he will also descend in personal and social esteem,* as seen in this contrast between glory and shame.

> The wise shall inherit glory,
> but shame shall be the promotion of fools.[11]

Shame, like glory (or honor), takes many forms and admits of different degrees, but in all cases it tends to be manifest in public. Surely, this verse can be applied to any specific act of folly, but it is best to interpret the saying in a more general, universal sense. In the same way that the wise will attain open recognition for their wisdom (though they may have to wait for it like an inheritance), so will the self-confident fool be recognized, much to the embarrassment of himself and whoever must be identified with him.

If his particularly favored form of folly is slothfulness, he may also lose his livelihood.

> The fool folds his hands together in sleep,
> and eats his own flesh.[12]

Here is a clear identification of self-confident folly with the sin of slothfulness. It is not that all fools are sluggards—some may be workaholics. Many of us, however, have a tendency toward self-indulgence and complacency simply as a weakness of temperament, much as cartoon characters like Dagwood, Beetle Bailey, and Garfield. Those who fit into this category have to learn to cope in a world that is unsympathetic with their desire to take it easier. One way or another, they must acquire enough self-discipline to get to work and to make a living for themselves and their families. The self-confident fool who is inclined toward sloth, however, is undone by his unearned self-esteem. He congratulates himself on his ability to avoid work, and his casual attitude toward life becomes his undoing.

On the other side of the spectrum is the materialistic fool who manages to acquire and maintain wealth. He may work hard for it, to the exclusion of everything else. *His money will be of no ultimate value to him because he will not be able to buy off the day of his death.*

> Those who trust in their wealth,
> and boast themselves in the multitude of their riches,

none of them can by any means redeem his brother,
nor give to God a ransom for him…
that he should live forever,
and not see corruption.
For he sees that wise men die.
Likewise the fool and the stupid perish,
and leave their wealth to others.[13]

Neither will money benefit him in the day of judgment, when God will call him to account for his use of it. As Jesus said in his parable of the rich man whose only worry was where to store all his wealth,

But God said to him, You fool, this night shall your soul be required of you. Then whose shall those things be which you have accumulated?[14]

The lesson Jesus is imparting goes beyond the truth that death comes to all; it looks beyond death to the judgment. It is only a hint, at least in this parable, but it seems clear enough. The story concludes with Jesus urging his hearers to be "rich toward God." The implication is that there will be a final accounting, and that one day it will be learned who is truly rich and who is not.

The self-confident fool will very likely experience disciplinary punishment, perhaps even at the hand of the law.

Judgments are prepared for scorners,
and stripes for the back of fools.[15]

The word "stripes," remember, is not about decoration, fashion, or rank. It refers to the painful wounds inflicted by blows of a rod, whose purpose is to discourage someone who has offended society from repeating some offensive behavior. A major international controversy was raised some years ago over a young American man who committed a minor crime in Singapore and was punished by caning. That is the kind of punishment in view here.

The stripes do not necessarily have to be literal, however. Stripes may also be a figure of speech for any disciplinary consequences of self-destructive or anti-social behavior, in particular sanctions imposed by others. The giving of strokes also represents civil and legal penalties for petty crime, mischief, and general wrongdoing. In our vernacular we might say, for example, that someone has "taken a beating" in court. The point is, the fool is not always going to have smooth sailing for his folly, and may well (to borrow a contemporary American proverb) get his posterior kicked for his offenses.

Yet for all this, the self-confident fool has enough moral sense left that it is still possible to reach him—not likely, perhaps, but possible. Therefore there are a few rare direct appeals to him to wise up.

> You simple, understand wisdom,
> and you fools, be of an understanding heart![16]

Be warned that when you are trying to reach the self-confident fool, you cannot be soft or subtle. You have to be blunt and confrontational. The Bible itself gets right in his face. The fool must be directed to the first principle of wisdom and understanding, namely, the fear of God.

> Understand, you stupid among the people.
> And you fools, when will you be wise?
> He who planted the ear, shall He not hear?
> He who formed the eye, shall He not see?
> He who chastises the nations,
> shall He not impose correction?
> He who teaches man knowledge, shall He not know?[17]

To put it another way, God is God. He knows all our ways, and it is folly to think we shall not give an account to Him for every thought, word, and deed.

The Gist

Aggravating. The self-confident fool is probably the single most irritating, frustrating, and difficult personality you have to deal with.

Unhappy. The self-confident fool will never be truly happy, and eventually will get a comeuppance—but don't hold your breath. It may not be until he faces God.

And yet. The self-confident fool is not as bad as he could get, and is still reachable.

For your consideration

Read the story below and answer the questions that follow.

In 2004, Dartmouth professor Sydney Finkelstein, reflecting research on fifty companies, published an article titled "Why Smart Executives Fail" in which he enumerated "7 Habits of Spectacularly Unsuccessful Executives":

1. They see themselves and their companies as dominating their environment, greatly overestimating their control over events and circumstances that are, in fact, beyond human control.
2. They treat their companies as extensions of themselves. The warning sign is when the leader sees no ethical conflict with using corporate funds for personal purposes.
3. They think they have all the answers and cannot be told anything.
4. They interpret disagreement as disloyalty and ruthlessly eliminate anyone who isn't completely behind them.
5. They are obsessed with the corporate image, but have little time for operational details.
6. They underestimate obstacles.

7. Often looking back to some defining moment that was key to launching their success, they stubbornly rely on what worked for them in the past and fix on it as though it were the absolute.

- Can you see any of the principles of character deficiency syndrome reflected in Prof. Finkelstein's findings?
- How do the above "7 Habits" compare with the behavior patterns of the self-confident fool?
- Which of these would you recognize as a danger sign in your own life?

11

Committed to Folly

"There are no guilty people in prison." This is a truism familiar to those whose work in law enforcement, the legal system, and our penal institutions. Now to say that *every* soul in prison proclaims his or her innocence is an overstatement—but not by much. It makes it difficult for those who try to work with them in a redemptive way to determine who really is innocent and should not be in prison at all. I know several people who work in jail and prison ministries, and I applaud all who do. But it is not a work for the simple. Prisoners do lie, and some of them do it convincingly well and have fooled many.

Roger Keith Coleman, however, seemed to be different. Convicted of the 1982 rape and bloody murder of his sister-in-law, he persisted in his denials throughout the investigation, trial, and subsequent string of appeals. The staff at Centurion Ministries who labored for almost two decades to try to overturn his conviction were not gullible people. They knew they were dealing with a man who had a history of attempted rape. What seemed to them the thinness of the evidence against him was combined with the overwhelming sincerity of his protests of innocence. All their efforts were to no avail. He was executed by the State of Virginia on May 20, 1992, two days after he appeared on the cover of *Time* magazine under the headline: "This man might be innocent; this man is due to die." His last words before being electrocuted were, "An innocent man is going to be murdered tonight." His supporters and all opponents of the death penalty nationwide mourned this apparent travesty of justice.

Efforts continued for years to clear the executed man's name posthumously (and, by implication, to condemn the system that convicted him). When DNA testing became viable and began to be instrumental in overturning many longstanding convictions, the governor of Virginia ordered tests to be done in the case of Roger Keith Coleman. In January 2006, the results of those DNA tests came in. They brought conclusive evidence that he was, in fact, guilty of the crime he vehemently denied with his last breath.

In an interview with the *Washington Post*, James McCloskey of Centurion Ministries appeared stunned by the outcome. "How can somebody, with such equanimity, such dignity, such quiet confidence, make those his final words even though he is guilty?"[1]

How indeed? Only someone who is absolutely persuaded that his guilt or innocence is a matter of self-declaration rather than fact could so maintain his innocence when he knows his guilt. Only someone who has no concern for judgment after death could face his imminent death with a bald-faced lie such as this. This is someone who has made a full commitment to folly.

To the Lower Depths of Folly

The Roman statesman Cicero observed that the function of wisdom is to discriminate between good and evil. The shortage of this kind of wisdom is the epitome of character deficiency syndrome, the downward spiral of folly. Before we explore this phenomenon further, a brief review of where we have been may be helpful.

First, remember that our English word "fool" translates several Hebrew words used widely in the Old Testament for individuals who are lacking in moral character. A fool is not someone who is silly or unintelligent, but someone who is *unwise*. He has never learned nor purposed to live by the axiom that "the fear of the LORD is the beginning of knowledge."

The different Hebrew words for fool, in their respective scriptural contexts, have very different shades of meaning while owning the same essential theme. Together they indicate at least four progressive stages or degrees of descent into the moral and spiritual depravity that are described by the term character deficiency syndrome.

The term *simple fool* identifies the least insidious stage, that of the naïve and immature soul who lacks the most basic understanding of moral cause and effect. In this case, we are dealing with someone who is immature, who lacks the judgment and discernment that should come with experience. Years ago, there was a tag line on a television comedy show: "Blow in my ear, and I'll follow you anywhere." That could serve as the motto for the simple fool. He is easily enticed. He is gullible. He sees how much fun it will be to misbehave. He never checks if there is a price tag. He is like the unhappy teenagers who made a spur of the moment decision as a prank to steal some stop signs from a lightly traveled road, but then a fatal accident occurred at the intersection where one of the signs was stolen. The teens now had to face the grim charge of involuntary manslaughter, learning sadly and too late the price of acting without thinking of consequences.

When the small town of Jamestown, New York, made national headlines, the city fathers cringed, for they were not the kind that boosted civic pride.[2] Nine teenage girls, including one only thirteen years old, had contracted the AIDS virus from one infected man. A twenty-year-old drifter, he had gotten the girls' attention by flattering their looks, and in some cases offering them drugs. That is not all. The public health authorities were estimating that one hundred or more people may have been put at risk of HIV infection because of this one reckless reprobate.

A few weeks after this story came out, a reporter went back and did a follow-up story of the impact of this dreadful news on the town. Some of the local youths who admitted they were engaging in "risky sex" said that all the warnings they had been getting about AIDS and sexually transmitted diseases were hitting home for the first time. One sixteen-year-old boy, who was tested after hearing about the local epidemic, made this astounding statement: "I didn't know it was that big a deal until it came to Jamestown." These young people have grown up in the age of AIDS, and neither its horrors nor its primary means of transmission has been hidden from them. Nevertheless, it never occurred to them that they could become its victims until some of them did. That is the universal mindset, not only of youth, but of the simple fool, and there are plenty of them—of us!—out there. The simple are slow to learn of things that hide behind the mask of pleasure but can destroy. Yet if their course can be interrupted before they become cynical or before disaster overtakes them, they can be "scared straight."

We hope the simple one will learn, before someone gets hurt, that the neglect of wisdom always carries a high cost. Even more important, we want him to learn that wisdom and morality, too, has some "sex appeal," so to speak—that there are tremendous rewards to paying the price of learning moral discipline.

If, however, the simple fool's tendency to follow his passions goes unchecked, he may descend to become the *self-confident fool.* The Bible has more to say about this character-deficient soul than any other. The Hebrew word *kesil* suggests someone who is full of himself. Like the simple one he is inclined to make the wrong moral choices, but even more so. The naive fool might stumble into a disastrous trap. The self-confident fool will stride boldly into it, convinced that he is the master of the situation.

Proverbs describes the self-confident fool as a soul with no moral understanding. He "has no *delight* in understanding." Not to belabor the issue, but understanding is not a matter of the intellect; it is about choosing to do right and not wrong. This fool reveals himself by three outstanding characteristics: he is extraordinarily stubborn, he is mouthy, and he thinks it is fun to cause trouble.

The self-confident fool may spend his life in the pursuit of vain riches and even attain them, yet die unsatisfied with any of it, leaving behind a legacy of unhappiness. He may, on the other hand, descend into poverty through slothfulness. Sooner or later, he is likely to face punishment for his misdeeds, along with shame and embarrassment. Worst of all, unless he repents, he may descend still deeper into that multilevel condition of folly we are calling character deficiency syndrome.

Yet he is not a completely hopeless creature—at least not yet. Wisdom pleads with the fool to "be of (or take on) an understanding heart."[3] A scathing series of couplets in Proverbs 26 flays the self-confident fool, yet verse 12 arrives with this surprising barb: "Do you see a man who is wise in his own conceit? There is more hope of a fool than of him." We are now ready to see more fully who that one is. It is a phrase that aptly introduces us to the fool in the third degree, the *committed fool*.

Here is the whole story in a nutshell: The naive fool doesn't *realize* that sin has consequences. The self-confident fool doesn't *believe* that sin has consequences. The committed fool doesn't *care* that sin has consequences.

The Hebrew word is *'evil* (eh-VEEL—no relation to the English word "evil," just coincidence). It refers to the full-fledged fool, a person who is morally perverse and insolent. He (or she, for folly has no gender bias) is one who has decisively rejected wisdom and made a commitment to destructive ideas and behaviors. We have already seen a related term, *'ivveleth* (ihv-vel-leth) in connection with the behavior of the self-confident fool. It is the primary Hebrew word for folly, sometimes translated "foolishness," and refers primarily to attitude and behavior. It is Folly with a capital *F*.

The Committed Fool: Identifying Marks

In the first place, *the committed fool has positively rejected reverent faith, moral absolutes, and the disciplines of an upright life.*

> The fear of the LORD is the beginning of knowledge,
> but [committed] fools despise wisdom and instruction.[4]

The word "despise" is the Hebrew *buz* (booz). It is a strong word. It indicates not mere neglect or disdain, but open contempt and mockery. The problem with the committed fool is not just that he is inclined through human weakness to miss the mark. We all do that. This individual has consciously set himself or herself against the moral order of God. "[Committed] fools *despise* wisdom and instruction."

Even at this point, one may detect degrees of folly. Usually, there is a particular *part* of wisdom and instruction (i.e., certain of God's commandments and principles of their application) that the committed fool will reject. Occasionally, however, one may come across an individual who reacts against *all* wisdom and instruction in principle. In all cases, the term describes a person who has made a conscious determination by the strength of his will to live as though he were independent of God's moral order and not constrained by its injunctions, whether in part or in whole. He despises it; that is, he declines to respect it, but rather holds it in contempt.

The fact that he has made this conscious choice does not necessarily mean that he will turn into a certifiable sociopath. He may well obey the laws of *man* in all civility and give all outward appearances of decency most of the time.

He will not, however, tolerate being rebuked by absolute divine laws that cut against his own will and desires. He does not agree that there are moral and spiritual principles that are binding on all people of all times and environments—or at least that are binding upon *him*. Neither will he appreciate hearing that he will ultimately face a personal judgment from the God who instituted those laws and principles. He is quite determined that these things are not true, if for no other reason than that he does not want them to be true. The focus here is not on an abstract philosophical stance, but on concrete behaviors and personal choices.

The committed fool's rejection of God's moral order is directly related to the moral perversity of his character. By the habit of his life, he has become used to ignoring God, so that it has become the wisdom of his life to be a fool. The prophet Jeremiah refers to this when he says,

> For my people are *foolish*: they have not known me;
> they are stupid children, and they have no understanding;
> *they are wise to do evil, but to do good they have no knowledge.*[5]

It is hard to know, in this case, which came first: the moral perversity or the rejection of God's laws. The two things go hand in hand.

Again, I want to emphasize that the point is not that every committed fool plunges headlong into every type of depravity. Felonies and misdemeanors and debaucheries are not the only marks of folly and rebellion. The point is rather that the rejection of "the fear of God" as his value system is traceable to his desire to do some evil while avoiding his moral obligation to do what is right and good.

It may be that there is some particular evil thing the committed fool desires to do because it holds the promise of pleasure or power or possession. On the other hand, there may be rather some righteous duty he does not want to perform because it is inconvenient or difficult, or perhaps not sufficiently rewarding. In either case, he does not want to be reminded of his moral obligations.

See if the following story sounds familiar. A fellow wants to move in with his girlfriend so he can enjoy free (or at least convenient) sex with her, along with housekeeping, laundry, and shared rent—but he does not even want to have a legally binding contract with her, let alone a lifelong covenant. That would tie him down He certainly does not want to hear about responsibility, paternity, or any other moral obligation. She, on the other hand, is willing to tolerate that arrangement because presently he meets her minimal needs for affection and security, while leaving her free to pursue her own career interests. Besides, she may be able to manipulate him into a more permanent arrangement in the future. To that latter end, she might even get pregnant with the thought that perhaps a baby on the way would move him closer to a binding commitment.

Both of these people are living in folly, playing fast and loose with their moral responsibilities, being honest neither to themselves nor to one another. In the process, they injure not only themselves and each other, but they also help drag down the collective morality of their own generation and damage the prospects of the children they may bring into the world. There was a time not long ago when few entered into an arrangement like this because it was so severely disapproved socially. Today, it is a socially accepted practice and in some spheres is positively expected, despite ample evidence that cohabitation provides neither future marital happiness nor a satisfying substitute for marriage.[6]

This is but one banal scenario of how people engage in folly while thinking they are making the best choices for their happiness. Not everyone who commits to a foolish decision is a committed fool. Many people live their lives in careless disregard for God's commandments, although they may mean well. That is the mark of the simple fool. But the mark of the committed fool is that he knows someone will get hurt through his choices and deeds and cares nothing about it. Committed fools are the ones who prey on the simple.

Most of us know or have had some dealings with this kind of character in a variety of settings. He was the crooked salesman who stuck us with shoddy merchandise. She was the coworker with the vile tongue and backstabbing ways whose mission in life seemed to be to keep the workplace in turmoil. He was the worthless creep who married into the family and brought heartache and division with him. She was the hypocrite who masqueraded as a friend while undercutting every relationship of those who trusted her. In Shakespeare, he is Iago and she is Lady Macbeth.

Jeremiah says, "They are stupid children." Stupid is the adjective form of *sekel* (se-KEL); it means senseless. In Ecclesiastes, this word is used in various forms as a virtual synonym for *kesil,* the self-confident fool. In this verse, however, the context makes clear that for Jeremiah, it is synonymous with the *'evil,* the committed fool. One Hebrew scholar says, "it denotes any deviation of the mind from what is true, good and right," and thus characterizes someone who acts "stupidly, absurdly, inconsistently,"[7] someone who lives in a spiritual stupor. In Jeremiah 5:21, the same word is translated "foolish" and defined there as being without a heart of understanding, having unseeing eyes and unhearing ears. This is only the beginning of the Bible's profile of a depraved character.

There is one more insight from this verse in Jeremiah: *"They are wise to do evil."* Here is the very definition of moral perversity. Perversity is not the same thing as perversion. Perversion is the twisting of some good thing into an evil, unnatural thing. This English word is so strongly associated with sexual deviancy that I have been careful to avoid its use in connection with character deficiency syndrome because it could be misleading. A perverse person is not necessarily a pervert. He is, however, a rebel, who in a more general sense has become an adversary to what is good and right.

What the prophet makes clear once again is that folly is not a deficiency of intellect—the use of the word "stupid" notwithstanding—but a perverse rejection of godliness. In other words, "they" (the unrepentant subjects of his diatribe) are not incompetent ignoramuses at all, but smart people. They turn the sharpness of their intellect toward finding ways out of their moral obligations, toward denying the claims of righteousness on their lives. They invent new approaches to defying God's law, and then justify themselves for doing it. They are the people who can give a persuasive explanation for why God's law is terrible and why it is good and necessary to break it.

The committed fool's character is a product of rebellion, and his characteristic behavior is equivalent to sin.

> Some became [committed] fools through their rebellious ways,
> and suffered affliction because of their iniquities.[8]
> The thought of folly is sin...[9]
> O God, you know my folly,
> and my sins are not hidden from you.[10]

As we have been saying all along, anyone and everyone who aims for this condition of character, intentionally or not, inevitably reaches it.

The word "thought" in Proverbs 24:9 ("The thought of folly is sin") is *zimmah*. It comes from a root verb meaning to meditate, to have in mind, to purpose. This is not a fleeting fancy or fantasy, but an intention to commit folly. According to this proverb, before the deed is ever carried out, even the plan and purpose to do so is described as sin. If, therefore, the plan and purpose is a sin, how much more must the deed be sinful! When Jesus impeached anger as murder, lust as adultery, and calculated swearing as taking God's name in vain (Matthew 5:21–37), he was not inventing a new principle or adding to the Ten Commandments. His preaching was saturated with the Wisdom perspective. Surely, he was aware of this proverb when he spoke, and he appears to be enlarging the principle it expresses. People can observe deeds, but only God knows the thoughts of the heart.

It is possible to come up with all kinds of reasons, insights, and excuses for why people do the crooked, dishonest, perverse, and perverted things they do. Ultimately, no one is responsible for what others may do, but each soul is responsible before God and the world for his own choices. To do right is a choice, and to do wrong is a choice—and it is a choice that the committed fool makes of his own accord. No one makes him do it. He does what he wants to do.

The committed fool is what he does.

> Though you crush a [committed] fool in a mortar
> like grain with a pestle,
> yet will his folly not depart from him.[11]

Here is a crucial insight into what separates the committed fool from other, less egregious types of fools. This is the outcome of the law of sowing and reaping in the life of the committed fool. Sow a thought, reap a deed; sow a deed, reap a habit; sow a habit, reap a character; sow a character, reap a life.

There is a clear progression laid out in the book of Proverbs. The simple one, naively failing to use any judgment or discernment, follows his passions. Self-discipline and sound morality appear to him to be tough, unappealing, and unrewarding. It is easier to seek direct gratification of his ego and his senses. This inevitably leads him away from what he perceives as self-denial and toward a positive rejection of specific moral standards. Thus Proverbs

14:18 provides the forecast for his life: "The simple inherit folly," *'ivveleth*, moral rebellion.

Eventually, the simple one loses his gullibility—some would call it innocence, but there is nothing truly innocent about it. He crosses over from simpleness to becoming a self-confident fool, depicted in Proverbs as being absolutely enamored with *'ivveleth*, full-fledged folly. It is something he seems inspired to achieve. He talks it, plans it, and eventually starts doing it.

At some point, he becomes committed to it. Just as the believer in Christ becomes a disciple of the Lord, *the fool becomes a disciple of folly*. It becomes his lifestyle, and it is his study. It grows until it is his love and passion. For the committed fool, the folly (whatever form it may take) becomes *his* folly, becomes ingrained into his character to the point that it is now an integral part of his personality. No longer is he merely morally deficient. He has become morally *pernicious*.

His rebellious attitude and behavior, then, is no longer merely a habit or even a lifestyle, but his identity. He has become what he does. For this reason, one may forget about helping him reform his behavior. Whatever kind of godless folly he has favored is now inseparable, as it were, from the molecules of his body. To use a different metaphor, he is no longer merely running the software of rebellion; he has rebellion for his operating system.

Perhaps you think I am exaggerating. Perhaps you think even Solomon is overstating the case, or at least using hyperbole to make his point. Not this time. There is no overstatement here at all, but a straightforward observation of principle. To illustrate my point (and Solomon's), I return to some comments by John Douglas, whose work in criminal profiling was mentioned in the first chapter. He describes a conversation with a gambler he had arrested, which gave him a seminal insight into the criminal personality. The gambler told him, "You can't stop us, John, no matter what you do. *It's what we are.*"[12] In another passage, Douglas refers to the work of behavioral psychologist Stanton

Samenow who, "after years of firsthand research...concluded in his penetrating and insightful book, *Inside the Criminal Mind*, that 'criminals think differently from other people.' Criminal behavior, Samenow believes, is not so much a question of mental illness as *character defect*."[13]

Recall the proverb that started this discussion to begin with: "Though you crush a fool in a mortar like grain with a pestle, yet will his folly not depart from him." Once again, it is important to divest the word "folly" (or "foolishness") of all our lighthearted associations with the comic and the ridiculous. Folly, as it is understood here, reaches to the uttermost depths of depravity in the crime of serial murder. At one point in his book, Douglas discusses the question of whether a serial killer can be rehabilitated.

It is not an abstract question. Douglas cites the case of a killer of two children, who was released from prison after serving only fifteen years of a twenty-five year sentence and proceeded to kill again. His argument, powerful both in its logic and indignation, is that to let such a person go free, one must assume one of two premises. Either he found prison to be "a wonderful, spiritually uplifting, eye-opening, and rehabilitative experience" that made him see the light and change his ways forever; or "prison life was so thoroughly punishing in every way, that despite his bad background and continuing desire to rape and kill children, he never wanted to be back in prison and resolved to do anything he could to avoid going back."[14]

> But if you don't accept either of these two premises, how... do you let someone like that out without considering the strong possibility that he's going to kill again?[15]

For the serial killer, in particular, a line has been crossed (perhaps several lines in succession) and a radical commitment made, so that he (it is almost always a male) is going to relieve the pressures of his life and find satisfaction in taking the life of other human beings. His terrible, secret urges become his terrible, secret identity.

Before going any further, I want to make clear the purpose of this discussion is *not* to say that all committed fools are serial killers or that they will become serial killers. I am using this extreme example of the most horrible criminal behavior imaginable to point out a truth that applies to all forms of human iniquity across the board—*that once a person has committed himself to moral rebellion, that form of wickedness becomes indelibly an element of his character.* Only a radical change of identity could possibly eradicate it.

But no, it is not necessary to become a serial murderer or even a criminal at all to qualify as a committed fool. On the contrary, *the committed fool may still be very religious, even a member of the clergy.* This is not my opinion, but that of the biblical prophets. Consider the words of the prophet Zechariah:

> A *foolish* shepherd...shall not visit those in the land that are cut off, neither shall seek the young one, nor heal that which is broken, nor feed that which stands still, but he shall eat the flesh of the fat, and tear their hoofs.[16]

This is a disturbing indictment: moral rebellion as the identifying characteristic of a spiritual leader! At first blush, the prophet appears to be scolding ministers who are basically negligent in their ministerial duties. But why does he call them *foolish*, thus accusing them of *'ivveleth*, moral rebellion?

Note first that the spiritual leader has rejected God's priorities for ministry. He is not seeking the lost, nurturing the immature, healing the broken, nor feeding the flock. Why is he not? The prophet does not charge him with incompetence, but with folly. He has made a commitment against God. He has adopted selfish, self-centered priorities. He will feed so greedily on the flock that he will even resort to "tearing off the hoofs"—an image of ruthless and insatiable rapacity.[17]

The message is clear enough. One does not have to search the prison rolls in order to find corruption of character. One might just as well find it at church. Folly is not necessarily crude, and the committed fool is not necessarily rude. At its heart, folly is a self-serving lifestyle. A person may be urbane, dignified, educated, respected—even religious—yet be a fool. To give oneself over to even one immoral issue, one point of moral rebellion, is to become a fool. This is why Ecclesiastes says,

> As dead flies cause the perfumer's ointment to stink,
> so does a little folly outweigh wisdom and honor.[17]

Whoever, therefore, thinks he can persist in some sin or immoral behavior and still control and confine its effects to one compartment of his life is deluded. It is a modern conceit that life is divided into discreet segments, each one separate from the other. God's Word affirms that life is a whole. What occurs in one of its departments affects all.

People may draw a veil between private and public character and think that they have walled off one from the other. The past few decades have been littered with the reputations and careers of some prominent ministers and statesmen who have had the veil torn aside to reveal ugly secrets they have tried to hide.

Beyond the risk of exposure, however, is the inescapable truth that God is one, morality is one, and ethical principles are inseparable from morality. From a biblical worldview, it seems inconceivable that anyone should think otherwise. Permit, please, one more illustration from the history of infamous crimes. In 2005, the identity of the BTK killer of Wichita, Kansas, was discovered, and his gruesome murders over decades revealed and judged in a court of law. What shocked the community is that he was an upstanding, reputable member of it—a respected family man, a civil servant, and a leader in his church. Now what difference does it make if a serial murderer is a decent fellow, other than that one horrible habit? A person's character may be at odds with his mind (the way he thinks about things), but his character is who he truly is. All the good aspects of a person's character cannot outweigh the folly that he harbors *unrepentantly* in his lifestyle. To that extent, he is a committed fool.

The Gist

The Committed Fool:

- Has positively rejected the fear of God and moral absolutes.
- Has acquired his character through the practice of rebellion.
- Is what he does. Folly is not only his behavior, it is his identity.

For your consideration

- How does one progress from being simple and easily mislead to becoming a committed fool? How long do you think the process takes?
- What do you think: Are some people born evil, or do they become that way? Or is it some of both?
- How does understanding character deficiency syndrome help explain the problem of recidivism (the tendency to relapse into criminal behavior after punishment)?

12

A Fatal Attraction

One of the most compelling metaphors for evil in modern literature is the One Ring in J. R. R. Tolkien's *The Lord of the Rings*. Vested with untold power by a Dark Lord, the Ring is coveted both by the one who made it and by every intelligent being that knows of it. It binds souls with the promise of attaining one's deepest desires, but in the end destroys all who seek to possess it. It is said:

> A mortal...who keeps one of the Great Rings, does not die, but he does not grow or obtain more life, he merely continues, until at last every minute is a weariness. And if he often uses the Ring to make himself invisible, he fades: he becomes in the end invisible permanently, and walks in the twilight under the eye of the dark power that rules the Rings. Yes, sooner or later—later, if he is strong or well-meaning to begin with, but neither strength nor

good purpose will last—sooner or later the dark power will devour him.[1]

At this point, we need to turn our investigation to consider the fatal attraction of folly, *'ivveleth*, the attitudes and behaviors of moral rebellion. What could possibly be so attractive about moral decay and the degeneration of character that it draws so many into its destructive flame? Up to this point in our analysis of character deficiency syndrome, we have focused upon a *person*, specifically the fool and his unhealthy character. Before we go further, we must give due consideration to *the folly that drives the fool*. In doing so, we will return to some of the proverbs we have seen before, as well as bringing in some passages from outside of the wisdom literature. It is important to understand the folly that makes a fool what he is, and how we might avoid its enticements.

The Rule of Folly

The first thing we have to come to grips with is that *people are attracted to folly because it makes them feel good*. It offers excitement, pleasure, the feeling of freedom, and momentary self-fulfillment.

> Folly is joy to him who is destitute of wisdom,
> but a man of understanding walks uprightly.[2]

People of healthy character *do right*. They keep their responsibilities and stay within God-ordained boundaries regardless of whether it is fun or entertaining or enjoyable. Yes, there are joys involved, but there are also hardships. In good times and in bad, they stay and keep the faith simply because it is the right thing to do.

We must admit, however, that all those morally perverse attitudes and behaviors that may together be classified as folly do have an attractive side that appeals to people at the point of their vulnerabilities. Lust is compelling, and so is greed. Likewise anger, revenge, bigotry, and egotism. It is true that when the true nature of these motives is exposed they do not look beautiful at all, but they never go out in public without a costume. Lust is all about good feelings and excitement, while greed is about getting what one wants. Anger flares when one's rights are threatened. Social and ethnic pride is acceptable, but no one admits to bigotry. Fame, popularity, wealth, pleasure, ego gratification—all these things are powerful enough motives that people will do despicable things to fulfill them.

Read the proverb again:

> Folly is *joy* to him who is destitute of wisdom,
> but a man of understanding walks uprightly.

Note that folly is contrasted with uprightness, which is universally and cross-culturally regarded—wrongly—as being dull. Notice also that people with weak character consider folly to be "joy," meaning either fun or fulfillment or both. The problem with teaching values in today's world is that righteousness does not often have effective public relations, while folly has an astronomical advertising budget!

The second observation we need to make on this point is that *participating in morally perverse behavior leads ultimately to the adoption of morally perverse values.* Let's revisit a couple of proverbs we've looked at before.

> The simple inherit folly.
> The folly of [self-confident] fools yields folly.[3]

We have already made the point that folly, in all its manifestations, is an aggressive force in a person's life. If a person yields to it, it will progressively take over. The Apostle Paul, combining theology and psychology in a masterful way, writes,

> Do you not know that to whom you yield yourselves as slaves to obey, you become the slave of whom you obey, whether of sin which leads to death, or of obedience which leads to righteousness?[4]

It may not be in the mind of the simple fool to become a moral rebel when he gives in to his lusts; and even the self-confident fool may not have planned from the beginning to become lawless and godless. It is seldom apparent how slippery the slope truly is between contemplating folly as a deed and embracing folly as a lifestyle. Indulging one's weaknesses can be dangerous to one's moral health.

What happens is this: When an individual continues to indulge in wrong behavior because of its pleasure and supposed benefits, he or she vests that wrongdoing, that evil thing, with value. If, for whatever reason, you allow yourself to do something that you yourself regard as wrong, even if you know it is evil, it becomes incorporated into your total value system as a *good* thing. It then has an effect of its own upon the whole. We think we can keep different segments of our lives in neat, leak-proof compartments, but the Bible says otherwise. The biblical saying is, "a little leaven leavens the whole lump," a little bit of yeast permeates the whole batch of dough. A little bit of moral compromise can affect the whole value system of an individual, of a family, of a society, of a nation. Evil does not stand still, and wickedness is infectious.

The end result is that folly, if it is not resisted and actively displaced by the practice of discipline and virtue, will take over one's life. Along the way folly installs its own new and perverse value system that calls right wrong and wrong right. Folly is an individual matter, and the perversities of an individual fool's value system may be idiosyncratic and even antisocial. Society as a whole still tries to keep weird, bizarre, and disruptive behavior in the margins.

When, however, enough committed fools populate a society, they can begin to sway the culture toward their own downward direction. The prophet Isaiah spotted this horrific development in his own society and condemned it. He was particularly alarmed because it was the elite class in his society that had adopted a twisted system of moral values.

> Woe unto those who call evil good and good evil, who put darkness for light, and light for darkness; who put bitter for sweet and sweet for bitter.[5]

Then he follows up with words that hauntingly echo the wisdom writings:

> Woe to those who are wise in their own eyes, and prudent in their own sight.[6]

It begins with people who believe they do not need God to tell them what to do, or the Scriptures to delineate authoritatively what is right and wrong. They proceed to devise for themselves a "modern" or "contemporary" or "revolutionary" system of values and morals. Lacking a transcendent point of reference, their moral improvisations eventually become so twisted and perverse that it becomes impossible to truly judge (on their terms) what is good and right, and what is evil and wrong.

Consequently, the sweet becomes bitter and the bitter becomes sweet—that is, people become attracted to what ought to be repulsive, and vice versa. Things that should repulse people now stimulate them, while at the same time they reject truth, real beauty, and the pleasures of purity. This is a truly abnormal moral condition—and one that I fear our own society is increasingly demonstrating in the present day. Listen to the arguments given in the public forums (including the school systems) for abortion rights, euthanasia, same-sex marriage, "tolerance" for what are euphemistically called "alternative lifestyles." Consider that all these things, once regarded with moral revulsion, are now regarded as mainstream values by many (it does not have to be a majority), and that whoever argues against them is considered out of step with the evolution of society.

As the revolutionary point of view gains ascendancy among the cultural elite, those who desire to maintain the moral order established for generations are put on the defensive. A process of relabeling is set in motion. Immorality is put forward as the "new morality," as the propagandists for folly seize the rhetorical high ground. Defenders of real moral absolutes fall into the trap by insisting on a return to "traditional values," as though acknowledging that there really is more than one moral standard. One can hardly blame them. Having been fiercely attacked for being "Puritans," "Victorians," or "Fundamentalists," and now being labeled as bigots and worse, they are only trying to rescue from complete vilification the standards that society used to honor and serve.

Look at the popular media, television, music, literature, movies. The memory has faded, but one of the most talked about films of the 1990s was *Primary Colors*. Adapted from a bestselling roman à clef, the film depicts the presidential campaign of a lusty southern governor whose disingenuous campaign for votes is punctuated by a number of extramarital affairs. Without commenting on the movie itself (or the thinly disguised events it purports to retell), I wish to point out what was in the mind of the people who made it. Director Mike Nichols had this to say about his philandering hero:

> Vital men have strong appetites and that's the package they come in. Powerful sexual urges go with powerful men who want to get things done.[7]

How is that as a defense of adultery in principle? The thesis is that real men, powerful, potent men, cannot confine their primal urges to marriage, nor can they be satisfied with one partner. We have to expect that the men who have what it takes to rule the nations of the earth are going to spread themselves around sexually. By implication, anyone who is faithful to his wife and honest in his dealings must be a wimp!

I am not citing this opinion because it is new—it is not. It is a rationalization for immorality that has been around for millennia. It caught my attention, though, because ever since then things like this have been said quite a bit in our generation. Here is an illustration of how folly inevitably distorts our reason even as it corrupts our morality. It has been repeatedly stated in these pages that folly is not a synonym for low intelligence. It must now be observed, however, that a fool's logic is likely to be as faulty as his character.

Folly as Deceit

Thus far we have seen that folly is attractive and that once it is accepted as a part of life, it begins to affect, influence, and even take over the whole. Now I want to point out that, according to the scriptures we've been studying, *the attractiveness of folly is deceitful*.

> The wisdom of the prudent is to understand his way,
> but the folly of [self-confident] fools is deceit.[8]

Moral soundness means to have a clear view of life and what it takes to be happy. Folly, moral perversity, holds only a counterfeit promise of happiness.

In this proverb, the prudent person is contrasted with the self-confident fool, the *kesil*. The prudent person is someone who is both morally aware and practical. He uses the mind God gave him to make his choices based on God's commandments. He regards the commandments to be absolute, and circumstances to be relative. He desires a happy life as much as anyone, but he pursues it by making decisions based on right and wrong, not feelings or apparent benefits. He does not let changeable circumstances knock him off the path of what he knows is right. His life is not always easy or pleasant, and sometimes the moral choices he must make even seem to add to his difficulties. On the balance, however, his life is a happy and satisfying one, and he leaves behind a legacy of honor for his posterity. This is what it means to live according to true wisdom.

The self-confident fool thinks he has a better plan. He thinks that God's commandments are too restrictive and that all absolutes are merely arbitrary. He believes that he needs no standard of right and wrong beyond his own opinions in order to gauge the situation of his life. "It can't be wrong if it feels right," he tells himself. He is deceived to think that moral rebellion will set him free.

This is why, whenever one deals with a self-confident fool, the first goal—and the dilemma—is to keep from being sucked into his self-deceiving universe, his self-constructed morality.

> Answer not a [self-confident] fool according to his folly,
> lest you also be like him.
> Answer a [self-confident] fool according to his folly,
> lest he be wise in his own conceit.[9]

The self-confident fool will not be reached simply through the reassertion of moral truth or the quoting of Scripture. If you do not confront the fool on his own terms, he will probably never listen to you. The danger of dealing with him lies not only in his own stubbornness, however, but also in the *'ivveleth* of which he is enamored. It necessarily entails the rejection of absolutes and the ethical confusion that results from that rejection. To adopt his frame of reference, therefore, is to become subject to the same confusion that afflicts him.

The Chains of Compulsion

We move on to a fourth observation: *Folly, in whatever form it may take for the individual, is addictive.* Here we must examine the addictive nature of *'ivveleth*, the behavior of moral rebellion.

> As a dog returns to his vomit,
> so a [self-confident] fool returns to his folly.[10]

This instinctual canine habit has always been disgusting and incomprehensible to humans. Likewise, an impartial observer cannot fathom why an individual keeps reverting to behaviors that are morally repugnant and clearly harmful to himself and to others, even to people he loves.

Unlike the dog, the self-confident fool has the capacity to reason and should be able to make a rational choice to not engage in risky, destructive behaviors—especially after he has already engaged in them and been injured in some way by the results.

Instead, in the deep recesses of his soul, he makes the choice to embrace the pleasure or benefit of a deed, bypasses the roadblocks of reason, and installs instead turnpikes of rationalization:

"It's not that bad."

"The benefit outweighs the cost."

"I have to love myself first."

"I can't help it. It's who I am."

"I come from a disadvantaged background."

"My family was dysfunctional."

"I was abused as a child."

One of the most disturbing news stories to close out the twentieth century and begin the twenty-first was the tragic story of Mary Kay LeTourneau. Herself the child of famous parents and having grown up in a profoundly unhappy family environment, the Washington State school teacher destroyed her marriage and shattered her own family when she "fell in love" with a boy who was a pupil in her classroom. She became pregnant by the fourteen-year old boy and gave birth to a baby girl, endured a trial for rape of a child that became a national spectacle, and was given a probated sentence on the condition that she stay away from the boy. Not many weeks afterward, she was found in the lad's embrace in an automobile on a country road. Her probation was revoked, she was put in prison, and then it was revealed that she was pregnant again by the same fourteen-year old boy. Her explanation? The boy was the "love of her life," their love could not be stifled by a court order or by social conventions, and they found it impossible to stay away from each other. Eventually, when she got out of prison, she married her junior but finally of-age lover.

I do not bring up this story in order to be sensational or titillating. I think it is sad beyond words (not to mention an alarming harbinger of what has become almost a social trend of adult women turning to adolescent boys for affection). It illustrates the incredible power of folly to deceive those who seek it and compel them to do patently stupid and disgusting things. One may argue in the case of a drug addiction that the physical component is overwhelming. Some try to explain compulsions like this in terms of brain chemistry, but folly does not need a physical component to become a compulsion. Here is the power of *'ivveleth*: like the One Ring, it so fastens its hooks on a person's affections and desires that it not only drowns out the voices of moral reason and conscience, it even cancels out practical reason and common sense.

It is not that the individual literally has no power of choice. If, however, he desires the evil thing, has no desire to avoid it, and external controls on his behavior are weak, then it is virtually the same thing as having no free will, and the result is the same. The dog returns to its vomit, and the fool returns to his folly.

Not only this, but folly is so compelling that it can be dangerous to try to dissuade someone who is given to it.

> Let a bear robbed of her cubs meet a man,
> rather than a [self-confident] fool in his folly.[11]

Why? First, because he may try to enlist you to join in his folly with him. Second, even if you don't join him, you are still liable to be affected by the collateral effects of what he does. In that case it is best if you simply stay out of his way and warn those who are in his way. If, however, you should urge him to quit or to change his course, the reaction you receive may be violent—for he is as protective of his choice as a mother bear of her cubs. He does not want to hear it—not from you, not from his mother, not from the judge, not from anybody.

In other words, the time to help someone out of this kind of trouble is before it ever gets this far. Ideally, this decline into corrupt character should be preempted before the person ever reaches it. Let us return to the observations of criminologist John Douglas (remember, his focus is much more specific than mine—violent crime—but his point is the same):

> People often ask me what can be done about our horrendous violent-crime statistics...The only way crime is going to go down is if all of us simply stop accepting and tolerating it in our families, our friends, and our associates...*Crime is a moral problem. It can only be resolved on a moral level.*[12]

Amen. As a moral problem, crime is thus a matter of personal responsibility for one's own actions, and Douglas affirms that strongly. At the same time, he looks to the roots of criminal choices and offers this opinion on how crime might be prevented.

> Twenty-five years of observation has also told me that criminals are more "made" than "born," which means that somewhere along the line, someone who provided a profound negative influence could have provided a profound positive one instead. So what I truly believe is that along with more money and police and prisons, what we most need more of is love. This is not being simplistic; it's at the very heart of the issue.[13]

Mr. Douglas is surely correct that a wholesome, loving family environment makes a huge difference in the direction of a life. Moreover, the very Bible passages we've been studying affirm the same thing—provided that one understands that love does not mean permissiveness. Consider this, one of the most famous (or infamous from some points of view) verses of the Bible:

> Folly is bound up in the heart of a child,
> but the rod of correction shall drive it far from him.[14]

Unfortunately, folly, particularly as that means rebellion against authority, is part of the inborn nature of all of us. In most of us, it begins to show up in earnest at the tender age of about two years. According to the principle stated above, the goal of correction in childrearing is not merely to punish bad behavior. It is rather to cause the child to associate pain rather than pleasure with the attitudes and behaviors of rebellion.

This has become one of the most controversial issues in our society, even among people who say they believe in the Bible. Before you start reacting one way or the other to this statement, examine this verse closely. Once again, the word folly here is *'ivveleth*, that most serious Hebrew word for corrupt character. (The KJV says "foolishness," which is misleading—see below.) But wait a minute—it does not say that a child *is* a committed fool, but rather that these rebellious tendencies *dwell* in the child. Another way to say this is that we all have, even from childhood, something in us that, left to itself, could turn us toward rottenness, even crime.

The goal of maturation is to grow out of our innate self-centeredness and into a mature others-centeredness. The parents' task is to guide that process of maturation. A significant part of that task is to prevent their child's innate selfishness and will-to-rebel from taking over.

It must be firmly emphasized that *the folly spoken of here refers not to foolishness as in childishness or silliness or immaturity, but to rebellion against moral authority.* Dr. James Dobson and others who have taken a biblical stance on childrearing have pointed out that parents must not punish children simply for being children. Childish immaturity must not be confused with rebellion. At the same time, the wise parent will not permit the child to sustain a challenge to the parent's authority. That is where the "rod of correction" comes in.

This concept of the "rod of correction" rankles some. They regard it as cruel abuse, as violence that begets violence. Nothing could be further from the truth. Moral rebellion, as we have seen, gives an immediate pleasure, but the long-term result is pain. The purpose of the rod of correction is to rattle the natural association between rebellion and pleasure by the application of immediate pain. It is kindness, not cruelty. We will all be better off if we associate moral rebellion with pain rather than with pleasure. This concept is developed in several proverbs, some of which are famous (or infamous in our day of "progressive" childrearing):

> Stripes that wound cleanse away evil,
> and strokes reach the innermost parts.
> He who spares his rod hates his son,
> but he who loves him chastens him early.
> The rod and reproof give wisdom,
> but a child left to himself causes shame to his mother.
> Do not withhold correction from the child,
> for if you strike him with the rod, he shall not die.
> Strike him with the rod,
> and deliver his soul from *Sheol*.
> Correct your son, and he will give you rest—
> indeed, he will give delight to your soul.[15]

It would be a mistake to think that punishment is the major emphasis of Proverbs in dealing with the subject of childrearing. Much more is said, as we have already seen, about positive teaching and training in wisdom. Yet as we also see in the proverbs collected above, there is no shying away from the principle of administering negative consequences when necessary.

Behind all of these verses is the concept that sooner or later, folly will be punished, and that it is better done sooner. When a child experiences the mild and temporary pain of chastisement for his misdeeds at the hand of a loving parent, the pain is corrective, not punitive. The second verse above (Proverbs 13:24) is famously misquoted: "He who spares the rod spoils the child."

In fact, the proverb is a rebuke to the father who excuses his refusal to discipline his son with firm consistency by saying he loves him too much. That is not love, it is self-indulgence, and in effect is the same as rejection of the child. It is tantamount to turning the child over to build his own self-indulgence into lifelong habits. This means he will eventually bring upon himself the harsher disciplines of life and circumstances, and perhaps of a society that cannot love him as parents can. Ultimately it subjects him to the judgments of God (hence the reference to *Sheol*, the realm of darkness and despair, the end of a misspent life), all for misdeeds that could have been corrected *early* if the rod had not been spared. The word "early" is related to the word for the dawn. It speaks of the importance of correcting misbehavior and rebellious attitudes at the earliest possible occasion—not only with reference to the time of the infraction, but more importantly, with reference to the life of the child. There is but a narrow window of life opportunity to set the basic shape of a character. Note also that it is not the rod alone that is necessary for correction, but "the rod and *reproof*"—not criticizing or scolding, but setting the child right through corrective teaching.

The "rod of correction" certainly *does* include the idea of corporal correction—spanking—but it is not exclusively that. It can also refer to *any* kind of painful but harmless (i.e., noninjurious) penalty that the parent (or the one who stands *in loco parentis*) may impart, which fits both the offense committed and the capacity for understanding possessed by the child. The wise parent will not have a stereotyped, knee-jerk response to every misdeed of each child, but will have an array of measures at his or her disposal. Some will be more appropriate than others, and some will work better with some children than with others. The wise parent will also focus on *behavior* rather than on feelings. Personal observation leads me to believe that too many parents use attempts to manipulate their children's emotions as a weapon with which to battle their wayward wills. Parental whining, wheedling, nagging, flattering, and fussing will not succeed as substitutes for the rod of correction, and may in some cases be more cruelly abusive (as regards long term effects) than physical beating.

To say much more about this would take us far afield from our main subject, but this much has to be said here: The purpose of the "rod of correction" is not to inflict punishment in retribution; it is to train character while it is still malleable. Once established, a sound character can continue to grow in health—"Train up a child in the way he should go"—but the window of opportunity is brief.

The Gist

Attraction. Folly is attractive because it offers people what they think they want, but its attractiveness is deceitful.

Adoption. Participating in folly leads to the adoption of corrupt values.

Addiction. Folly is addictive.

Avoidance. Loving correction of children by their parents can help keep them off the path of folly.

For your consideration

- Are you a fan of The Lord of the Rings books or movies? If so, discuss the following question with a fellow fan: How would you compare the compulsion to own The Ring with the fatal attraction of folly?
- If not, then read Romans 6:14–23, and answer or discuss this question: How does Paul's discussion of the bondage to sin relate to Proverbs description of the fatal attraction of folly?

I3

The Fool vs. Wisdom

It should be clear by now that the committed fool is no child and that his folly, unlike that of the simple, is neither immature nor naive. This degree of folly is deliberately chosen by persons grown up enough to know the difference between right and wrong and able to understand the full ramifications of their choices. Generally, it is not something people enter into suddenly, though some do begin their fool's quest at a younger age than others. Usually, it is a more gradual process: it grows on them. Once they do make the decision to cross the line, wherever they draw it, they become set against righteousness. Now it becomes the fool versus wisdom.

We are now going to look at how the committed fool sets himself against godly wisdom as we examine what the Bible says about the fool's *attitude,* the fool's *mouth,* and the fool's *anger.*

The Committed Fool and His Attitude

> He who answers a matter before he hears it,
> it is his folly and shame.
> The way of a fool is right in his own eyes,
> but he who listens to counsel is wise.
> Every prudent person acts out of knowledge,
> but a fool lays open his folly.
> Fools mock at making a sin offering,
> but among the upright there is favor.
> It is an honor for a man to cease from strife,
> but every fool is quick to quarrel.
> If a wise man contends with a foolish man,
> whether he rage or laugh, there is no peace.[1]

The first characteristic of the committed fool's attitude is that *his mind is closed.* Consider again:

> He who answers a matter before he hears it,
> it is his folly and shame.[2]

The virtuous are often accused of closed-mindedness. The reality is that no one is more prejudiced, more bigoted, more difficult to persuade than the committed fool.

Snap judgments and hasty replies are identified with both folly and shame. The word for "shame" here is a very strong term for utter disgrace and loss of honor.[3] The point is not that everyone who does this is a fool, but that this is the *characteristic behavior* of the fool. This is the way the fool is, and whoever does this is acting as disgracefully as a fool.

Second, *the committed fool's ethics are egotistical.*

> The way of a fool is right in his own eyes,
> but he who listens to counsel is wise.[4]

The committed fool considers himself competent both to construct his own standard of right and wrong and to evaluate it by his own subjective intellect, experience, and feelings.

The phrase "wise in his own eyes" is significant and appears a handful of times in Proverbs (including references to the self-confident fool, the sluggard, and the rich man), once in Isaiah (5:21), and even in Romans (11:25, 12:16); but the key passage for background is this one:

> Do not be wise in your own eyes.
> Fear the LORD and depart from evil.[5]

To be wise in one's own eyes is the same as leaning on one's own understanding; it is the opposite of trusting in the Lord with all one's heart, acknowledging God in all one's ways, fearing God and departing from evil.

Franz Delitzsch summarized it well in his classic Old Testament commentary. The language is somewhat archaic, but what he says is on target and the message is up-to-date. He first observes, "There are objective criteria according to which a man can prove whether the way in which he walks is right." By "objective criteria," he means rational ethical principles. For the faithful, they are derived primarily from the Ten Commandments, the Sermon on the Mount, and the Bible as a whole. Secular people may also share such objective standards, even if their standards rest on a less stable base.

> But *the fool knows no other standard than his own opinion.* However clearly and truly one may warn him that the way which he has chosen is the wrong way and leads to a false end, yet he obstinately persists. *But a wise man* is not so wise in his own eyes as not to be willing to listen to well-meant counsel, because, however careful he may be regarding his conduct, yet he *does not regard his own judgment so unerring as not to be inclined ever anew to try it and let it stand the test.*[6]

In other words, the wise individual does not rely on his own subjective wisdom to guide his life, but has checkpoints outside of himself to verify the rightness of his actions. He will check himself by the Word of God, but he will also check himself by others whose judgment he trusts to make sure he is interpreting God's Word and will correctly.

Meanwhile, the fool, who is by definition devoid of moral wisdom, believes himself to be inherently competent to direct his own life independently of all other counsel. If he refers to the Bible or to others at all, it will be to justify the course he has already decided to take. Here then is the paradox of wisdom: Those who have it do not presume to think their own wisdom is enough, while those who do not have it imagine that they have more wisdom than all of mankind before them.

Third, *the committed fool is shameless about his deeds.*

> Every prudent person acts out of knowledge,
> but a fool lays open his folly.[7]

At first glance, Proverb 13:16 looks like a version of "actions speak louder than words." Yes, but there is more to it than that. The proverb contrasts the thinking person who uses careful, deliberate judgment to make decisions with the committed fool who "lays open his folly." There is a word picture here of a merchant or vendor unrolling and spreading out a cloth in which he has wrapped his goods. He opens up the bundle in the marketplace for display. This is what the fool does with his behavior and attitudes. Anyone with good sense, if he were going to practice such things, would want to keep them to himself. Not the fool. He is proud of it.

In other words, the fool's ego demands that at some point he parade his character deficiency before the public eye. If he was ever ashamed of his motives, plans, and deeds, he is so no longer. He is unworthily, shamelessly proud of them and makes trophies of his "conquests."

His egotism and exhibitionism also give him away when it comes to matters of religion, faith, and conscientious observance.

Whether he is a religious pretender or openly irreligious, this statement holds true:

> Fools mock at making a sin offering,
> but among the upright there is favor.[8]

The Hebrew word *asham*, translated "sin offering," can be mean "transgression" or "guilt." The reference seems to be to the sin offering (Leviticus 5:1–6), which was brought along with restitution for the offense. It was a religious rite that included confession of sin, atonement, and personal reparation for damages. It was brought not after a public judgment, but as a matter of conscience when the individual realizes he has violated the standards of God and the community.

This verse is actually more ambiguous in Hebrew than it appears to be in translation—it is possible to read it two ways. You can read it as is rendered above, that the committed fool scoffs at the idea of confessing his sins. You can also read it the other way around, so that the sin offering mocks *him*, that if he were to bring such a sin offering even the offering would laugh in his face for his hypocrisy. Either way the verse is interpreted, it speaks of the bold irreverence of the committed fool. He cares nothing about his moral guilt, so why should he have anything but disdain for having to account to either God or man for his self-centered values and actions?

The fourth thing about the committed fool's attitude is *that he is belligerent and contentious.*

> It is an honor for a man to cease from strife,
> but every fool is quick to quarrel.
> If a wise man contends with a foolish man,
> whether he rage or laugh, there is no peace.[9]

One should always count the cost before one crosses this person, for there will be a price to pay. He will not let an issue go without a fight.

It is not possible to reason with the committed fool, particularly in a dispute. If he cannot win his point, he will not lose the fight—and he fights dirty, whether in private discourse or public debate. He will not listen to reasonable arguments, even if he has to laugh them off or storm against the one bringing them. If he sees that the argument is lost, he will turn against his opponent with invective, name-calling, and perhaps even brute force.

It is also worth noting, even in passing, that the word "honor" appears here as something that the fool does not have. Shame is associated with the committed fool, and when he is placed near those who have honor, it only highlights his deficiency. Proverbs 19:11 sharpens the contrast further, while highlighting forbearance as a quality of wisdom.

> The discretion of a man makes him slow to anger,
> and it is his glory to pass over a transgression.

A committed fool simply cannot see it that way. Anger to him is both a natural right and a powerful tool for accomplishing his will. The fool's glory is to make everyone who offends him pay dearly for the offense.

The Fool and His Mouth

There is a whole series of proverbs that focuses on the fool and his mouth and how he uses it. In the Bible, the mouth is, as it is in our own language and culture, a figure of speech comprehensive of what we say and how we say it, of our typical conversation and our customary choice of words. The mouth has always been a leading indicator of a person's character.

> The heart of him who has understanding seeks knowledge,
> but the mouth of *fools* feeds on folly.
> A prudent man conceals knowledge,
> but the heart of *fools* proclaims folly.
> The tongue of the wise uses knowledge rightly,

but the mouth of *fools* pours forth folly.[10]
Even a fool, when he holds his peace, is counted wise,
and he who shuts his lips is esteemed a man of
understanding.
In the mouth of the foolish is a rod of pride,
but the lips of the wise shall preserve him.
The wise in heart will receive commandments,
but he who has foolish lips shall fall.
He who winks with the eye causes sorrow,
and he who has foolish lips shall fall.
Wise men lay up knowledge,
but the mouth of the fool invites destruction.[11]

The committed fool's mouth is careless, reckless, hurtful, and excessive. The first few proverbs are actually about the *kesil*, the self-confident fool, and we have seen them before. They are pertinent here also because the product of the self-confident fool's mouth is *'ivveleth* or full-blown folly, the characteristic behavior of the committed fool. This is what the self-confident fool aspires to, and it is what he will become if his heart is not turned back.

"The heart of him who has understanding seeks knowledge, but the mouth of [self-confident] fools feeds on folly." On one hand, there is the person with understanding, who is engaged in the purposeful quest for truth. This man or woman is therefore going to be looking for the right words to say—or indeed, whether anything should be said at all in a given situation. There are some times when, if one opens his mouth at all, it had better be filled with something appropriate. For example, the understanding person will not try to comfort a grieving family with something like, "I hope his life insurance policy is paid up," or "I know somebody else who died being treated by the same doctor."

The foolish mouth is, at best, a careless mouth, and foolish words are careless words. There is a vivid word-picture in this proverb. Unlike the understanding heart that seeks knowledge, the foolish mouth is like the aimless but fervent grazing of a flock or herd out in the pasture, whose only demand is that whatever is there be ample and tasty. In other words, the fool is not trying to understand the situation; he just wants to have something to say. His mouth "feeds on folly": the output of his words will reflect the input of his thoughts, which we have already seen are not directed by the fear of God.

"In the mouth of the foolish is a rod of pride, but the lips of the wise shall preserve him." The committed fool is given to proud words that can sting and wound. The "rod" spoken of here[12] is not the firm "rod of correction" by which corporal punishment was issued to felons, but a slender and flexible switch that gives stinging, perhaps cutting blows. Yet the wise person is able by his own words to fend off his hurtful remarks.

We may also say that foolish mouth is a reckless mouth, for it calls out—publicly announces, blurts—what it knows (or thinks it knows) with no concern for time, place, or consequences. Gossip, slander, libel, or maybe just a tasteless remark—all comprise the stock in trade for the committed fool.

"The tongue of the wise uses knowledge rightly, but the mouth of fools pours forth folly." A foolish mouth is excessive. The committed fool doesn't just use words: he pours them forth. His mouth is like waters flowing from a perpetual source, and there appears to be no stopping them.

It's important to note that *the committed fool's mouth also reveals him.* As it says in 17:28, "Even a fool, when he holds his peace, is counted wise; and he who shuts his lips is esteemed a man of understanding."

This is one of those proverbs that isn't actually about the fool, but uses him as an object lesson. The point is that even the committed fool, if he would only keep his mouth shut, would be thought by everyone (who does not know him) to be a person of character, integrity, and discernment.

There is little chance of that happening. The other side of this equation is that as soon as he opens his mouth, he reveals his true colors to everyone within earshot. By now we know that a fool is not going to keep his mouth closed willingly. Why? Because he is a fool. It is not his nature to keep his mouth closed.

Finally, *the committed fool's mouth is his downfall.* Proverbs 10:8 and 10:10 share the same second line: "The one (who has) foolish lips shall fall"[13]—not just with a bump, but with a terrible crash. The Hebrew word for "fall" here is not a little trip or a stumble. It speaks of utter destruction.

Verse 8, which starts out, "The wise in heart will receive commandments," suggests that the destruction comes because the committed fool will not accept any authority beyond his own. The commandment does not have to be God's law. It might be orders from a superior, instructions from someone who has more expertise, or even advice from one who has better understanding. As for the fall, the destruction, perhaps it comes because of the boastful pride that the fool's words reveal.[14] Or perhaps the words themselves, most unfitly spoken, have finally provoked the wrath and retaliation of someone more powerful than he.

The reference to the winking eye in 10:10 relates the foolish mouth to the crooked mouth of the worthless troublemaker described in chapter 6, verses 12–15, who "winks with his eyes, scrapes with his feet, signals with his fingers." He is a deceiver whose perverse purpose is to sow strife. So in Proverbs 6:15, his fate is told: "Therefore shall his calamity come suddenly. Suddenly shall he be broken without remedy."

In Proverbs 10:14, we first see a wise soul who "stores up" knowledge like a farmer preserves his harvest for winter. Where does that kind of forethought come from? It comes out of a righteous drive to protect and preserve himself and his loved ones. What is this contrasted with? With the reckless, destructive speech of the committed fool, whose only instinct is to magnify his own ego. His mouth is literally said to be "near ruin" (NIV, "invites ruin"; MLB, "hastens ruin"; ESV, "brings ruin near").

The Fool and His Anger

If the fool's mouth invites and hastens ruin, *his anger completes his self-destruction.*

> He who is soon angry behaves like a fool.
> He who is slow to wrath is of great understanding,
> but he who is hasty of temper displays folly.
> A fool's wrath is immediately known,
> but a prudent man overlooks an insult.[15]

The main thrust of the first two proverbs is to commend the quality of longsuffering and self-control. Yet once again, by using the characteristic behavior of the fool as the fulcrum of the proverb, they give us a key insight into the fool himself. The committed fool is quick to take offense, and he is quick to arch his back and show his fangs. He will do it immediately, without regard even for the *tactical* value there might be in concealing his anger (let alone the moral ramifications involved).

Do not misunderstand this. The meaning is not that *everyone* who has a quick temper is a committed fool, but rather that a quick temper is the characteristic *behavior* of the committed fool. Just because someone has a short fuse does not mean he has fallen into full-blown moral rebellion. If, however, we have already recognized the other warning signs of the fool, we know that if somebody crosses him (or her, because folly has no gender bias), that this person is likely to fly into a rage. (And at the same time, the reader also knows how *he* appears if *he* flies into a rage.) Likewise, we have a warning to be wary of anyone with a hair-trigger temper and to watch for other indications of more serious character deficiency. In any case, it is surely realistic to think twice before we commit ourselves to someone who is given to anger.

The third proverb confirms what is implied in the first two—that outbursts of wrath proceed from the inward character of the fool. "A fool's wrath is immediately known, but a prudent man overlooks an insult." The second line implies a typical provocation: someone has trod on his pride. The prudent person overlooks an insult, but not the fool. He reacts immediately (the Hebrew literally reads, "today"). Never one to conceal his ego, the committed fool, is compelled to demonstrate his wrath on the spot whenever someone offends his pride or arouses his indignation. This may well be the point at which he meets his disaster. If he has an enemy who knows how to trigger his anger response, he can be easily lured into a trap. That is one of the one of the most successful strategies of war, whether it is between nations, or inner city gangs, or business executives in a Fortune 500 corporation. Make him lose his self-control, and he has already lost.

> He who has no rule over his own spirit
> is like a city that is broken down and without walls.[16]

The Fool and His Fate

The committed fool can be a source of deep consternation to those who are conscientious and godly. He seems to get away with all sorts of malfeasance, from blasphemy to corruption to murder. Worse, he actually appears to prosper because of his misdeeds. It is enough to make even a psalmist sing the blues.

> But as for me, my feet were almost gone,
> my steps had almost slipped.
> For I was envious of the foolish:
> I saw the prosperity of the wicked.
>
> They are not in trouble as other men,
> neither are they plagued like other men.
> Therefore pride encircles them like a chain,
> violence covers them like a garment.
>
> When I considered how to understand this,
> it was too painful for me,

> Until I went into the sanctuary of God:
> then I perceived their end.[17]

The word "foolish" here is different from those we've considered before. It is *halal* (hah-LAL), the same root for the word "praise" (as in "hallelujah"). The reference here is to the arrogant, boastful, and self-congratulatory nature of the godless. The psalmist Asaph's description of the wicked in this psalm, however, runs closely parallel to the profile of the committed fool described in Proverbs.

To all appearances, the committed fool lives a happy and successful life, while preventing the success and preying on the happiness of others. Such appearances are deceiving. Their fate lies in the hands of a just God. Solomon and the other sages of Israel help us to understand in practical terms why we should not envy the "prosperity" of the fool.

In the first place, *we must remember—and trust in—the law of sowing and reaping*.[18] In the chain of sayings below, "fool" translates *'evil*, the committed fool, and "folly" *'ivveleth*, the moral rebellion characteristic of the fool.

> Understanding is a fountain of life to him who has it,
> but the instruction of fools is folly.
> The lips of the righteous feed many,
> but fools die for lack of heart.
> He that troubles his own house shall inherit the wind;
> and the fool shall be servant to the wise of heart.[19]
>
> A fool [is compelled to go] to the correction of the stocks.
> His own iniquities shall take the wicked[20] himself,
> and he shall be held with the cords of his sins.
> He shall die without instruction,
> and in the greatness of his folly he shall go astray.[21]
>
> And a highway shall be there, and a way,
> and it shall be called the Way of Holiness;
> The unclean shall not pass over it—

it is for those who will walk that way.
Fools shall not stray there.[22]

"Understanding is a fountain of life...the instruction of *fools* is folly." The instruction of fools is not the instruction they give but what they receive, the principles by which they live. It is the return of their investment in life—they get back what they have put in. The NIV translates this line: "folly brings punishment to fools."

The contrast is made with one of the richest images of abundant life in the Bible, *the fountain of life*. The fountain of life nourishes the understanding soul, and also all who are touched by his life. But the committed fool, whose life is characterized by one form of moral rebellion or another, will receive more of the same. He will become more and more confirmed in his way of life, not merely as a habit but as a principle.

"The lips of the righteous feed many, but fools die for lack of instruction." Here we see an image of spiritual anorexia—committed fools starving themselves to death in the midst of plenty. Their starvation is not physical but spiritual, and they have no excuse because they could have had the good life through wisdom, but they rejected it. The end result of their lifestyle is death.

One way the fool's folly catches up with him is when he transgresses the laws of society and must face its punishments for crimes and misdemeanors. Thus, "a fool [is compelled to go] to the correction of the stocks," the ancient Israelite version of jail.

Even if he does not actually indulge in criminal behavior (or isn't caught at it), it will still catch up with him by way of habits he cannot break and consequences that he cannot undo. Finally, he will die in his sins.

"He that troubles his own house shall inherit the wind, and the fool shall be servant to the wise of heart." This verse is a small but powerful poem with urgently compelling imagery. In these few words, we can perceive the whole tragic story of a head of a house who is a committed fool. Though his selfishness, obstinacy, shortsightedness, and sheer perversity, he throws his whole family network into an uproar. Ultimately, he loses it to someone who has some measure of wisdom.

This grim proverb is not just about individuals. It is also about marriages, families, businesses, even nations and civilizations. Moreover, not only is it a clear warning to the committed fool, it is also a *promise* to all those who suffer under one kind of incompetent and incorrigible authority or another: We shall not forever be governed by fools. Their house will inevitably, inexorably come tumbling in around their heads. (Of course, we hope and pray we are not in the house when it does!)

Neither will we forever have to walk the same road with fools, according to Isaiah 35:8, because when God's kingdom comes and His will is done on earth as it is in heaven, the crooked, wayward path of these moral rebels will be separated away from the way of life. We are spared the gory details of their eternal fate. That is only implied in the positive assurance that some day the righteous will be free from their vexation forever.

There are other biblical passages that provide for us some *case studies of committed fools who met their fate.*

One is reported to us by Eliphaz the Temanite in the book of Job. Eliphaz is probably not the best witness to call to the stand at this point because he's something of a fool himself. He thinks—wrongly—that Job's sufferings are the punishment of God for unconfessed sin. In this passage, he is trying to scare righteous Job into admitting that he is a hypocrite and rebellious fool. Eliphaz claims that he has personally seen what happens to such a person, how a fool's prosperity ended in disaster for himself and his whole household. He says to Job,

> For wrath kills the foolish man,
> and envy slays the simple one.
> I have seen the foolish taking root,
> but suddenly his house was cursed.
> His children are far from safety,

and they are crushed in the judgment,
neither is there any to deliver them;
Whose harvest the hungry eat up,
and take it even out of the thorns,
and the robber swallows up their substance.[23]

It may be that Eliphaz draws too general a conclusion out of
one incident when a particular fool got what he justly deserved.
He may even be exaggerating the fool's fate. Still, in the whole
book of Job, there is never a refutation of this particular point.
Nevertheless, considering the context—that this case study
is being used to browbeat a righteous man into confession of
sins he has never committed—the words of Eliphaz are terribly
hard to take. At the end of the book of Job, God Himself says
to Eliphaz, "My wrath is kindled against you, for you have not
spoken right of me as my servant Job has." Fortunately, we don't
have to rely only on one witness for the destruction that falls on
the committed fool.

In fact, King David, a man after God's heart, not only witnessed
it, he *experienced it personally*. He writes in Psalm 38:4, 5 about the
unbearable burden of folly that got far out of hand. The choppy
style and vivid, concrete metaphors convey the emotional stress
better than prose ever could.

For my iniquities have passed over my head,
Like a heavy burden—too heavy for me.
Putrid have my wounds become—
Corrupt, because of my folly.

Everything in these verses repeats and confirms what we
have already seen. Iniquity and folly are synonyms here. They
have taken on a life of their own and have gotten out of control,
"passed over my head." David had never intended things to go so
far as they went. Now he is suffering psychological and apparently
even physical distress. His guilt is like an infected wound become
gangrenous. However, while he has *pursued* folly (like a self-

confident fool), he has stopped short of *committing himself* to it. Now he wants out, and he cries out to the only One who can help him out of it.

This is truly what separates the committed fool from others. Anyone who still has some moral sense left in him, when he finds himself and the people he loves up to their necks in the consequences of his wrongdoing, will at least pause and reconsider his ways. Not the committed fool. Repentance is not part of his vocabulary.

> The foolishness of a man perverts his way,
> and his heart frets against the LORD.[24]

The New International Version aptly translates the same verse this way:

> A man's own folly ruins his life,
> yet his heart rages against the LORD.

When the harvest comes in for the committed fool, it does not lead him to repent and dedicate his life to serving God. No, instead he bitterly blames God for his problems and is driven even further away from Him.

The Bible teaches that there are only a few basic motives for human self-destruction.[25] Lust is one, greed is another. I am convinced, however, that at the deepest root of the life of those who descend to becoming committed fools, there is one dominant motive: bitterness. Bitterness because of injuries inflicted by others, sure, but especially bitterness for injuries they suppose were inflicted by God. Bitterness is a terrible and powerful drive and moves many not only to reject the Way of Life, but also to become scornful of it. That is the terminal stage of folly, but before we investigate it, there is one other aggravated aspect of *'ivveleth* that we must pause to review.

The Gist

Fool Spotting:

- The committed fool is close-minded, egotistical, shameless, and belligerent.
- The committed fool's speech is reckless, hurtful, and excessive; self-revelatory; and may be his downfall.
- The committed fool's anger is destructive—to others, and ultimately to himself.

The Fool's Retribution: The committed fool, though he seems to prosper, will ultimately be undone by his rebellion.

For your consideration

It was an election year nightmare for this governor of a large state. His reputation as a corruption-busting prosecutor had gotten him elected. One of his key targets was high-end prostitution—therefore, it came a shock to his constituents when federal authorities indicted him for involvement in a high-priced call girl ring. Evidence showed that he was engaging in illegal activities even during his prosecution of the same kind of activity. Pundits and the public were not impressed by his self-righteous performance in press conferences after his arrest. They were even less impressed with his post-conviction "apologies" in which he minimized his offenses and maximized his virtues.

How would you evaluate the public character of a politician in such a situation as this?

14

The Degradation of Folly

It is my duty now to introduce you to another character, a special case under the general category of the third-degree fool. One would have to consider him the clown in this miserable circus of moral depravity. He is the *nabal* (nah-VAHL), the *shameless fool*. Nabal comes from a root word that means to fade, to wither, to fall like desiccated fruit. Whatever vestige of a moral conscience he ever had is dried up and shriveled into uselessness. *The nabal is a man or woman with a withered soul.*

The *nabal* is the fool's fool. Like the *'evil*, the committed fool, he has decisively rejected wisdom and made a commitment to destructive ideas and behaviors. More than this, he has so given himself over to his lower nature that he has made himself odious to the world. He is self-centered, ignoble, irreverent, boorish, rude, vile. He is the third-degree fool gone to seed. Earlier we discussed the difference between the perverse and the perverted. This fool is a true pervert. He has a perverted mind, and his lifestyle reflects it. There's a related Old Testament term: *nebalah* (ne-va-LAH), which is usually translated "folly," but that is truly a gross understatement. More accurately, it is villainy or vice. We are talking serious sin here.

The Degradation of Folly

How serious? How degraded do you think human folly can become? Let me walk you through a biblical description of *the degradation of folly*—but put on your mental hip boots before we go.

Nabal is a synonym for incorrigible wickedness and unbelief.

> They have corrupted themselves,
> their mark is not the mark of (God's) children;
> they are a perverse and crooked generation.
> Do you thus repay the LORD, O *foolish* people and unwise?[1]

Did you notice those modifiers? Corrupt, perverse, crooked, unwise—they all go with *nebalah,* shameless folly. When the prophet Isaiah needed a word to describe faults that provoked God's inescapable wrath, he chose this one:

> Therefore the LORD shall have no joy in their young men, neither shall he have mercy on their fatherless and widows; for every one is a hypocrite and an evildoer, and every mouth speaks [shameless] folly. For all this his anger is not turned away, but his hand is stretched out still.[2]

Once again, shameless folly is keeping company with hypocrisy and evildoing so egregious that God has determined not to turn away his anger.

Every parent wants to make sure his child does not turn out like this.

> He who begets a [self confident] fool does it
> to his own sorrow,
> and the father of a [shameless] fool has no joy.[3]

It seems to be more understandable when we see character deficiency syndrome at work in families that scarcely seem worthy of the word "family." We can understand why children growing up under parents who are either abusive or absent would become rebellious toward society at large. Indeed, it surprises us is when we see someone who has overcome such a terrible background to become an outstanding example of high character and achievement. It is not common, but it happens.

On the other hand, what truly alarms us, and rightly so, is when we see decent people produce rotten offspring, a son or daughter who becomes a parasite and even a menace to society. This reality, unfortunately, is not as rare as it should be. It has already been affirmed in an earlier chapter that parents have a powerful role in shaping their children's lives. It is also, however, only a limited role with a limited window of opportunity to exercise it. Every individual chooses his own moral course in this world—how much more those who are well raised to know right from wrong. Some exercise their option so as to become reprobates, to the profound grief of their parents.

The proverb above is a reminder to parents that, "It could happen to you." It is an exhortation to every parent to seize the day, to begin right away to do the things—through example and precept—that inculcate moral character in their children. It urges every father and mother to do all they can to prepare their children for the day when they must make their own choices for their lives. While parents cannot choose their children's moral destiny, they can nurture it. Intentions, hopes, and best wishes will not do the job. Being a parent is a full time occupation and duty, not a pastime to be enjoyed in one's leisure hours.

To make things worse in this fallen world, God seems to have created some children to be more difficult to handle than others! We are all faulty and fallible people, and even our best efforts may fall short. Therefore, to give less than our best to rearing our children comprises a kind of folly all its own. The fruit of the folly of parental failure is a fool—even a shameless fool.

It is a gross insult to be compared to the nabal. You do not even want to act or talk like a shameless fool, not even one time in an isolated incident.

> If you have been *foolish* to exalt yourself,
> and if you have planned evil,
> put your hand over your mouth.[4]

In this verse there are a couple more revelations about what constitutes the behavior of the shameless fool—self-exaltation and the planning of evil. An intriguing combination of traits, are they not? Self-exaltation is putting oneself forward or congratulating oneself for a position or achievement that has not been earned or deserved. To plan evil is broad in what it may mean, but it is aggressive in its intent. The shameless fool does not wait around for a temptation to float by. He would rather design temptations that would ensnare or injure others. The exhortation: "Cover your mouth," i.e., "Shut up! Stop! Don't say another word. You have already gone too far."

One does not even want to hear a shameless fool speak *well*.

> Excellent speech is not fitting for a [shameless] fool...[5]

The word *excellent* here may mean just that, or it may mean "high-handed and arrogant." One way or the other, the conscientious person does not want to be around when the shameless fool opens his mouth. His arrogant boasting and crowing are sickening. On the other hand, if his speech is truly excellent—that is, if he actually has something to say that is decent, pleasant, and unpolluted by obscenity—there is probably something underhanded going on. If his conversation is on an uncharacteristically high level, let everyone watch their step and cover their backs, because someone is being set up for some kind of fall.

We do not want to hear the shameless fool speak well, nor do we want to see him *do* well. This is a hard thing for any decent

individual to accept—that we should not wish someone well—
but this is exactly what wisdom is teaching.

> For three things the earth is disturbed,
> and for four it cannot bear up:
> For a slave when he reigns [as king],
> and a [shameless] fool when he is filled with food;
> For an odious woman when she is married,
> and a handmaid who takes the place of her mistress.[6]

Even though only one line of this poem refers to the nabal, in
order to understand its full impact we need to examine the whole
thing in some detail.

"The earth" (or "the land") here is a poetic figure of speech
for society. It trembles and feels oppressed by an overwhelming
burden when any one of these characters comes forth able to fulfill
his or her personal desires. Four kinds of people are assembled
as examples of the influences that society should dread. The
proverb identifies a slave who takes over the throne, an unloved
or rejected woman who gets married, a servant girl who displaces
her mistress, and a *nabal* who has eaten and drunk to satisfaction.

What a quizzical poem! At first glance, one would wonder
why putting these people in any of these situations should be
regarded as a bad thing. It would seem that at least some of
these ascents might even call for applause. Do these situations
not depict the overthrow of injustice? This is a most politically
incorrect proverb!

The connecting link between these four issues is that they
are all an overturning, not of injustice, but of righteous order.
They represent *the overthrow and displacement of equity by envy—
people receiving not what they deserve, but what they covet*. In these
situations, the newly elevated persons are likely to indulge in
"paybacks." It occurs with enough frequency that it must be a
rule: when people who feel that they have been put down finally
get to the top, their first and sometimes only order of business is
to get revenge upon the people they envied.

Leaving aside the question of how a slave could ever be qualified to rule a nation, history has provided several examples of lowly or oppressed people who overthrew their established authorities. Some, like Napoleon, Lenin, Mao, and Castro, were able leaders. Others are little more than historical footnotes. Are there any examples of such people who did not become tyrants as great as or greater than the rulers they displaced? Perhaps, but as I write this, I can think of none.

The line about the "odious woman" is sure to strike someone as being sexist. Psychologically, however, it rings true. In that Middle Eastern culture, marriages were (and continue to be) arranged. The "odious woman" is one who has been repeatedly rejected, particularly because of her prickly and unsociable personality. The word "odious" does not refer to her physical attributes but to her social relationships. She is hated by her peers, and no one wants to be around her. Rejection is a kind of reproof that rarely produces reform. It is more likely to generate resentment and a desire for revenge. Woe to the poor husband who himself is such a poor catch that he must contract for marriage to such a woman. He is in for a hard life.

There is an explicit biblical example of the handmaid who displaces her mistress: Hagar, the Egyptian servant girl who bore the firstborn son of Abraham as a surrogate mother for Sarah. Her only qualifications for such a promotion were her fertility and proximity. It was an arrangement that quickly soured into a domestic disaster, and ultimately into an everlasting enmity between peoples.[7] A large part of the blame can be traced to the inopportune elevation of a person to a position that she had neither earned nor deserved in terms of character.

To give Hagar her due, she surely was a resourceful and resilient individual who, when put into the most desperate situation imaginable, did not reject God but cried out to Him and was heard by Him. This actually upholds the central point, however, for it was not her elevation that brought forth admirable character qualities, but her catastrophic demotion and suffering.

Having said all this, why should we begrudge the *nabal* his full stomach? Because when the shameless fool has enough to eat, it means he is living without care, without hardship. He has been successful (and that in itself is a scary thought, considering what he may have done in order to become a success). He feels no reproof for his deeds, and therefore he feels no restraint. Why should he change? Why should he even hold back? Thus he becomes more arrogant, more obnoxious, and more dangerous than he was when he was hungry. Therefore, "the earth shakes" when this unworthy person is elevated and happy.

Truly Despicable

Why is this person so despised? So far we've only seen hints of it in the scriptures we've read together. It is striking to me as I have studied the scriptures how this individual is so loathed by the biblical writers that no one, not even Solomon, wants to write an exposition about him. We do, however, see several anecdotal episodes in which particular actions are labeled as *nebalah*, shameless folly. As we shall see, this is not a particular misdeed or even a kind of trespass, but an aggravation that can be found in any and every category of sin.

They called it *shameless folly* when Jacob's daughter Dinah was date-raped by Shechem, the son of Hamor.[8]

According to the Torah, if a woman who is already betrothed in marriage is unfaithful to her husband to be, it is a capital offense because it's the equivalent of adultery. This crime is also called *shameless folly*.[9]

When the city of Jericho was destroyed, the LORD commanded all its plunder to be destroyed. One man, Achan, took for himself some of the cursed gold and involved his whole family in the conspiracy. His sin brought judgment first upon the army of Israel, and ultimately on the head of Achan and his whole family. Joshua called it *shameless folly*,[10] referring both to the character of the deed itself and the calamitous results it brought.

There is a horrifying story from the lawless days before Israel had a king how a mob gathered and demanded that a fellow Israelite who was passing through the town be brought out so they could sodomize him. They did end up committing mass rape and assault against his concubine. They so brutalized her that she was dead by daybreak. Three times in the story this atrocity is called *nebalah*.[11]

A classic illustration of *shameless folly* occurred in the life of David while he was a fugitive from King Saul. A wealthy man whom David and his band of men had voluntarily helped not only refused them the hospitality required by tradition, he openly slandered David and his men. The offense so infuriated David that he came very close to committing a dreadful atrocity against the man and his household just to get even. Would you like to guess the name of this fool? Nabal.[12]

Years later, King David's oldest son Amnon, encouraged by the callously amoral advice of his best friend, raped his own half-sister Tamar—an act described as *shameless folly*. This sin set in motion a chain of events which resulted in murder within the royal family, a *coup d'etat*, and ultimately civil war.[13]

We have previously mentioned Job's "friends." In their spiritual arrogance, they presented themselves as though they were God's own representatives, speaking on His behalf. In his anguish, Job spoke rashly and repented. In their complacency, Eliphaz and his accomplices committed slander and never retracted it. Their absurd pride contrasts starkly with Job's humility. God rebuked Job's three friends, shockingly defining their attitude and conduct as *shameless folly*.[14]

While we are talking about the *shameless folly* of those who claim to speak for God but do not, we shall mention also Ezekiel's characterization of the self-willed, self-styled, self-appointed, false prophets, who lied to the people about their inspiration and deliberately deceived them.[15] Before we get to that, however, there is something more to consider.

Theology of a Fool

Observe this famous passage from the Psalms:

> The *nabal* has said in his heart,
> "There is no God."
> They are corrupt.
> They have done abhorrent works.
> There is none who does good.
> They have all turned away.
> They have alike become filthy.
> There is none who does good, no, not one.
> Have all the workers of iniquity no knowledge,
> who eat up my people as they eat bread,
> and call not upon the Lord?[16]

The shameless fool is an atheist at heart, whether he is a formal atheist or not. (By the way, the point of this psalm is not that all atheists are fools, but that all shameless fools are atheists at heart.)

What is spoken here is not a mere avoidance of God. It is a positive statement of unbelief. There are layers of unbelief, and the shameless fool lies at the bottom. He does not merely doubt whether there is a God, nor is he merely unconscious of God's pervasive presence. He does not merely worry that there may be no divine Providence when he is in need. He does not just hope that no God is watching him. *In his heart he believes—he has complete faith—that he will never have to give an account to God.* He "says" there is no God. He declares it. He has decided it is so. He may not have studied it as a philosophy or adopted it as an opinion of his mind, but he has made a decision in his heart.

But wait—if only God knows the heart, how can it we know so generally that the shameless fool is an atheist? Behold his deeds. Examine his lifestyle. *Behavior reveals character.* This is the recurring theme of all the wisdom literature. Test his fruit and you will find corruption: "They are corrupt…They have all turned away." He has taken all the virtues that make for a functional, harmonious life, and so turned them toward selfish ends that they have become devoid of moral worth.

He bears the fruit of *abomination*: "They have done abhorrent works." Because he is hostile to holiness, he commits deeds that God has pronounced detestable, ranging from idolatry to sexual perversion. "They have alike become filthy." Such a lifestyle is a social pattern, and there is a group identity that is forged through shared participation in immorality.

He bears the fruit of *omission*: "There is none who does good…There is none who does good, no, not one." He does not do the good that God's law requires. His deeds are not beautiful, beneficial, pleasant, or agreeable. The psalmist marvels instead at his *extreme perversity*. He is one of the "workers of iniquity," a phrase in Hebrew that could be translated "troublemakers."

He bears the fruit of *extortion*: "[They] eat up my people as they eat bread." He is a predator who preys on those who play by the rules. He bears the fruit of *autonomy*: "[They] do not call upon the LORD." He considers himself self-sufficient, self-determining. He is a thoroughgoing humanist, whose self-perception is that he has no need to pray or to call on God, even in case of dire emergency. Neither does he consider any oath taken in God's name binding. Thus if he tells the truth, it is only because he chooses to do so. If he decides to lie, his lie must be uncovered and his testimony impeached by those who uphold the law. He will not confess it because he has no regard for any moral authority above himself.

If there is a fate worse than death, it is to become the reproach of these fools.

Deliver me from all my transgressions.
Do not set me as the reproach of the [shameless] fool.[17]

The Psalmist dreads the thought that the consequences of his sins will make him the laughingstock of shameless fools. When these godless no-goods find a godly person who has stumbled into hard times, they are as merciless as jackals. They relish the opportunity to feast upon the reputation of a good person who is revealed to have feet of clay. Even the most upright among us is fallible. Decent people may dabble in folly and get caught in it. None but the dead are immune to temptation, and any runner still in the race may stumble and fall. When he does, he certainly is doing no worse than any other sinner, nor are his faults more egregious.

The ungodly, however, are not inclined to give them the same latitude of excuse that they allow one another. Led by the scornful and the shameless, they rejoice over the discovery of the prominent minister who gives in to temptation, the godly family that falls apart under life's pressures, the gifted and devout young person who is drawn into sinful worldliness. Such foibles feed the cacophony of the talk shows, while popular comedians ridicule the fallen righteous to the callous cackles of their audiences.

The bitter unbelief of Job's wife gives a glimpse into the nature of the taunts of the shameless fool.

> Then said [Job's] wife unto him,
> Do you still retain your integrity? Curse God, and die.
> But he said to her,
> You speak as one of the foolish women speaks.[18]

So hurtful are her remarks that he reacts with a verbal slap to the face. A "foolish woman" (one word in Hebrew, the feminine form of *nabal*) would have to be a female of the most debased moral character. There really is no modern synonym that fits here—*not even an obscene one!* With all the expansive vocabulary of abusive language in our day, no contemporary slur quite comprehends the depravity of the word Job uses here. He does not actually call his wife this vile name, but only says *her words* are the words of such a woman. His point is not to retaliate with an insult but to correct with a rebuke. How does one of the foolish women—a partaker of this shameless sort of folly—speak? She encourages a person swamped in trouble and grief to denounce God and give up hope. Such a woman speaks thus out of her own bitter unbelief and hopelessness—because she has already said in her heart, "There is no God." There is thus no point or purpose in suffering, and oblivion is better than pain. Job expects better from his wife, who truly does know better.

Job later describes the humiliation of an honorable man who becomes the target of the jeers of the foolish:

> But now [shameless fools] that are younger
> than I hold me in derision,
> whose fathers I disdained to set with the dogs of my
> flock.[19]

Now that he, a once-revered citizen, has fallen, *they* are eager to torment *him* and to magnify his misery as much as possible:

> They were the children of [shameless] fools—
> Yes, the children of worthless men!
> They were filthier than the dirt.
> And now I am their song, and I am their byword.[20]

This, to Job, was the ultimate insult added to his many injuries that made his misery too terrible to bear: to be the byword of shameless fools, to be the punch line for their jokes, and the subject matter for their jeering gossip.

For Job, the shameless fool is a worthless individual, someone who makes no positive contribution to society and may well be part of the criminal element. To the psalmist Asaph, the shameless fool is nothing less than an enemy of God dwelling even among God's own people. He cries out for deliverance from blasphemers, and the nabal is right in the middle of the group.

> Remember this: that the enemy has vilified You, O LORD,
> and a foolish people have blasphemed Your Name.
> Arise, O God, plead your own cause!
> Remember the daily insults toward you from the [shameless] fool.
> Forget not the voice of your enemies.
> The clamor of those who rise up against you
> increases continually.[21]

This fool's existence is an active threat to peace, reflected in the psalmist's plea to God for protection: "For the dark places of the land are full of the dens of violence."[22] Where such fools have gained a foothold, there will be no peace, no security. There will be dark places where the threat of violence lurks ready to pounce at any time. These shameless people are responsible not only for criminal activity in general, but specifically for the violence that shatters the peace. A misguided and even malicious political correctness seeks to blame violence and oppression on the "intolerance" of people who want to preserve "traditional" values. Political correctness claims that the social structures that are propped up by such values create criminals.

Not so. The *denial* of moral absolutes creates criminals, once it filters down to everyday living. The refusal of parents to provide godly training and discipline to their children creates criminals. The self-centered, unbridled pursuit of pleasure, wealth, power, or esteem—along with a willful disregard for truth, righteousness, compassion, and love of neighbor—that is what creates criminals.

One does not have to be a criminal to qualify as a shameless fool, however. One may even be among the most religious. Even though the *nabal* is the enemy of God who in his heart denies God, there are those among them who will venture to speak in the name of God. They are indicted by the prophet Ezekiel:

And the word of the LORD came to me, saying, Son of man, prophesy against the prophets of Israel who are prophesying, and say to those who prophesy out of their own hearts, 'Hear the word of the LORD.' Thus says the Sovereign LORD: Woe to the *foolish prophets*, who follow their own spirit and have nothing! O Israel, your prophets are like the foxes among ruins…They have seen falsehood and lying predictions, saying, 'The LORD says,' when the LORD has not sent them. Yet they fully hoped to establish their word…Therefore, thus says the Sovereign LORD, because you have spoken falsehood and have seen a lie, therefore take notice: I am against you.[23]

Perhaps it seems contradictory that someone who says in his heart there is no God should go forth speaking in His name. It is indeed contradictory. It is not that the insights from Psalm 14 do not apply here. It is rather that consistency is not a matter that concerns any kind of fool, let alone the *nabal*. The God in whose name the shamelessly foolish prophet speaks is "God" as invented in his own imagination, "Christ" in his own image. To what end? To undercut the influence of the godly and intimidate them into standing down from conscientious convictions; and meanwhile, enabling people to feel comfortable and complacent in popular, profitable, and politically influential sins. To do this in a day of peril, as did the false prophets in the days of Ezekiel, is nothing short of villainous. "Like the foxes among ruins," they are in it for themselves and will get what they can get with no care of what they leave behind.

It is a dreadful and dangerous thing to speak in the name of God, and every true prophet knows that. The *foolish* prophet— i.e., a prophet who is a shameless fool—is not worried what God will think because he has already established his own authority and believes that his own thoughts and desires must be God's as well. In every age there have been so-called spokesmen for God who are willing to put up their own word for God's, and there is no shortage of this kind of religionist today. To these, God speaks through his true prophet: "I am against you." That should strike fear into their hearts. It does not. To the shameless fool, those are only words spoken by a crank.

As the Scripture does not dwell on a description of the shameless fool, neither does it dwell on his end. It simply assumes that he will be destroyed in the end. He thus serves as a byword for anyone who meets an ignominious fate. The following proverb was spoken by the prophet Jeremiah, describing the futility of the shameless fool's life:

> As the partridge which sits on eggs that do not hatch,
> so he who gets riches unrighteously
> shall leave them in the midst of his days,
> and at his end shall be a fool.[24]

David lamented over Abner, a former adversary who had defected to him but was treacherously murdered in jealous revenge by David's highest ranking officer.

> *Died Abner as a fool dies?*
> Your hands were not bound,
> nor your feet put into fetters;
> As a man falls before wicked men,
> so did you fall.[25]

David's lament is worth comment: Abner was a highly esteemed man in his day, a renowned general and statesman—honored, if not always honorable. He should have died gloriously in battle or peacefully surrounded by loved ones. Instead he was stabbed to death outside the city gate like the victim of a pointless street crime, like *a shameless fool*. It's not offered as a universal truth, but as a typical occurrence. It is not that shameless fools actually die this way but that it is a way to die that is fitting only for a shameless fool. Whether it occurs in violence or otherwise, his passing marks the end of a noxious life.

The Fool's Last Hope

The Scriptures paint such a dark picture of the committed fool and his degenerate counterpart, the shameless fool, that one might think there is surely no hope at all of seeing any repentance or reformation of character in either of these individuals. Even so, there is mercy from God that can find its way even into the hardened heart of the committed fool. It is (to borrow the title of the book by Sheldon Vanauken) *A Severe Mercy*. The only thing that the Hebrew sages could see that would shake this fool loose from his extreme self-confidence and self-absorption is extremity. It has often been said that there are no atheists in foxholes. Let's revisit a verse we saw earlier and see it in its fuller context of Scripture.

> Fools, because of their rebellion
> and because of their iniquities,
> suffered affliction.
> Their soul abhorred all food,
> and they drew near to the gates of death.
> Then they cried to the LORD in their trouble,
> and He saved them out of their distresses.
> He sent His word and healed them,
> and delivered them from the things that destroyed them.[26]

The committed fool brings suffering upon himself through his own misdeeds. Whether the affliction is sent directly from God or whether it is the natural consequence of his own lifestyle is left as an open question. What is clear is that it is not the result of bad luck, nor is it one of those unfair blows that life sometimes deals to good people. The fool has brought it on himself through his deliberate and habitual folly.

Alcoholics and drug addicts who return to sobriety often speak of "hitting bottom"—coming to a crisis in their lives they can no longer bluff their way out of. Here we learn that it is possible for the committed fool to hit bottom. The psalm depicts a wasting disease. His suffering is acute and life threatening. The sufferer has lost all appetite and refuses to take any nourishment at all. He is in the last stages of his terminal illness.

In his extremity, he lets go of his rebellion and bitterness toward God. Like the prodigal son in Jesus's parable, he "comes to himself,"[27] as though he had been in a daze or under a spell and not in his right mind. He cries out to the LORD—a familiar phrase in the Old Testament, and an important one. It is true that prayer is not for emergencies only. If one prays only under duress it does not speak of a healthy relationship with God. Nevertheless, even those who do not have a healthy relationship with God may be heard if they cry out to Him in their desperation. "Whoever calls on the name of the Lord shall be saved."[28] God responds, first with promise ("He sent his word"), then with healing, then with deliverance—an undoing of the ways that brought the fool into his distress.

It is significant that the salvation of the fool is offered as a testimonial, not as an infallible promise. The great point of the psalm is the goodness of God and His willingness and ability to respond to those who cry out to Him in distress. It is not an encouragement to try to manipulate the Lord just because He is faithful and gracious. Rather, it is an encouragement to us all not to despair in the direst circumstances, even if we have sinned gravely, because God can change things.

Certain observations may be made of this psalm relative to the specific subject of character deficiency syndrome:

The passage offers hope even for a committed fool to be redeemed *because it has happened.* That is what the psalm itself affirms—it is a testimony of things that God has done in the past and can still do today.

Probably the most remarkable thing about this passage is that it is the *only* one in all the wisdom literature that seems to offer any hope at all that this kind of fool can be saved.

The clear implication is that the committed fool will only repent when he is completely overwhelmed with the troubles brought on him through his own sin. The committed fool has a hard heart that will not be softened without being broken. Who would want to experience such ruin before turning to God?

Scripture does not *guarantee* that any committed fool actually will turn to the Lord, even if he is overwhelmed by his troubles. *Perhaps* he will come to himself, but he likely will not. (Remember the case of Roger Keith Coleman.)

Yet if he does come to his senses and cry out for mercy, God in His sovereign freedom is good and will hear him and rescue him.

Who is wise and will observe these things? "They will discern the steadfast love of the Lord," declares the psalmist.[29] By definition, mercy is completely voluntary on the part of the one who gives it. The steadfast love and mercy of God may be discerned in many ways, including His care for those who love Him. It is also seen in the way He redeems those who despise Him, changing their hearts and redeeming their character.

The Gist

The shameless fool is basically a committed fool who has given himself over to his lower nature.

Shameless folly is not a particular misdeed, but an aggravation that can be found in any and every kind of sin.

When it says, "The Fool has said in his heart, There is no God," (Psalm 14:1; 53:1), it is to explain why the shameless fool acts as he does.

There is only one verse in the whole Bible that specifically indicates that a committed fool may call out to God to be saved—but there is one!

For your consideration

- Psalms 14:1 says, "The [shameless] fool has said in his heart, There is no God." Ezekiel calls out the false prophets who claim to speak in God's name but do not, and calls them [shameless] fools. How can someone who believes there is no God turn around and speak in His name?
- Do you personally know of someone who seemed in many ways to be a committed fool, but got turned around, became a believer and began to serve God? Do you know of someone who seemed to be serving God but later turned around and became bitter toward God?

15

Terminal Folly

By this point, the subject matter is so abjectly depressing that I cannot blame the reader who may get discouraged about staying with this study to the end. Please do not give up, because we will see light again before we are finished. There is, however, one more tragic stop on this journey, and it is indeed the heart of darkness. It is the terminal stage of character deficiency syndrome, the scornful fool. Fortunately, it will not take much time to come to grips with this subject. The Scripture itself deals with him tersely, but not dismissively. Its description of him is both pointed and powerful.

The Hebrew word is *luts* (rhymes with 'boots'). It is translated "scorner" in the King James Version, also "scoffer" and "mocker." It refers to a contemptuous person who scorns spiritual truth and openly flouts godliness, moral righteousness, and whatever is sacred. He is an evangelist for folly. "Scorner" may be an archaic word that has all but fallen out of our language, but I prefer it.

"Scoffer" suggests skepticism mingled with pride, and a "mocker" may be little more than a cynic with a penchant for sarcasm. The character of this stage of folly certainly includes these attitudes, but they revolve primarily around a strong element of contempt for the truth. The word "scorner" to me highlights that contempt better than other translations.

The lines between the committed fool and the scorner may seem blurred. One way to look at it is that *the scorner is that committed fool who has passed the point of no return.* For this person, folly and the rejection of moral absolutes is more than a personal choice or a lifestyle. It is a worldview, and even a mission in life. He or she has not merely rejected God's standards but has decided that God is the Enemy, the Great Satan who must be opposed in this world.

Relatively few individuals adopt this viewpoint with regard to the whole of life. Most scorners seem be so in a limited sense, usually toward some specific issue or relationship. The main thing to understand is that they are rooted in bitterness and hatred toward God. At some point in their lives, God disappointed or angered them. Now they want to get back at Him. In order to understand the nature of character deficiency in the scorner, we are going to examine the extreme case as it is depicted in the scriptures.

The Unrepentant Scorner

What shall we say about the character of the scorner? In the battle between good vs. evil, the scorner has placed himself squarely against God and His standards of right and wrong.

> Blessed is the man who walks not in the counsel
> of the ungodly,
> nor stands in the path of sinners,
> nor sits in the seat of the *scornful*.[1]

Clearly, anyone who wants to abide in the pleasure of God will have nothing to do with the scorner. Notice who forms a team with the scorner: the "ungodly" and "sinners." There is a progressive, stair step parallelism in the poem, indicating that the scorner is the most egregious offender of the three.

"Ungodly" is *rasha'* (rah-SHAH), usually translated "wicked." If you follow the way this word is used in the Old Testament, this person is ungodly and wicked not only in terms of subjective, personal unrighteousness and immorality. This person engages in moral turpitude and criminal behavior that ranges from dishonesty in business and corruption in politics all the way to premeditated murder. We have seen before that this same word—whether translated "wicked" or "ungodly"—is synonymous with the most aggravated behavior of the committed fool. If this fellow is bad, the next one is even worse.

Sinner" is *chatta'* (khat-TAH). Even though *chatta'* is derived from the principal word for sin (meaning "missing the mark"), it is not used as a general word for everyone who commits a sin (i.e., all of us). It specifically refers to notorious sinners, people who are marked by a prolonged series of sinful deeds, or by a particular act that has outraged the community. These "sinners" are people who are recognized on the street as (to grossly understate the matter) very bad role models. Among their number we would probably find the *nabal* of the previous chapter.

The scorner fits into this company and, in the context of this psalm, is regarded as the worst of the bunch. Why? Because the scorner is an implacable enemy of righteousness. *He is someone who will use the rules of law in order to overturn the rule of law.*

For this reason, the scorner is a dangerous foe in a court of law. As the prophet Isaiah observed, these are the scoundrels:

> Who make a man an offender for a word,
> And lay a snare for him who upholds justice
> in the public gate,
> And turn aside the just with empty arguments.[2]

In the context of this passage, the prophet assures the world that God will judge the tyrant and the scorner. His point is that the scorner's clever manipulation of the law will see its comeuppance at the judgment seat of the Almighty.

Isaiah observes that the scorner may be quite sophisticated in the use of the court system. The use of legal technicalities and disingenuous rhetoric to ensnare the innocent and set free the guilty did not originate in the modern era, but is as ancient as law itself. The scorner is both willing and able to use and abuse the court system unscrupulously in order to prevent justice from being done, and especially in order to hinder the people of God and the work of God. Why? Others may do so primarily (or entirely) for personal gain. The scorner will do it as a way to get back at God.

It gratifies the scorner to be the way he is, and to reject God and righteousness.

> How long will scorners delight in their scorning...?[3]

This is a rhetorical question. There is no need to answer it. It is a way to point out that the scorner enjoys his role as a self-appointed prophet of unrighteousness and unholiness. Some are recognized authors, some are celebrated media figures, and some are locally known cranks. What is common to them is that they savor the limelight and relish the storms of outrage triggered by their blatant conduct and public remarks. They seem to find their greatest satisfaction in provoking Christians to speak and act in an unchristian manner and in drawing the "bluenose moralists" into a raucous debate.

Not only does the scorner delight in scorning, he is aggressively arrogant.

> Proud, haughty, Scorner is his name,
> who deals in the wrath of pride.[4]

I am presenting you a very literal translation of this proverb in order to bring out the motives, attitudes, and behaviors of the scorner. Pride is the motive, haughtiness is the attitude, and angry aggressiveness shows up in the behavior. The Amplified Bible puts it this way: he "deals and acts with overbearing pride."

One classic commentary explains the verse thus:

> For not only does he inwardly raise himself above all that is worthy of recognition as true, of faith as certain, of respect as holy; but acting as well as judging frivolously, he shows reverence for nothing, scornfully passing sentence against everything.[5]

Anyone who has studied Bible or religion in a university knows that the attitude and approach of the scorner is no longer merely an influence, it is a scholarly standard. Let no one wonder why character deficiency syndrome has become a rampant beast ravaging our society. The raging unbelief which lies at its core is enshrined in many of our most respected halls of learning and in some of the most prestigious theological seminaries.

The scorner's distinguishing characteristic is moral obstinacy.

> A scorner seeks wisdom and finds it not;
> but knowledge is easy to him who understands.[6]

> A wise son hears his father's instruction,
> but a scorner does not hear rebuke.
> A scorner does not love one who reproves him,
> neither will he consult the wise.[7]

> He who reproves a scorner gets himself shame,
> and he who rebukes a wicked man, a stain.
> Reprove not a scorner, lest he hate you;
> rebuke a wise man, and he will love you.[8]

The scorner may protest loud and long how he has studied the Bible and it didn't make sense, or how he prayed and was never answered, etc. The problem is not that it is difficult to find God, but that the scorner did not want to find Him. He does not really desire to know God, and he does not earnestly hope to discover the point and purpose of morality and righteous living.

Every generation seems to have its own infamous infidels, and certainly the infidel everyone loved to hate in the 1960s and '70s was the publicity-seeking atheist Madeline Murray O'Hair. This manifestly bitter woman is gone now, the victim of a murder/theft conspiracy perpetrated by close associates. Mrs. O'Hair, who earned her notoriety by using the courts to cast Bible reading out of public schools in America, claimed that she had read the Bible and knew it better than most Christians. She certainly knew enough of it to torture it beyond recognition, often throwing poorly educated and unequipped believers into utter confusion in circus-like public debates.

The point is that just because one studies the Bible does not mean that one is trying to learn from it. Comedian W. C. Fields was known for his cynical outlook that gave his comedy a sharp satirical bite. He was also known as a devout skeptic of all religion. Late in his life a friend found him perusing the pages of a Bible and asked him whether he was turning to faith in God. "No," he replied, "I'm looking for loopholes." Even if a scorner were to seek wisdom, he would not find it because it is not what he wants it to be.

The scorner does not receive correction or listen to wise advice—not from his own father, nor even from the wisest counselors—and he never has. That is why he is in the moral condition he is in.

I call to your attention once again in these proverbs the close connection between the mocking scorner and the godless. Both are reprobate. What this means is that they will not repent of what they do, think, or believe. Confront him if you must for his egregious behavior and his outrageous speech, if only to stanch his impact on others. Understand, however, that any attempt to restore the scorner to right thinking and right living will be met with vituperative mockery, insult, and hatred. "Do not cast your pearls before swine, lest they turn and attack you."[9] Give your attention instead to the teachable and toward reaching and saving the simple.

There are some who, upon reading this, will object that Christians are obligated to give witness of the gospel and seek to persuade everyone, even the scorner. I am not saying we should not. I am merely pointing out the plain teaching of Scripture that it is a waste of time to reason with the scorner. Even Jesus told his disciples that there comes a time to break contact and go on to another place where people will listen.[10] No one can be forced into faith, and it is not only unwise to attempt to coerce another person's conscience, it is wrong. *To leave the scorner to his scorning is to respect him as a soul.*

Someone will perhaps bring up an example of an atheist or skeptic who turned to faith—someone like C. S. Lewis, for example. I reply that not all who call themselves atheists, agnostics, and skeptics are scorners. They are often honest and earnest. God has His own ways of bringing closed minds and hearts to a place where they are ready to listen to the truth. In one way, the above proverb gives a way to identify the scorner and separate him from someone who can still be redeemed: If he genuinely *listens* to you, he is not (yet) a scorner. There is still some wisdom in him that can be reached. There is still some gracious movement of the Spirit of God in his heart.

The scorner, however, by definition is someone who will not listen. He has not merely failed of belief, he has decisively rejected it. Any attempts to persuade him will be regarded by him as an act of war against his person. The advice of Proverbs is that whoever wishes to reach the scorner with truth and correction must proceed at his own risk.

The Influence of Alcohol

Proverbs reveals a peculiar and perhaps surprising connection between alcohol and the spirit of the scorner.

> Wine is a mocker [scorner], strong drink is raging,
> and whoever is deceived by it is not wise.[11]

I learned this proverb as a youth (from the King James Version quoted above), but I did not understand it very well. It was vigorously applied by our mentors, who used it to exhort us that "drinking is bad for you," but they did not explain what the verse actually means. What is so wrong with alcohol when the entire world seems to think it is a good thing?

The New International Version clears up some of the confusion: "Wine is a mocker and *beer a brawler.*" This helps. The "strong drink" of ancient times was not distilled liquor (the technology to produce this did not exist until more recent times), but beers made from various grains. Archeologists have discovered beer recipes dating back to the Sumerian kingdom more than two thousand years before Christ. Even in ancient times, they noticed that "beer is a brawler" (the Hebrew word suggests a noisy disturber of the peace).

Any policeman or highway patrolman will tell you that the meanest drunk they have to deal with is the beer drunk. People who are intoxicated on beer frequently have nasty attitudes. They tend to be more belligerent and combative than other drunks. This was also confirmed to me by a friend of mine who has battled alcoholism, whose beverage of choice for a long time was beer (he hated the taste, but it was easy to get). The problem was, whenever he got drunk on beer, he inevitably got into fights. Now this is a really amiable, good-natured guy when he is sober—but drunk on beer, he kept getting drawn into brawls. "Strong drink is raging," "beer is a brawler." It is something that can be observed anywhere that the beverage is consumed in excessive quantities.

There is a physiological reason for this phenomenon. It is the narcotic lupulin, which is imparted to beer by one of its main ingredients, hops. Lupulin is a compound that includes a lupulic acid called humulone, whose chemical formula closely resembles that of cannabinol, the hallucinogenic ingredient in marijuana. Moreover, the hop oil that flavors the beer contains geraniol, a powerful member of the alcohol family of chemicals. The net result of the use of hops in every beer recipe is to fortify the alcoholic "buzz" with a sting that brings out the most aggressive aspects of a personality.

Perhaps this is why the most successful advertising and marketing of beer has been in conjunction with sports, especially professional football. Certainly, it helps to explain why some communities and teams have banned or restricted the sale of beer in their sports stadiums. "Beer is a brawler."

It was not until I was preparing this study on character deficiency syndrome that the full force of this verse dawned on me. An increased understanding of the techniques of Hebrew poetry and its use of parallelism in the proverbs began to illumine this proverb in particular.

"Beer is a brawler." An excess of beer can turn an ordinarily affable person into someone with a terrible temper who is willing to tear up rooms and smash faces. Likewise, "wine is a mocker." The apostle Paul warns, "Do not get drunk on wine, which leads to debauchery." It has the power to change a decent person into someone who may commit any kind of indecency, who is openly contemptuous of truth and moral goodness. It will turn even a decent person into a mocker, a scorner, a terminal fool.

My friend whom I mentioned above later moved on from beer to harder and quicker forms of intoxication. He spent his working days in an alcoholic haze and spent the nights drinking himself into a stupor. After some problems with traffic violations he began going to AA meetings and, as far as I knew, was beginning to gain sobriety.

Late one night, I received a call from him in which he threatened to do violence to others and to himself. With alarm and a healthy measure of fear to keep me wary, I went to his house to find him sitting at his kitchen table sipping placidly from a Coca-Cola can. His eyes were slightly glazed, but he was otherwise calm, and his conversation was lucid—no slurred speech or any of the other familiar signs of drunkenness. He was not agitated as he had been on the phone, and I thought that it would be possible to reason with him.

I was wrong. As we talked about his problems, he parried every statement I made with remarks that ranged from off-the-wall absurdities to bitterly sarcastic denunciations. After a while, I asked him how long it had been since he had taken a drink of liquor. He took a sip from his soft drink can and said, "Just now." I will never forget the coldness in his eyes. I realized at that moment that I was not talking to my friend, but to a scorner. Alcohol had turned a decent human being into a terminal fool who, on that damp winter night, seriously contemplated murdering someone who made him angry and then taking his own life so he would not have to pay society for his crime.

"Wine is a mocker...and whoever is deceived by it is not wise." It is a deceiver. Alcohol promises to be the fluid of happiness, excitement, pleasure, joy, and love. Yet when it takes over, no other substance known to man so universally brings or accompanies more misery, heartache, and devastation. There is no wisdom there, and multitudes find in it instead the final destiny of every fool.

Judgments on Scorners

Late in the book of Proverbs, there is a blanket warning issued, apparently, to every fool of every type:

> A man often reproved who hardens his neck
> shall suddenly be broken beyond healing.[12]

If this warning applies to anyone, it applies to the scorner, who has reached the terminal stage of folly unfazed by every rebuke he has received in life. Once a person has reached this stage in his life, there is nothing more to add to his condemnation.

> The thought of folly is sin,
> and the scorner is an abomination to men.[13]

We have already looked at the first part of this proverb in connection with the third-degree fool and his folly. We have already seen that the true character of folly is not just a matter of having a few faults—it is sin. Remember that by definition, folly, as deliberate moral rebellion against the Creator and Judge of the Universe, is a doomed endeavor. To *contemplate* folly, to desire, seek, and plan it, is a sin of the mind. Now we can see what finally happens to the thought and plan of foolishness if it is allowed to follow its own course all the way to the end.

"The scorner is an abomination to men." The Hebrew construction of the phrase "abomination to men" allows for a double meaning: On the one hand, it means that the scorner will be repulsive to people of better character, and they will steer clear. On the other hand, it means that he is the *cause* of abomination; he pollutes the faith and morals of others and draws them into his own moral cesspool. He is a willing and willful stumbling block in the path of others. Jesus said, "Offenses must come, but woe unto that man by whom the offense comes."[14] Jesus added that when the time of his judgment comes, the offender is going to wish someone had drowned him rather than making the Lord's little children stumble.

God—merciful, gracious God—returns the scorn of this reprobate.

> Surely the LORD scorns the scorners,
> but he gives grace unto the lowly.[15]

It is important to get the last part of that verse in because I promised you that before we finished, we would see the light again. I want to make sure you at least get a glimmer. God reflects back scorn to those who mock Him. He rejects their pride and sends it right back to them. This is not the same thing as saying that God rejects sinners. No, He loves sinners, and He gives grace to those who come to Him with their need—but not those who come with an attitude of rebellious accusation against Him. The most devastating act of the judgment of God in this present age (i.e., before His climactic judgment of the world arrives) is *when he gives sinners what they want and turns them over to their own desires.*

Certain passages in the New Testament indicate that scorners will be prominent in the Last Days. In 2 Peter, we read about "scoffers." The Greek word[16] resembles our phrase "child's play" and literally describes someone who treats serious matters as a plaything. Here is what Peter says about them:

> First of all you should understand that in the last days *scoffers* will come, scoffing and following their own evil desires. They will say, "Where is this 'coming' He promised? Ever since our fathers died, everything goes on as it has since the beginning of creation." But they deliberately forget that long ago by God's word…the world of that time was deluged and destroyed. By the same word the present heavens and earth are reserved for fire, being kept for the day of judgment and destruction of ungodly men.[17]

The scoffers spoken of here certainly resemble the scorners of Proverbs. Along with the familiar, self-seeking lifestyle of the fool, the scorner adds to it the role of being (to coin a phrase) a *jeer leader* for infidelity. He harangues the godly, seeking to overturn truth by ignoring manifest facts.

The main point to be made here concerns not the profile of the scorner, but the judgment that will come upon him. The righteous can put up with his mocking mouth only for so long before they are crying out for God to shut him up. The Word of God assures us that the scorner will be taken care of in due time.

What believers need to realize is that their scoffing is not going to change God's program.

In C. S. Lewis's space fantasy *Perelandra*, the protagonist Ransom must endure a night of psychological torment by an inhuman adversary—an alien spirit who has taken over the body of a dead man—who keeps him from sleep by repeatedly, eerily calling out his name: "Ransom...Ransom...Ransom." When Ransom demands to know what he wants, "the Un-man" replies, "Nothing." Then the cycle begins again. The Un-man cannot hurt him, but he will not be quiet. So it is with the scorner. He cannot truly hurt the child of God by his scoffing, but he will not be quiet, and thus both wearies and discomfits those who are serious about faith and righteous living.

Sooner or later, the scorner will face judgment on two levels—man's judgment, and then God's.

Man's judgment? That is what the Bible says.

> When the scorner is punished, *the simple* is made wise.
> Smite a scorner, and the simple will beware.
> Cast out the scorner and contention shall go out,
> and strife and dishonor shall cease.[18]

When the scornful fool's behavior crosses the line into antisocial lawlessness, society must take action. The scorner's case does not call for discipline and rehabilitation, but direct retributive punishment. Two kinds of punishment are implied here: the levy of a financial penalty or fine, and the inflicting of blows. The scorner must feel the pain of his misdeeds.

There is a deterrent effect in the punishment of the scorner, but it is not upon the scorner—it is upon *the simple fool*. The simple can be made to see that this is where he could end up, and perhaps become less enchanted with folly. The scorner will not change, but his chastisement will put the fear of God into the simple.

There is also a direct beneficial effect when the scorner is "cast out." That may mean being cast out of a place by being fired or expelled or just kicked out. It may mean being cast out of society by being imprisoned, or in extreme cases where a capital crime has been committed, executed. The beneficial effect is the restoration of peace because the scorner is a perpetual agitator who is not only in a personal uproar, but keeps everyone else in an uproar as well. Cast out the scorner and strife will cease.

There is, of course, a limit to the judgment man can impose—even scorners have civil rights! The prospect of God's judgment ought to make us stop and think. "The fear of the LORD is the beginning of wisdom." Remember, we live in a "limited liability" society, but God presides over a moral universe of *unlimited* liability.

Judgments are prepared for scorners.[19]

The word for "judgments" here[20] is never used of the verdict or sentence of a human court of justice, but always of the judgments of God. They are prepared for scorners. In fact, the prophet Isaiah's prophecy of the final judgment is addressed directly to the scornful fool and includes him prominently in the picture of the devastating ultimate sentence.

> Now, therefore, be not *scorners* lest
> your bonds be made strong;
> for I have heard from the LORD God of hosts a destruction
> even determined upon the whole earth.[21]
> For the ruthless one is brought to nothing,
> and the *scorner* is ended,
> and all who watch to do evil are cut off.[22]

Is there any New Testament parallel to this teaching? There is, and it is one of the most chilling, most discussed, and least understood statements to come out of the mouth of Jesus Christ:

> Therefore I say to you, every kind of sin and blasphemy
> shall be forgiven of men, except blasphemy against the

Holy Spirit shall not be forgiven of men. And whoever may speak a word against the Son of man, it shall be forgiven him. But whoever should speak against the Holy Spirit, it shall not be forgiven him, neither in this age nor in the one to come.[23]

It is true that neither the words "fool," "scorner," nor "mocker" show up in this passage. It must be clear, however, that the nature of this sin and the finality of this judgment certainly fit what we know of the terminal fool.

This sin cannot be committed incidentally or accidentally. It is the most deliberate choice anyone can make. It is not just a rejection of the intellectual concept of God, nor a temporal rejection of the person or mission of Jesus. It is the heart's rejection of God the Spirit, who reveals God in grace directly to the heart and mind of the sinner. The person who blasphemes the Holy Spirit has had a direct encounter with God through that Spirit. The truth has been made known to him, he knows whom he has encountered—and he not only turns away, he opens his foolish mouth to mischaracterize, belittle, and slander the experience.

These words of Jesus must be the most horrifying words of judgment he ever spoke. The damnation described here is unconditional, irrevocable, and eternal. Where does the grace of God come in? In view of all the folly we have dissected, is there any good news left in the world?

Yes. Thank God, yes.

The Gist

Beyond reach. The scorner is a committed fool who has passed the point of no return.

Bitter. The scorner is bitter toward God, and desires to embitter others as well.

Booze. Alcohol, drunk in excess, can turn a decent person into a scorner who will do evil things he otherwise would never think of doing.

Banned. God declares a definitive judgment on scorners.

For your consideration

- Do you think scorners have more or less influence on society today? If they do have an influence on society, then what does it mean that "the scorner is an abomination to men" (Proverbs 24:9)?
- The author finds a possible connection between the scorner and the "unpardonable sin" defined by Jesus. Do you agree or disagree?
- How does the excess consumption of alcohol differ from other forms of the sin of gluttony? If you use alcohol as a beverage, what measures do you take to insure you do not drink to excess? How seriously do you regard the danger?

16

God's Wisdom for Fools

Funny how when you think you're right,
everybody else must be wrong
'Til someone with fool's wisdom
somehow comes along
His voice was strange, and the words he said
I didn't quite understand
But I knew that he was speakin' right
by the leather-backed book in his hand[1]

In our study of character deficiency, the reader has perhaps become conscious of certain deficiencies in the study itself. You may be sure this writer is acutely aware of several.

In the first place, since I have purposely restricted the scope of my analysis to the theme of folly primarily in the book of Proverbs, I have necessarily neglected much more that should be said regarding moral character. I do not regard this as a weakness, however. To focus intense attention on one issue may throw all other issues out of focus for the moment, but it ultimately brings greater clarity to the "big picture." Therefore I offer without apology what might indeed be an "unbalanced" portrait of disorderly character. I encourage the reader to find the balance for himself within the wider scope of doctrine and Scripture.

A second deficiency I note with regret: that there are larger dimensions of the struggle between wisdom and folly that I have only hinted at in order to give attention to the central theme of *moral* character. I have stressed repeatedly that folly is not a matter of intelligence. This is not the same as saying that folly is not a matter of the mind, for *there is an intellectual dimension to folly*. If this theme had been a major part of the discussion, I would have proposed that the four-stage syndrome describes the descent into infidelity as well as character deficiency. I would also have acknowledged that moral folly and intellectual folly do not necessarily converge in the life of a given individual. Some have departed from faith into unbelief without becoming overtly immoral, and conversely some have become moral fools yet still clung at least nominally to a profession of faith. Yet on a societal and cultural level, I submit that intellectual and moral folly must and actually do go together, and result eventually in decay at the root of civilization. That ambitious argument, alas, lies outside the scope of this book.[1]

---

[1] I therefore commend to the reader the excellent book by Nancy R. Pearcy, *Total Truth* (Crossway: 2004). While Pearcy's thesis is not exactly coextensive with mine, the reader might make some suggestive connections. Consider, for example, the biographical sketches Pearcy gives of the fathers of philosophical pragmatism in Chapter 8, "Darwins of the Mind." It is not hard to see something like the descent from simpleness to committed folly in the stories of the intellectual evolution of John Dewey and Oliver Wendell Holmes, Jr. Beyond this, Pearcy also demonstrates (in Part 3, "How We Lost Our Minds") how American evangelicalism intellectually disarmed itself, and in the process became philosophically, theologically, and religiously "simple."

A third deficiency has been revealed by the subject matter itself. At the end of the previous chapter, we were left with a tragedy—not a satisfying classical tragedy, but the depressing, modern kind. Classical tragedy is directed toward a cathartic experience in which the audience leaves the theater sad but satisfied. Loose ends are tied, questions answered, tensions resolved, and catharsis occurs. There is mental and emotional cleansing. Think: *Hamlet.* Modern tragedy is consistently anticathartic. In a modern tragedy, there is no moral clarity; there are no resolved tensions, not even real conclusions. There are only endings. The dilemmas remain in place, even after the demise of the tragic characters. Think: *The Godfather II.*

Such is the course of the fool who follows his folly all the way, the way that seems right to him. Its end is "the ways of death." There is no resolution, no satisfaction, no catharsis. There is only a sad finality, and if it is the end of the *nabal* or of the scorner there is not even pity, but only a momentary sigh of relief that we are finally done with him.

What, then, is the answer of the wisdom literature to those who are caught and sucked down in an inescapable whirlpool of folly? All along the way, there have been admonitions, reproofs, and warnings to turn around. The problem is that folly deceives us. As James says,

> Each one is tempted when he is lured away and seduced *by his own desires.* Then desire, having conceived, gives birth to sin, and sin, when it reaches full term, brings forth death.[2]

These words not only remind us of the proverb that "even the thought of folly is sin,"[3] but also that the very appeal of folly is that it offers us what we want and delivers just enough to keep us coming back for more. This is the deceptive element of folly that we have spoken of before. How, then, can anyone break free from folly if he is self-deceived?

Surrender to Cynicism?

Someone might suggest the problem is that we have put such emphasis on the negative that we have lost sight of the positive. It is a point that is perhaps reflected at the end of Ecclesiastes:

> Let us hear the conclusion of the whole matter: Fear God and keep His commandments, for this is the whole duty of man. For God shall bring every work into judgment, including every secret thing, whether it be good or evil.[4]

This is offered as "the conclusion of the whole matter," but what is the matter?

Ecclesiastes is written by an anonymous *koheleth* (preacher) who identifies himself as "the son of David, king in Jerusalem." I will leave debates on the authorship and date of the book to others. But it cannot be questioned that the perspective of the book is of a man who wields economic, political, and intellectual power and prestige such as few (if any) besides Solomon could have held. Yet while he is facile in the production and use of proverbs, he is not at all the same optimist who brought forth the book of Proverbs. Ecclesiastes conveys a hard, biting edge, a bitter cynicism that is announced early—"Vanity of vanities, all is vanity"—and carried throughout the book. In Ecclesiastes, life is futile, meaningless, and frustrating, and wisdom does not alter the situation. Wisdom only aggravates the futility of it all because it sharpens the awareness of the emptiness.[5]

Is this a contradiction of the Wisdom Ethic, that wise living is the Way of Life? Not at all, for at least two reasons. First, while "folly" in Ecclesiastes carries essentially the same sense as in Proverbs, "wisdom" owns a different shade of meaning, if not a different meaning altogether. It has lost sight of its own motto, "Trust in the LORD with all your heart, and lean not on your own understanding," and lost its joy and hope along with it. Now it carries an element of disillusionment. Having cut loose from its anchor of faith, all that is left to wisdom is its analytical perceptiveness regarding the big picture and a shrewd realism toward the details. That is not enough to make for a happy life.

Second, and more fundamentally, Ecclesiastes takes the perspective of life "under the sun," a vividly concrete expression for naturalistic humanism. This is not a "perfect" naturalism (atheism) but a conflicted and impotent theism. There is a belief in God, but it consists of little more than a memory and a tradition. The preacher knows and believes that there will be a judgment. He has, however, lost all sense and belief of God's living presence. He does not place much stock in an afterlife. He proceeds through most of his investigations as though God were not there; and when he does perceive God's hand, it only increases his frustration. He determines that wisdom works well enough to solve problems and improve the quality of life, but he despairs of ever discovering true meaning and purpose. Right up to the end of the book he still cries, "All is vanity!" Wisdom has been reduced to pragmatism, even in religious observance. It is better to be wise than a fool, it is better to be good than bad, but ultimately there is no point to either if this life is all there is.

Thus when "the conclusion of the matter" is written, it is not with a blessing upon obedience or a promise of happiness, but with an almost grim admonition to live right for duty's sake. These are the words of a wise man who has tasted of folly as he had of wisdom, and found that the experience of folly had changed the taste of the wisdom and made it insipid. Gone is his zest for living in the Way of Wisdom. Regret has supplanted joy.

And yet, even with all its bitterness, cynicism, and regret, the last words of Ecclesiastes are true words and in full harmony with everything else that has been spoken of wisdom. The essence of wisdom is about devotion to God, about having faith in Him and keeping faith with Him by obeying His commandments. Moreover, within the framework of obedience and accepting the limitations of life under the sun, there is the possibility of real joy and real meaning.

Is Wisdom Christian?

A more serious problem, a theological one, is that the question of whether the Old Testament concept of wisdom and folly is applicable to Christians. It would seem to be obvious how saturated are the Gospels and the teachings of Jesus with wisdom; how Jesus "grew in wisdom" from his youth (Luke 2:40, 52); how Jesus compared himself and his message to Solomon (Matthew 12:24); and how early followers of Christ like Stephen were extolled for being filled with the Spirit and wisdom (Acts 6:3, 10). How, then, could the question even come up?

Some who raise the question simply discount the authority of the Old Testament. Others see a dichotomy and incompatibility between the law and the gospel. Wisdom is a way of life that is consistent with God's law, to keep the commandments and to abide under the benefits of the covenant. Objectors can point to numerous passages in the New Testament, especially in the writings of Paul, which indicate that the gospel of Jesus Christ has superseded and even supplanted the law as the governing factor in the Christian life. They can also point to passages that seem to say that wisdom and folly have exchanged roles, so that wisdom has been rendered foolish by the "foolishness of God."

Clearly, if this objection is upheld, it undercuts the entire thesis of this book. If faith in Jesus Christ has made God's law void and the development of virtuous character irrelevant, what could then be the point of trying to understand character deficiency syndrome? For sin is sin, and Jesus Christ receives sinners regardless of the depth of their depravity. "Believe on the Lord Jesus Christ and you shall be saved"—is that not enough to say?

It is undeniably true that the New Testament alters the function of the law in relation to the life of the righteous, but the above objection either exaggerates or misconstrues both the nature and the extent of that change. We have already seen at various points in our discussion how folly is discussed in the New Testament in a manner completely consistent with what we see in Proverbs. It is not at all within the scope of this book to demonstrate[2] fully the relationship of God's law to the Christian believer. What I do need to show is that there is a harmony, even a continuity between the way of wisdom as it is extolled the Old Testament sages and as it is promoted by New Testament apostles. In so doing, I believe we shall see how *Jesus Christ is the ultimate answer and solution of God to the problem of human folly.*

First, however, it will be necessary to tackle straight on the question whether wisdom is even Christian. Who would raise such a question at all? Apparently the apostle Paul:

> For Christ did not send me to baptize, but to evangelize—not in wisdom of word, in order that the cross of Christ might not be nullified. For the message of the cross is to those who are perishing foolishness, but to us who are being saved it is the power of God. For it is written, "I will destroy the wisdom of the wise, and I will bring to nothing the discernment of the discerning."
>
> Where is the wise, where is the scholar, where is the debater of this age? Did not God make foolish the wisdom of the world? For since in the wisdom of God the world did not know God through wisdom, God was pleased through the folly of the proclamation to save those who believe...We proclaim Christ crucified—to Jews indeed a stumbling block and to Greeks folly, but to those who are the called, both Jews and Greeks, Christ, God's power and God's wisdom. Because the folly of God is wiser than men, and the weakness of God is stronger than men.[6]

---

[2] One book I recommend toward that end is Thomas R. Schreiner, *The Law and Its Fulfillment: A Pauline Theology of Law* (Baker, 1993). It is a full exposition of the subject and brings up to date the defense of the classic Protestant doctrine of the law (especially with regard to the writings of Paul) against the most serious challenges and alternative views of contemporary scholarship. Schreiner's approach is scholarly and responsible but also accessible to the serious student and layperson who wishes to understand the issue better.

Some see in these words Paul's disavowal of all wisdom and rationality that man can possess. That would include the *biblical* concept of wisdom, defined and portrayed in these pages as relating to moral character. It seems to some that Paul has exchanged rational and moral wisdom for a non-rational, experiential, existential kind of wisdom that "we speak...among those who are mature."[7] Some trace this mindset to Paul's supposed sense of failure in Athens before he came to Corinth. They believe he arrived in Corinth with a sour taste in his mouth, determined not to repeat his "mistakes" in Athens, and properly disillusioned with every approach to preaching the gospel that tries to speak to the mind rather than to the heart.[3]

Is Paul really rejecting wisdom and promoting, to borrow the phrase from Francis Schaeffer, an escape from reason? Absolutely not.

The apostle writes to rebuke a spirit-killing trend of factions and partisanship that has emerged in the church in Corinth. One of the buzzwords in the Corinthian church was "wisdom,"[8] and some were saying that one of Paul's failings was that he did not have it. Paul's response here is to take aim at *their* concept of wisdom and bring it down.

Like old Agur in Proverbs, Paul demurs to those who are pressuring him to frame his message in "wisdom of words." At first glance, his reply seems to be merely a bit of self-deprecation, perhaps to deflect criticism that his preaching was neither sophisticated nor witty. In fact, he is cutting to the core of the pretensions of all the Corinthian factions—including the one that calls itself "of Paul."

---

[3] There is a great deal wrong with this opinion that I cannot deal with here. See my essay "Paul and the Humanists: An Examination of Acts 17:16–31" at http://www.seriouschristian.org/PaulinAthens.pdf, especially the postscript, "Did Paul Retract His Approach in Athens" for a discussion of this issue and why it is important.

He freely acknowledges that he did not come among them in order to teach them either a religion or a philosophy, but to deliver news of a Savior. Central to his message was the death of Jesus Christ on the cross. It is not that the cross was the singular and only element of his preaching,[9] but that he refused to gloss over its shame or minimize its significance in order to make the gospel more palatable to hearers. (Contrast Paul's attitude with that of many supposed "evangelicals" of our own day who try to make their churches more "seeker friendly" by obscuring the cross—not only in their architecture but, far more disturbingly, in their message.)

Paul not only did not try to hide the cross, he put it forward in such a way that his hearers had to respond to it. Their response to the cross would determine whether they believed in his gospel or rejected it. What is it about the cross—not as a religious symbol but as a reference to the bloody death of Jesus, all the events that pertain to it, and the meaning of those events—that it should be given this kind of prominence? Four things.

First, the cross stands as the pivotal act of God in salvation history, the decisive moment in a plan God formulated before time but only revealed in the coming of Jesus.[10] Through the cross Jesus Christ has accomplished atonement for sin, the redemption of mankind, and our reconciliation with God. Second, as a consequence of the gracious act of God on our behalf through Christ's death on the cross, the very message of the cross becomes the instrument of power through which God *effects* the forgiveness of sins, the redemption of a soul, and reconciliation with the sinner. This life-changing energy is applied by the Holy Spirit, "so that your faith might not be in man's wisdom, but in God's power."[11] Third, the cross of Jesus Christ demands that all who would follow Him must take up their own cross. It is a summons to lay down all self-interest, to accept persecution, to embrace suffering, and to follow Christ in a life of love and service to others in His name.[12]

Fourth and most significant to the present discussion, the cross is a direct challenge both to religious and philosophical kinds of humanism: "to Jews indeed a stumbling block and to Greeks folly." The racial divide between Jews and Gentiles is not in view here. Paul is speaking of the reasons why people stumble over the cross. The cross is the breaking point for all the pride of man and tests us whether we will reject our self-sufficiency and surrender to the grace of God.

The message of the cross opposes the spiritual pride even of *good* people and demands that they let go of the conceit that they are righteous because they are religious and nice. They must approach God the same as any sinner in need of forgiveness, because that is what they are. The cross also opposes the intellectual pride of *smart* people and demands that they let go of the delusion that they are virtuous enough to be saved because they have knowledge. They must approach God as the simple who know nothing because that is what they truly are. It is what we all are.

In Romans, Paul builds a systematic case that everyone needs a Savior, be they "Jew or Greek." With searing logic he proves by Scripture and by experience that everyone has broken God's law—whether they know it from the full light of the Torah (as the Jews) or the dimmer but still effective light of conscience (as the Greeks). He illustrates his case by quoting a psalm. We have seen it before. Do you recognize it?

> There is none righteous, not even one.
> There is none who understands.
> There is none who seeks after God.
> All have departed the Way.
> Together they became worthless.
> There is no one doing good.
> There is not so much as one.[13]

Perhaps it will be easier to recall if we supply the missing first line:

The [shameless] fool has said in his heart, There is no God.

But why would the apostle use this passage about not just any fool, but the shameless fool, to describe *all* of us? Has he become overheated in the course of argument?

Earlier we showed the close connection between folly and sin, that they are virtually synonymous. Therefore, *if no one is righteous, then no one is wise*—not in any way that justifies him before God. So Paul uses this psalm about the darkest form of folly to drive home his point that,

All have sinned and come short of the glory of God.[14]

Measuring ourselves against one another, some of us seem to come out pretty well.[15] When we sin, we take comfort that there are sinners worse than we are, who either sin more or who have done something worse than we have done. In the unfiltered light of the righteousness and holiness of God, however, none of us are better off than the loathsome *nabal*. None of us really has any understanding. We have all departed from the Way of Life to follow our deceptive desires. In the words of the prophet, "All we like sheep have gone astray; we have turned every one to his own way."[16]

The wisdom and righteousness of the law convicts us all of sin and labels us as fools, but Paul refuses to indict the law with blame or charge it with fault. There is nothing faulty about God's law. The law is good and necessary, but it is rendered impotent by "the flesh," that absolute weakness of character inherent in all of us that not only fails to perform what God's law requires, but in fact, inevitably rebels against it.[17]

It is here that the cross of Jesus Christ becomes the decisive issue and the dividing line between Christianity and every other religion and way of life.

> For all have sinned and come short of the glory of God,
> being justified freely by his grace through the redemption
> which is in Christ Jesus, whom God set forth as a
> propitiation by his blood [i.e., the cross]…that He might
> be just and the Justifier of the one who has faith in Jesus.[18]

This is the gospel with which Paul confronts everyone, even
if they are religious and good or secular and sophisticated. Both
groups demand irrefutable proof, the one through a religious
"sign," the other through intellectual "wisdom." To the one the
cross is unthinkable, a defeat for the omnipotent God: "He
saved others, he cannot save himself." To the other the cross is
nonsense, the denial of everything we know in the natural world
order. How can the death of one be the salvation of many? How
can the dead be raised? "But to those who are the called (i.e., the
saved)…Christ, God's power and God's *wisdom*."

Paul drives home his argument with a quote from Isaiah 29:14.

> For it is written, "I will destroy the wisdom of the wise, and
> I will bring to nothing the discernment of the discerning."

In the original Hebrew, the verbs are passive, but the Greek
translation Paul quotes (the Septuagint) makes it clear that God
Himself destroys wisdom and discernment among men. How
can this be? What is in view is not the destruction of wisdom
per se, but of human pride and man's independence from God.
Likewise, it is not wisdom itself that Paul rejects, but every kind
of wisdom (remember the phrase "wise in their own eyes"?) that
makes people reject their own salvation—in other words, that
which elsewhere is called *folly*.

At this point (verse 20) the argument becomes a triumphal
taunt song, a victory chant over the battlefield of men's souls:
"Where is the wise, where is the scholar (or scribe), where is
the debater of this age?" Paul cites the conventional rabbinical
categories of learning, giving them a universal significance
beyond the Jewish world. Where are *all* the pretenders to the

wisdom of the world, Paul demands? With all their knowledge, they are powerless to deliver one fool from his folly—but the gospel is able. Why is Paul so confident?

> Because the folly of God is wiser than men, and the weakness of God is stronger than men.

Paul is not implying that God is foolish and weak. Neither is he asserting that God's wisdom is so incomprehensible to man that one must fall back into a mystical experience in order to know it. This is not even a figure of speech for a spiritual mismatch, as when boys boast they can beat their foe with one hand tied behind their back (though this gets closer to the truth). It is rather that the cross of Christ is the Great Paradox. Further down in the passage Paul says:

> But God chose the foolish things of the world that the wise might be shamed. And God chose the weak things of the world to shame the strong. And God chose…the things that are nothing, so that He may bring to nothing the things that are, so that no flesh may glory in His presence.
>
> But of Him you are in Christ Jesus, who was made to us wisdom from God, and righteousness and sanctification and redemption, so that as it has been written, "He who boasts, let him boast in the Lord."[19]

Again we are confronted by the ultimate reality: God is God, and we are not. God has chosen to provoke the pride of man, to force each of us to choose whether we will go in the way that seems right to us, or to trust in Him with all our hearts and lean not on our own understanding.

How Do Christians Get Wisdom?

Recall now the admonitions in the early chapters of Proverbs to "get wisdom, and with all your getting, get understanding." The getting is not by a following a programmed series of steps, but walking step by step in the Way of Life. It begins with the fear of God.

The fear of God involves an element of crisis: to encounter the holy and majestic glory of God through His Word and His Spirit, and to come to a realization of who He is. There is also an element of commitment to walk in His ways. And there is an element of faith to understand that the hand of God is at work in the world and in one's own life, even if it may not be easy to trace. At the core, though, the fear of God is that sense that one is always in the presence and under the eye of the God who is an all-consuming fire, whose face not even Moses was permitted to see because "no one may see Me and live."[20] On the Day of Pentecost, when confronted with the reality that with his resurrection, "God has made that same Jesus, whom you have crucified, both Lord and Christ," some three thousand believed, were baptized, and "fear came upon every soul." [Acts 2:36, 43]

The fear of God is the front door to wisdom, but it is not the whole house. Living in the fear of God, one must study and practice obedience to His commandments. The first commandment the child will learn, even before he learns the fear of God (and by which he will likely come to learn it) is the fifth: "Honor your father and your mother." Getting wisdom means accepting instruction from parents—obediently in childhood and respectfully into adulthood. When the youth has reached maturity and must make his own decisions, he needs to seek out the counsel of those wiser than he. That, of course, requires a humble self-assessment, as does the necessity of accepting correction and paying heed to painful rebuke. Principles such as these are not only not excluded from the apostles' teachings, they are repeated and emphasized in Ephesians 6:1–4 and Colossians 2:20, 21.

All these things are reasonable measures and work for the building into one's life the disciplines that are the building blocks of success. Acquiring wisdom requires a struggle, but the rewards are worth the hardship.

Folly, however, exerts a terrible draw upon our desires. Wisdom is hard, but folly is easy. Does wisdom have the power to overcome the gravity of folly, or are we left to our own self-motivation and self-discipline to rise above it? If wisdom is only a principle, an abstraction for virtuous character and good decision-making, then we have little help. If wisdom could not even sustain Solomon, then where do the rest of us stand? In the end none of us understands, none of us seeks after God, and we all depart from the Way of Wisdom. Nor will it do to say, "Nobody's perfect." Wisdom's rewards go only to the wise, and the consequences of folly will fall on all who dabble in it.

Remember, though, how wisdom is personified in Proverbs 8, in the great Song of Wisdom. Portrayed as a woman, Wisdom stands at the busy intersection of civic and business affairs and cries out "to all mankind,"[21] promoting truth, righteousness, and prudence as the means to success in life. Now look again at this stanza:

> The LORD possessed me in the beginning of His way,
> before His works of old.
> I was set up from everlasting, from the beginning,
> before the earth ever was…
> When He prepared the heavens, I was there.
> When He appointed the foundations of the earth,
> then I was by Him as a master craftsman,
> and I was daily His delight,
> rejoicing always before Him,
> rejoicing in the habitable part of the earth,
> and my delight was with the sons of men.[22]

It seems here that Wisdom is no longer merely an attribute of the Creator, but a full partner with Him in the Creation.

It is not probable that these words were written with a Trinitarian view of God in mind. Yet when the writers of the gospels and epistles of the New Testament read this passage in the light of the amazing person of Jesus Christ, they saw a revelation of Him beyond what its writer could have understood. They recognized that in the soaring poetry of Solomon in praise of wisdom, the Holy Spirit had revealed something about Christ that explained the inexplicable.

In Christ "are secured all the treasures of wisdom and knowledge."[23] Jesus Christ *is* "the wisdom of God."[24] All the qualities predicated of Wisdom and more belong to Christ. Wisdom is not merely a personified attribute of God from which the God-fearing can draw inspiration. Wisdom is a Person, the incarnate Son of God, who, like Wisdom, stands in the public places and calls all who hear to "Come to me."[25] As if it were not already crystal clear, Jesus says to his disciples in John 14:6,

> I am the way, and the truth, and the life; no one comes to the Father but by me.

Added to this the Apostle Paul declares that all who come to Jesus in faith are so closely related to him that they can be said to be "in Christ Jesus,"

> who was made to us wisdom from God, and righteousness and sanctification and redemption, so that as it is written, "Let him who boasts, boast in the Lord."[26]

In its context, this statement means that Jesus Christ is the one Source for all the issues that make up our salvation—including and especially wisdom, divine direction in the Way of Life. No one may earn or attain any one of them outside faith in Jesus Christ, yet they are freely available to all who believe in Him. *To receive Him by faith is to get wisdom.*

This does not mean that the believer is a passive recipient of all wisdom's benefits and has nothing left to do. To believe in the Lord Jesus Christ is to submit to and receive a transformation of identity. In Chapter 11 we raised the problem of the committed fool: What if folly is not just a matter of *behavior*? What if it has become the very *identity* of the person? In our world we single out the big offenders against the laws of God and man and, compared to them, we do not seem so bad. However, in the light of the holiness and righteousness of God, we are all shown to be fools. Our consciences sometimes accusing, sometimes excusing us, we find ourselves powerless to do the good we want to do, while we keep getting drawn back into doing the wrong we want not to do.[27]

In Jesus Christ, however, there is an actual change in who we are and what we are. This change is expressed in different ways throughout the gospels and epistles: new birth, regeneration, new creation, the new man in Christ.[28] These terms and images are not mere metaphors for conversion, even if we define conversion as a subjective change in self-identity that can result in objective changes in behavior. The meaning is more radical than that. *The new birth is nothing less than an objective change in identity that results in subjective changes in self-image, decision-making, moral behavior, and ultimately, in moral character.*

In what sense can this identity change be said to be objective, since family, friends, and acquaintances still relate to the same human personality? In this sense: that the change of identity is a real reassignment, engineered by the One who has both the sovereign authority to decree it and the unrestricted power to put it into effect.

In other words, the new creation in Christ is not merely a peak experience, an upsurge of religious emotion, or a figure of speech for a fresh start in life. It is a radical makeover of that individual who has encountered the full meaning of the cross and is overpowered by it. The person he used to be—the sinner, the fool—dies with Christ. A new person, owning a new nature and new resources of wisdom, takes his place, being raised as from the dead together with Christ to live a new life. He becomes a child of God.[29] To realize this change of identity is so crucial for us that Paul prayed that God would give believers "the spirit of wisdom and revelation" to comprehend the magnitude and power of that change.[30]

Does this look like an overstatement? If so, the overstatement is in the scriptures themselves, for I have done little more than to paraphrase and summarize what they say. I believe it is more likely that too many professing Christians are living far below their privilege. As one sharp-witted Christian put it, most Christians are so subnormal that when they see one who is normal, they think he is abnormal.[31] Perhaps too many have a faith that rests in the wisdom of men rather than in the power of God. Those who have believed in a gospel that gives them a hope of heaven without changing their character need to examine whether they have believed in a false gospel, or whether they have not yet truly believed in the true gospel.[32]

The Wisdom from Above

The doctrine of the New Person in Christ is *not* an overstatement. It is what salvation is about. But then what relevance does our study of character deficiency syndrome still have? Much indeed. The answer is found in the way wisdom operates in the New Person. It is not automatic. The new birth changes our identity and imparts a new power principle, but it is still only a birth. No babe is born full-grown. Moreover, the new creation that takes place only impacts the spirit of the person, the "inner man."[33] It does not change his environment, conditioning, or material makeup. All these other things await the Last Day to be redeemed. *We have the mind and wisdom of Christ by access, but that does not mean we have immediate, full possession of it.*[34]

How, then, does wisdom operate in these conditions, and where does folly intrude? Paul expresses it as a war between the Spirit and the flesh. In 1 John it is a struggle against the world. Throughout the New Testament, there are warnings to beware of deceptions and temptations authored by the devil. For our present study, however, James in his epistle frames the issue as a choice between the wisdom from above and an alternative "wisdom" (i.e., way of life) of a non-heavenly character.

> Who is wise and understanding among you? Let him show out of his wholesome lifestyle his works in meekness of wisdom. But if you have bitter jealousy and strife in your heart, do not boast and lie against the truth. This is not the wisdom that comes down from above, but is earthly, natural, demonic. For where jealousy and strife are, there is unrest and every evil thing. But the wisdom from above is first pure, then peaceful, gentle, deferential, full of mercy and of good fruits, unprejudiced, and without hypocrisy. But the fruit of righteousness is sown in peace for those who make peace.[35]

James uses the word "wisdom" in essentially the same way it is used in Proverbs. Wisdom displays its virtuous character in good works and meekness (the opposite of arrogance). It displays the inner qualities that befit godliness. Notice that the deeds themselves do not constitute wisdom, but the character of the deeds.

Wisdom is contrasted with a false wisdom that is "earthly, natural, demonic." (This is the one verse in the Bible where the three enemies of faith—the world, the flesh, and the devil—are apparently brought together, at least by implication.) In particular, see that the competing forces of wisdom and false wisdom are known, not in the abstract, but in their fruits, especially in relationships between people.

It is clear from James (and any other part of the New Testament) that character deficiency syndrome is far from a dead issue under the New Covenant. The development of virtuous character is demanded in Christ as much as in the law, if not more so. Folly is no less destructive and no less tempting to those who are walking in the Way. Choices must be made. Just as in

Proverbs, so in the New Testament: wisdom is the Way of Life in which we must purposely walk and be trained. Paul writes:

> Be therefore imitators of God as beloved children...For you were once darkness, but now are light in the Lord. Walk as children of light—for the fruit of the Spirit is in all goodness and righteousness and truth—proving what is well-pleasing to the Lord. And have no fellowship with the unfruitful works of darkness, but instead reprove them...So be careful how you walk, *not as unwise but as wise*, redeeming the time, because the days are evil. Because of this *do not be foolish, but understanding what the will of the Lord is.* And do not be drunk with wine in which is dissipation, but be filled with the Spirit.[36]

With regard to the life of wisdom, what, then, is new in the New Covenant? God the Father is still the Source of wisdom, the Determiner of all reality, the King who has set the terms for our life and existence, and the Author of our salvation. But now God the Son, Jesus Christ, has been revealed, bringing wisdom near and making it personal. Now living wisely is a matter of following not laws, but Him. Wisdom is still the Way of life, and Jesus said, "I am the way, and the truth, and the life." Now also the Holy Spirit has been poured out upon the people of God, empowering the walk of the wise. The law still describes the will of God in which we must live, but now we have the motivation and power by the Spirit to live it.[37]

So is fulfilled the promise of the Lord for those who find wisdom:

> He keeps the paths of justice,
> and preserves the way of His saints.
> Then you shall understand righteousness
> and justice and equity
> and every good path.[38]

The Gist

Jesus Christ is God's answer the problem of human folly.

- The gospel does not make the teachings of wisdom irrelevant.
- All have sinned and have become fools through sin.
- Jesus Christ, the Wisdom of God, brings salvation from the folly of sin.

Wisdom is the way of life of those who believe in Jesus Christ.

- To receive Christ by faith is to "get wisdom."
- The new birth is an objective change in identity that results in an experiential change in moral character.
- Wisdom does not displace folly automatically, nor does folly become less destructive for the believer.
- The life of wisdom is a walk, and every decision is a step; and for the believer in Christ, it is a walk enabled by the Spirit of wisdom.

For your consideration

- What objections might be made to a Christian using the principles of wisdom vs. character deficiency syndrome as a guide to life?
- How might the following scriptures relate to our study of character deficiency syndrome?

"I am the way, and the truth, and the life; no one comes to the Father but by me." John 14:6

"But of Him are you in Christ Jesus, who was made to us wisdom from God, and righteousness and sanctification and redemption, so that as it is written, 'Let him who boasts, boast in the Lord.'" 1 Corinthians 1:30, 31

"But the wisdom from above is first pure, then peaceful, gentle, deferential, full of mercy and of good fruits, unprejudiced, and without hypocrisy. But the fruit of righteousness is sown in peace for those who make peace." James 3:17, 18

"So be careful how you walk, not as unwise but as wise, redeeming the time, because the days are evil. Because of this do not be foolish, but understanding what the will of the Lord is." Ephesians 5:15–17

Notes

Preface to the First Edition

1. Proverbs 26:14; 24:33; 12:27; 19:24; 24:30–31; 26:15; 22:13; 26:13; 26:16; 10:26; 15:19; 13:4; 19:15; 20:4; 16:26; 21:25; 26:34
2. The essay can be read on the worldwide web at http://www.leaderu.com/orgs/probe/docs/char-def.html

Chapter 1

1. Hebrews 4:13
2. Psalm 22:28, NIV
3. Acts 17:26–28, author's translation
4. Proverbs 14:34, NIV
5. First Timothy 2:2, NIV. The context refers to praying for the ruling authorities, who have the responsibility for keeping law and order. See also 1:8–11.

6. John Douglas and Mark Olshaker, *Mind Hunter* (NY: Pocket Books, 1996), 344.
7. Proverbs 1:6
8. Proverbs 1:7
9. Ringo Starr, "It Don't Come Easy."

Chapter 2

1. Proverbs 1:1
2. See Exodus 34:5–7.
3. Deuteronomy 32:39
4. Deuteronomy 30:11–14
5. Deuteronomy 32:4
6. Deuteronomy 30:15–20
7. Or "leads others astray" (so ESV, NIV)
8. Proverbs 15:24; 14:12 (and 16:25); 10:17; 6:23
9. Proverbs 9:10
10. Proverbs 16:22; 3:18; 13:14; 14:27
11. Proverbs 3:16–18. Compare Deuteronomy 28:1–14.
12. Proverbs 14:34
13. First Kings 4:29–34, 10:1–13
14. Proverbs 12:28
15. Proverbs 2:6, 9
16. Proverbs 8:8, 20–21
17. See Romans 6:23.
18. Proverbs 10:2; 11:4–6, 18–19; 13:6
19. Proverbs 16:8; 21:21
20. Wisdom is *chakᵉmah* (kha-kᵉ-MAH); righteousness is *tsᵉdakqah* (tse-da-KAH)
21. Proverbs 8:12. Prudence = *armah* (ar-MAH)
22. Prudent = *'arum* (ah-ROOM) in Proverbs 12:16, 23; 13:16; 14:8, 15, 18; 15:5; 22:3; 27:12.
23. Prudent = *nabun* (nah-VOON) in Proverbs 16:21; 18:15.
24. Proverbs 8:22–31. Many Christian theologians, from the days of the early church fathers to the present, have seen in this

passage at least a foreshadowing, if not explicit revelation, of the preincarnate Logos of God (John 1:1–3), i.e., Christ Himself. We shall bring up the issue in Chapter 16.
25. Proverbs 23:23; 11:3
26. Proverbs 2:11–13
27. Proverbs 10:29; 11:3, 6; 13:6
28. Proverbs 19:1; 12:17, 19; 8:7
29. Proverbs 3:3; 14:22; 16:6; 20:28
30. Proverbs 1:4
31. Proverbs 4:5–9
32. Proverbs 3:13–15
33. Proverbs 4:1–4
34. Matthew 7:1–2
35. Matthew 7:6

Chapter 3

1. Proverbs 30:1–6
2. Proverbs 16:4; 21:30
3. Proverbs 20:24; 16:33; 21:31; 29:26; 21:1
4. Proverbs16:1, 9; 19:21
5. Proverbs 20:12; 15:3, 11; 16:2; 21:2
6. Proverbs 6:16–19
7. Proverbs 16:5; 3:32, 33
8. Proverbs 10:6, 7, 11
9. L. Russ Bush, *A Handbook for Christian Philosophy* (Zondervan, 1991): p. 273.
10. 10. Proverbs 11:27, 31
11. Proverbs 26:27; 28:10
12. Mark 10:30; Luke 18:30
13. Heb. *shilem* (shee-LAYM), to recompense, requite, reward.
14. Proverbs 13:13, 21; 28:18, 14
15. Proverbs 20:22
16. Proverbs 22:12

17. Proverbs 17:13; 17:5
18. Proverbs 24:17, 18
19. Proverbs 25:21, 22
20. Romans 12:20. See also v. 19.
21. Proverbs 29:18; 28:5; 25:26; 29:27; 28:4; 11:11, 10
22. This is the only place where the King James Version translates the word *pare'* (pah-RAY) thus. Compare Exodus 32:25, "made naked."
23. Proverbs 21:3; 28:9, 14, 13
24. First Samuel 15:22
25. Proverbs 4:23
26. See Proverbs 14:10, 13, 30; 15:13, 15; 17:22; 18:14.
27. See Proverbs 16:23; 20:5; 28:26; 17:20.
28. Proverbs 20:9, 27; 17:3
29. Proverbs 18:12; 16:18, 19; 21:4; 29:23; 11:2; 13:10; 15:25; 22:4
30. Proverbs 3:5–6
31. Deuteronomy 6:5
32. George F. Santa, *A Modern Study in the book of Proverbs: Charles Bridges' Classic Revised for Today's Reader* (Mott Media, 1978), p. 30.
33. Proverbs 3:7–12

Chapter 4

1. Evan Trembley Hoax, http://www.snopes.com/inboxer/missing/trembley.asp
2. Proverbs 14:15
3. Proverbs 22:3 and Proverbs 27:12
4. Proverbs 21:23
5. Proverbs 24:26
6. Proverbs 25:11
7. Proverbs 27:14. Some interpreters, however, see this as a reference to someone going overboard to flatter his

neighbor in order to gain some advantage—a ploy that the proverb says won't work.

8. Proverbs 25:20

9. Proverbs 18:8 and 26:22. The KJV translates "tasty morsels" as "wounds." It's a rare word, occurring only here in the OT, and early translators thought it was from the root meaning "to wound." In fact it's related instead to a verb that means, "to swallow greedily," and that is reflected in most modern translations. It therefore describes the seductive appeal of gossip rather than its destructive effects.

10. Proverbs 26:18–19

11. Proverbs 30:33

12. Proverbs 26:27

13. Proverbs 11:15

14. Proverbs 6:1–5. See also 22:26, 27. Compare 20:16, advice given from the other side of the lending equation.

15. Source: Flim Flam Dot Com, http://www.flimflam.com, 1999. The name of this purported organization (WCC) has been changed before and may currently be operating another banner.

16. Proverbs 14:18

17. Proverbs 1:10–15

18. See, for example, the story of David's oldest son, Amnon, and how it was his best friend who encouraged him to commit terrible acts (2 Samuel 13).

19. See National Fatherhood Initiative, www.fatherhood.org .

Chapter 5

1. Proverbs 9:13–15

2. Hebrew: *kᵉsiluth* (k'-see-LOOTH), the feminine form of the noun for self-confident folly.

3. Proverbs 9:16–18. "*Sheol*" is the realm of the dead.

4. Proverbs 7:7–9

5. Proverbs 7:10, 11

6. Proverbs 7:12–15
7. Leviticus 7:15–18. Some commentators, however, think the reference is more to Canaanite practices than Hebrew.
8. Matthew 23:24
9. Kenneth Woodward, "Sex, Morality, and the Protestant Minister," Newsweek (28 July 1997), 62.
10. Genesis 3:1
11. Proverbs 7:16–18
12. Proverbs 7:19–20
13. Proverbs 7:21

Chapter 6

1. Matthew 18:7, NIV
2. First John 1:6
3. Proverbs 7:22, 23
4. *Sheol* (she-OHL; often pronounced SHEE-ohl by English speaking readers): The underworld, the place of the dead.
5. Proverbs 5:3–6
6. Proverbs 5:8–11
7. Proverbs 6:33–35
8. John 9:2
9. Proverbs 6:24–29, 32
10. This whole story is told in 2 Samuel 11–12.
11. Psalm 32:3–4
12. Psalm 51:8–9
13. See 2 Samuel 13–20.
14. Psalm 32:1–2
15. Proverbs 5:15–20
16. See Song of Songs 5:1.
17. See Galatians 5:13 in the light of 1 Corinthians 7:3–5.
18. Song of Solomon 8:6
19. Song of Solomon 2:7; 3:5; 8:4

Chapter 7

1. Proverbs 1:22
2. Proverbs 5:12, 13
3. Proverbs 1:32
4. Proverbs 9:18
5. Proverbs 1:20, 21
6. Proverbs 2:6
7. See Proverbs 8:22–31.
8. Psalm 119:97–100
9. Psalm 119:105
10. Psalm 119:9, 11
11. Proverbs 4:5–8
12. Proverbs 4:1–4
13. Proverbs 6:21–23
14. Proverbs 22:6
15. *chanak* (khah-NAK)
16. 1 Kings 8:63; Ezra 6:17
17. Proverbs 20:7
18. Judith Rich Harris, *The Nurture Assumption* (NY: Touchstone, 1999).
19. David Blankenhorn, *Fatherless America: Confronting Our Most Urgent Social Problem,* quoted in Gilbert Meilaender, "The Eclipse of Fatherhood," *First Things* 54 (June/July 1995): 39.
20. Wade F. Horn, *Father Facts 3* (Gaithersburg, MD: National Fatherhood Initiative, 1998). The National Fatherhood Initiative has maintained its study of the positive and negative issues associated with fatherhood, and more current studies can be found here: "Father Facts," National Fatherhood Initiative (http://www.fatherhood.org/father-absence-statistics).
21. Ibid.
22. Ibid.
23. Proverbs 19:25a; Proverbs 21:11a
24. Proverbs 8:5

25. Proverbs 9:1–3
26. Proverbs 9:4–6. Italics set these words apart as a first-person speech made by Wisdom personified.
27. Psalm 19:7
28. Psalm 119:130
29. Second Timothy 3:16
30. Romans 1:16
31. *anoetos* (a-naw-ay-TOSS). See also "foolish" in Galatians 3:3, 1; Timothy 6:9.
32. Psalm 116:6

Chapter 8

1. 1. Psalm 92:5, 6
2. 2. Proverbs 12:1
3. Proverbs 17:24
4. *aphron* (aph-RONE)
5. Romans 1:19, 21, 22
6. *asunetos* (a-su-nay-TOSS)
7. Proverbs 14:8
8. Ecclesiastes 2:12
9. *sikluth* (seek-LOOTH) and *sekel* (se-KHEL)
10. Ecclesiastes 2:13, 14
11. Ecclesiastes 12:14, 15a
12. Ecclesiastes 6:8, 9
13. Proverbs 18:2
14. Ecclesiastes 10:2
15. Ecclesiastes 7:2–5
16. Ecclesiastes 5:1
17. Ecclesiastes 5:1–5, 7. Compare Proverbs 20:25.
18. Exodus 20:7.
19. Galatians 6:7
20. Luke 11:40. Here the Greek word for "fool" is *aphron*, the unthinking person.

21. Proverbs 10:23
22. Heb.: *zimmah* (zeem-MAH).
23. Leviticus 18:17; 19:29; 20:14, 17.

Chapter 9

1. Greek: *aphrosune* (af-ro-soo-nay): mindlessness; lack of good sense. In the Jewish context in which Jesus spoke, it indicates a stubborn refusal to make right moral choices.
2. Proverbs 17:16. "Fool" in the scripture references in this chapter refer to the self-confident fool unless otherwise noted.
3. Proverbs 1:22
4. Proverbs 23:9
5. Proverbs 14:16
6. Proverbs 13:19
7. Proverbs 17:10
8. Deuteronomy 25:1–3
9. Proverbs 1:32
10. Ecclesiastes 5:3
11. Proverbs 14:33; 13:16; 29:11; 12:23. "Folly" and "foolishness" in these proverbs is *'ivveleth*, here referring to disorderly behavior, plans, intentions, and attitudes.
12. Proverbs 29:11
13. Proverbs 12:23
14. Proverbs 25:11
15. Proverbs 15:2, 14. "Foolishness" is *'ivveleth*.
16. Ecclesiastes 10:2
17. Second Corinthians 11:16–23
18. Second Corinthians 12:6, 12
19. Proverbs 19:1
20. Ecclesiastes 7:9
21. Proverbs 10:18
22. Proverbs 18:6; Ecclesiastes 10:12; Proverbs 18:7
23. Ecclesiastes 9:17

Chapter 10

1. Proverbs 17:21a, 25. Again throughout this chapter, unless otherwise noted, the word "fool" designates the self-confident stage in Character Deficiency Syndrome. "Foolish" here is the adjective form of *kesil*.
2. 2. Proverbs. 13:20
3. Proverbs 17:12. "Folly" is *'ivveleth*.
4. Ecclesiastes 5:4
5. Proverbs 19:10, 26:1, 3–12
6. From the root "to shoot." So the ASV, NAS, RSV, NRSV, ESV, NIV, and most other modern translations.
7. Proverbs 29:30
8. Proverbs 14:24
9. See Proverbs 8:17–21.
10. Leviticus 19:18. See also Matthew 22:39–40, Romans 13:9–10, Galatians 5:14, James 2:8.
11. Proverbs 3:35
12. Ecclesiastes 4:5
13. Psalm 49:6–10
14. Luke 12:20. "Fool" here is aphron (aph-RONE), a senseless, unthinking person.
15. Proverbs 19:29
16. Proverbs 8:5
17. Psalm 94:8–10

Chapter 11

1. Quoted by Bridget Johnson, "Stolen Innocence," Opinion Journal (opinionjournal.com), January 18, 2006.
2. Information excerpted from Associated Press reports from October 1997.
3. Proverbs 8:5
4. Proverbs 1:7

5. Jeremiah 4:22
6. See for example Scott Stanley, "The Complex Risks Associated with Cohabitation," *Family Studies,* April 3, 2014. For a view from a clinical psychologist, see Meg Jay, "The Downside of Cohabiting Before Marriage," New York Times Sunday Review, April 14, 2012.
7. William Wilson, *Wilson's Old Testament Word Studies,* p. 172.
8. Psalm 107:17, NIV
9. Proverbs 24:9
10. Psalm 69:5
11. Proverbs 27:22
12. John Douglas and Mark Olshaker, *Mind Hunter* (NY: Pocket Books, 1996), 58. Italics in the original text.
13. Ibid, 344. The emphasis is mine.
14. Ibid, 348.
15. Ibid, 349.
16. Zechariah 11:15, 16
17. Compare this passage to Ezekiel 34, and to the words of Jesus in John 10:11–15. These verses do not exhaust the theme of God's controversy with those who minister to their own appetites in His name, but they illustrate the point while sharing the common image of the shepherd.
18. Ecclesiastes 10:1. "Folly" here is *sikkluth* (seek-LOOTH), emphasizing poorly chosen behavior by one who is stubborn, thickheaded, and unrepentant.

Chapter 12

1. J. R. R. Tokien, *Lord of the Rings: The Fellowship of the Ring.*
2. 2. Proverbs 15:21
3. Proverbs 14:18a, 24b
4. Romans 6:16
5. Isaiah 5:20
6. Isaiah 5:21

7. Quoted by Linda Gorov, *Boston Globe*, in "Is *Colors* about the Clintons?" *Houston Chronicle*, Wednesday, March 18, 1998.
8. Proverbs 14:8. "Fools" here is *kesil*, the self-confident fool.
9. Proverbs 26:4, 5
10. Proverbs 26:11
11. Proverbs 17:12
12. Douglas, 383. Emphasis is Douglas's own.
13. Ibid.
14. Proverbs 22:15. Compare Proverbs 20:30
15. Proverbs 20:30; 13:24; 29:15; 22:15–17.

Chapter 13

1. Proverbs 18:13; 12:15; 13:16; 14:9; 20:3; 29:9
2. Proverbs 18:13
3. Heb.: *kalimoth* (ka-lee-MOHTH)
4. Proverbs 12:15
5. Proverbs 3:7
6. Franz Delitzsch, *Commentary on Proverbs*, s.v. 12:15. The emphasis is mine.
7. Proverbs 13:16
8. Proverbs 14:9
9. Proverbs 20:3; 29:9
10. Proverbs 15:14; 12:23; 15:2. Italics indicate *kesil*, the self-confident fool, as distinguished from *'evil*, the committed fool.
11. Proverbs 17:28; 14:3; 10:8, 10, 14
12. Heb. *khoter* (kho-TEAR); primarily a twig, branch, or shoot
13. Many translations change the adjective to a noun.
14. See Proverbs 16, 18
15. Proverbs 14:17a, 29; 12:16
16. See Proverbs 25:28. See also 22:24, 25.

Although anger is not a pleasant thing to be around, it is nevertheless a powerful emotion that creates a compelling presence. It is easier to fall under the influence of such a person that would seem rationally possible. Of course, rationality has nothing to do with it.

17. Psalm 73:2–3, 5–6, 16–17
18. See chapter 3, the section titled, "It's Moral Reciprocity… Not Karma."
19. Proverbs 16:22; 10:21; 11:29
20. Heb. *rasha'* (rah-SHA), wicked, ungodly, unholy.
21. Proverbs 7:22c; 5:22, 23
22. Isaiah 35:8
23. Job 5:2–5
24. Proverbs 19:3
25. See 1 John 2:16 for a succinct list of those root motives.

Chapter 14

1. Deuteronomy 32:5, 6a
2. Isaiah 9:17
3. Proverbs 17:21
4. Proverbs 30:32
5. Proverbs 17:7
6. Proverbs 30:21–23
7. See Genesis chapters 16 and 21.
8. Genesis 34:7
9. Deuteronomy 22:21
10. Joshua 7:15
11. Judges 19:23; 20:6, 10
12. First Samuel 25 (see especially v. 25)
13. Second Samuel 13:12
14. Job 42:8
15. Ezekiel 13:3
16. Psalm 14:1–4 and Psalm 53:1–4. Compare Romans 3:9–12, 23.
17. Psalm 39:8
18. Job 2:9, 10

19. Job 30:1
20. Job 30:8, 9
21. Psalm 74:18, 22–23
22. Psalm 74:20
23. Ezekiel 13:2–8
24. Jeremiah 17:11
25. Second Samuel 3:33, 34
26. Psalm 107:17–20. The "fools" here are what we have described as the committed fool (Heb.: *'evil*).
27. Luke 15:17
28. Joel 2:32, Acts 2:21, Romans 10:13
29. Psalm 107:43

Chapter 15

1. Psalm 1:1
2. Isaiah 29:21. The scorner (*luts*) is specifically mentioned in verse 20, and is the subject of this verse.
3. Proverbs 1:22
4. Proverbs 21:24
5. Franz Delitzsch, *Commentary on Proverbs*, s.v. 21:24
6. Proverbs 14:6
7. Proverbs 13:1; 15:12
8. Proverbs 9:7–8
9. Matthew 7:6
10. Matthew 10:14, Luke 10:10–11
11. Proverbs 20:1. See also 23:29–35 for a vivid poetic description of the folly of drunkenness.
12. Proverbs 29:1
13. Proverbs 24:9
14. Matthew 18:7
15. Proverbs 3:34. See also James 4:6, which quotes the Septuagint version of this verse.
16. *empaiktes* (cm-pike-TAYSS)

17. Second Peter 3:3–7, NIV. See also Jude 18.
18. Proverbs 21:11a; 19:25a; 22:10
19. Proverbs 19:29a
20. *sh'phatim*
21. Isaiah 28:22
22. Isaiah 29:20
23. Matthew 12:31, 32

Chapter 16

1. Malcolm Wild and Alwyn Wall, "Fool's Wisdom" (Thankyou Music, 1973)
2. James 1:14, 15. Emphasis mine.
3. Proverbs 24:9a
4. Ecclesiastes 12:13, 14
5. See Ecclesiastes 2:12–23.
6. First Corinthians 1:17–21, 23–25. See the full passage in 1:10–31.
7. First Corinthians 2:6
8. As witnessed by the number of times the word keeps coming up as a controversial issue in the first four chapters of 1 Corinthians, and by the pointedness of its usage—even in sarcasm (4:10).
9. See, for example, 1 Corinthians 15:1–7. See also Romans 1:1–6. The essential content of all apostolic preaching included the death, resurrection, and ascension of Jesus, all in the context of the fulfillment of prophecy. This is what scholars refer to as the *kerygma*, which is the word I have here translated "the proclamation" in 1:21.
10. In the immediate context, this is referred to specifically in 1 Corinthians 2:7, 8.
11. First Corinthians 2:4, 5
12. For this theme in 1 Corinthians, see Paul's testimony in chapter 9.

13. Romans 3:10–12. Paul is quoting Psalms 14:1–3 (and 53:1–3) from the Septuagint.
14. Romans 3:23
15. See 2 Corinthians 10:12.
16. Isaiah 53:7
17. Romans 7:7–25. See also Galatians 3:21, 22.
18. Romans 3:23–25
19. First Corinthians 1:27–31
20. Exodus 33:20
21. Proverbs 8:4, NIV
22. Proverbs 8:22, 23, 27, 30, 31.
23. Colossians 2:3
24. First Corinthians 1:24
25. See Matthew 11:28 and John 7:37.
26. First Corinthians 1:30, 31
27. See Romans 2:15; 7:19.
28. See John 3:3,5; Romans 6:8; 1 Corinthians 2:4; 4:20; 2 Corinthians 4:6; Ephesians 4:24; Titus 3:5; James 2:5; 1 Peter 1:23; 1 John 5:3.
29. See Romans 6:1–11; 8:14–17. See also John 1:12, 13.
30. Ephesians 1:15–23
31. Attributed to Vance Havner.
32. Yes, there is such a thing as a false gospel: 2 Corinthians 11:3, 4, 13–15; Galatians 1:6–9. And yes, there is such a thing as ineffectual faith: 2 Corinthians 13:5; James 2:26; 1 John 2:19.
33. See Ephesians 3:16.
34. Compare 1 Corinthians 2:9–16 with 3:1–3.
35. James 3:13–18. Compare Galatians 5:13–26.
36. Ephesians 5:1, 8–11, 15–18
37. Romans 8:4
38. Proverbs 2:8, 9